# BUREAUCRACY AND DEMOCRACY

# BUREAUCRACY AND DEMOCRACY

## ACCOUNTABILITY AND PERFORMANCE

**SECOND EDITION**

William T. Gormley, Jr.
*Georgetown University*

Steven J. Balla
*George Washington University*

CQ PRESS

*A Division of Congressional Quarterly Inc.*
*Washington, D.C.*

CQ Press
1255 22nd Street, NW, Suite 400
Washington, DC 20037

Phone: 202-729-1900; toll-free, 1-866-4CQ-PRESS (1-866-427-7737)

Web: www.cqpress.com

Cover design: Tony Olivis

☺ The paper used in this publication exceeds the requirements of the
American National Standard for Information Sciences—Permanence of
Paper for Printed Library Materials, ANSI Z39.48-1992.

Printed and bound in the United States of America

11   10   09   08   07        1   2   3   4   5

**Library of Congress Cataloging-in-Publication Data**

Gormley, William T.
   Bureaucracy and democracy : accountability and performance /
William T. Gormley, Jr., Steven J. Balla. — 2nd ed.
      p.  cm.
   Includes bibliographical references and index.
   ISBN 978-0-87289-347-4 (alk. paper)
   1. Bureaucracy—United States.   2. Administrative agencies—United
States.   I. Balla, Steven J.   II. Title.

   JK421.G6447  2007
   352.6'30973—dc22

                                                    2007027755

*To Rosie*
—B.G.

*To Desi*
—S.B.

# Contents

Tables and Figures   xi

Preface   xiii

**Chapter 1: Bureaucracies as Policymaking Organizations**   1

The Contours of Public Bureaucracy   5

Accountability and Performance in Public Bureaucracies   8

Accountability and Its Many Faces   11

    The Evolution of Accountability   13

    The Limits of Accountability   14

The Push for Performance   15

    The Government Performance and Results Act   17

    The Program Assessment Rating Tool   19

    Agency Reputations in the Real World   21

Accountability and Performance: Theories and Applications   24

**Chapter 2: Bureaucratic Reasoning**   28

The Bounded Rationality Model   31

Simplified Problem Solving   34

    Problem Disaggregation   34

    Standard Operating Procedures   35

    Sunk Costs   38

    Simulations and Tests   39

Implications for Policy Analysis   40

Motivation   41

    Empathy and Commitment   42

    Representative Bureaucracy   43

    Attitudes toward Risk   44

    Organizational Advancement   45

    Promoting Organizational Cohesion   47

Consequences of Bounded Rationality   49
   A Narrow Search   49
   Problem Disaggregation   50
   Approximations   50
   Standard Operating Procedures   52
Conclusion   53


Chapter 3: The Bureaucracy's Bosses   55
Delegation, Adverse Selection, and Moral Hazard   57
Why Bureaucracy?   59
   Why Delegation Varies   62
   Implementing Child Care Legislation   65
Managing Delegation   67
   Presidential Power   68
   Congressional Control of the Bureaucracy   78
   Judicial Review   85
Principal-Agent Theory and the Bureaucracy's Clients   89
Principals and Principles   91


Chapter 4: The Bureaucracy's Clients   94
The Benefits, Costs, and Politics of Public Policy   96
The Rise and Fall of Iron Triangles   99
The Venues of Client Participation   104
   The Notice and Comment Process   104
   Advisory Committees and Other Venues of Collaboration   106
   Political Intervention   109
   Client Participation and the Internet   110
Client Influence on Bureaucratic Policymaking   115
   Business Organizations   117
   Public Interest Groups   119
   State and Local Governments   121
Clients and the Institutions of Government   124

Client Participation: Three Lessons and Beyond    125
    Who Participates Varies    125
    Venues Vary    126
    Influence Varies    126

**Chapter 5: Networks    128**

Network Theory    130

The Tools Approach    134

Intergovernmental Relations    137
    Environmental Protection    137
    Health Policy    141

Public-Private Partnerships    144
    Contracting Out    144
    Energy Policy    145
    Mental Health Policy    145
    Welfare Policy    146
    Corrections    147

Partnerships without Contracts    147
    Environmental Protection    148
    Education    148

Interagency Networks    149
    The Cabinet    149
    Office of Management and Budget    150

Interagency Coordination    151

Czars    153

Networks' Effectiveness    155

Tools' Effectiveness    158
    Grants-in-Aid    158
    Regulation    160
    Information    161

Networks: Some Conclusions    163

**Chapter 6: The Politics of Disaster Management  166**

Hurricane Katrina: A Crisis with Precedent  168

FEMA's Evolution  169

Katrina Strikes  172

Applying the Theories  173

The Coast Guard and Other Success Stories  177

September 11, 2001: A Crisis without Precedent  179

The First Response  180

Bureaucracy after 9/11  182

The Iraq War  185

Bureaucratic Theories and Future Terrorist Attacks  187

Avian Flu Pandemic: A Crisis in the Making?  190

National Strategy for Pandemic Influenza  192

Using the Theories to Forecast  193

Evaluating Bureaucracy in Light of the Theories  197

**Chapter 7: Why Are Some Bureaucracies Better Than Others?  200**

Rating the Performance of Agencies  201

Explaining Variations in Performance  202

Tasks  203

Relationships  208

Political Support  209

Leadership  213

Bureaucracy in the Twenty-First Century  217

**Appendix: Web Resources  221**

**Notes  225**

**Index  251**

# Tables and Figures

**Tables**

| | | |
|---|---|---|
| 1.1 | "Full Immunization" of Two-Year-Old Children, New England States | 20 |
| 1.2 | Evaluating Bureaucratic Accountability and Performance | 25 |
| 2.1 | Changes in Air Quality and Emissions, 1986–1995 | 35 |
| 2.2 | Workers' Compensation Claims, Maine | 37 |
| 2.3 | Types of Bureaucrats | 42 |
| 3.1 | Number of Pages in the *Federal Register*, 1960–2006 | 61 |
| 3.2 | Implementation of the 1990 Child Care Law | 66 |
| 3.3 | Implementation of the 1996 Child Care Law | 67 |
| 3.4 | Review of Agency Regulations by Office of Management and Budget, 1981–2006 | 77 |
| 5.1 | Number of States Authorized to Run Environmental Programs | 138 |
| 5.2 | Agencies Shifted to Create the Department of Homeland Security | 156 |
| 6.1 | Jokes about the Government's Bungled Response to Hurricane Katrina | 169 |
| 6.2 | Confirmed Bird Flu Cases and Deaths | 191 |

**Figures**

| | | |
|---|---|---|
| 1.1 | The Government of the United States | 6 |
| 1.2 | Organizational Chart of the Food and Drug Administration | 9 |
| 1.3 | Forms of Executive Branch Accountability | 12 |
| 1.4 | 1956 Poster of Smokey Bear | 23 |
| 2.1 | EPA Organizational Structure | 51 |
| 3.1 | The Size of the Federal Bureaucracy, 1821–2005 | 60 |
| 3.2 | Explaining Variation in Delegation | 63 |
| 4.1 | The Benefits, Costs, and Politics of Public Policies | 97 |
| 4.2 | The "Iron Triangle" of Politics | 100 |
| 4.3 | Positive and Negative Images in Media Coverage of Nuclear Power | 102 |
| 4.4 | Client Commenting before and after Online Docketing at the DOT | 114 |
| 5.1 | Networks with Different Characteristics | 133 |
| 6.1 | Organizational Highlights of the Creation of the Department of Homeland Security | 184 |
| 7.1 | Report Cards for Selected Federal Agencies | 202 |
| 7.2 | Mean Reading Scores: Success for All Schools vs. Control Schools | 218 |

# Preface

It is not easy to describe what government bureaucracy does and why it is important. It is also tough to explain to family and friends why you are writing a book that attempts to do just that. Why not choose a more glamorous topic? Why force yourself to master dozens of acronyms, decipher bureaucratese, and grapple with such concepts as satisficing, delegation, diffuse costs and benefits, and networks? Despite these difficulties and occasional taunts from skeptics, we have persisted in seeking to bring to life a subject matter often viewed as tedious and impenetrable.

There is no doubt that myths about public bureaucracy abound. Many people believe the bureaucracy simply carries out public policies made by politicians. In reality a large number of our most important policies are formulated and implemented in the bureaucracy. Many people also believe the bureaucracy is a huge, inanimate, insensitive, rule-driven machine that produces enough red tape to choke progress on any front. In reality the bureaucracy can be remarkably responsive to outside pressure—partly because agency officials enjoy considerable discretion and partly because they often use this discretion to solve problems and improve conditions for individuals and organizations throughout society.

We hope students reading this book will develop an appreciation of these myths and realities and will come to view the bureaucracy as important, problematic, redeemable, and intriguing (all at the same time!). Bureaucracy is important because agency officials determine whether public policies succeed or fail. It is problematic because bureaucrats are unelected public officials and because many factors conspire against superior performance in executive branch organizations. It is redeemable because bureaucrats and agencies are capable of significant reform. And it is intriguing because the bureaucracy is far less predictable than simple myths, metaphors, or theories imply.

Bureaucratic accountability and performance are our specific focus in this book. We aim to lay out just how the bureaucracy is accountable, as well as to whom, under what circumstances, and with what results. In thinking about these issues, we draw on insights from several different academic disciplines, including political science and public management. Political science offers a plethora of empirical research and an appreciation of the importance of the bureaucracy's external environment. Public management provides a wide array of useful concepts and a rich understanding of the interior life of agencies.

Analytically, the book is organized around four prominent social scientific theories—bounded rationality, principal-agent theory, interest group mobilization, and network theory. These frameworks have a lot to say about normative issues regarding bureaucratic accountability in a democratic political system. In selecting these four theories for special emphasis, we have tried to ensure close attention to a range of factors affecting the variations that inevitably emerge in agencies' performance. Bounded rationality helps us capture the pragmatic side of bureaucratic problem solving and the bureaucracy's remarkable capacity to make reasonably good decisions with limited time and information. Principal-agent theory highlights the challenges of delegation from politicians to bureaucrats and the difficulties of bureaucratic surveillance. Interest group mobilization draws our attention to the important role societal organizations play and the circumstances under which they are most active and effective. Network theory stresses relationships inside and outside government that cannot be reduced to hierarchical form. In a new chapter on the politics of disaster management, we demonstrate how useful these four theories can be in understanding the bureaucracy's response to some of the most important challenges it faces, including terrorist attacks, natural disasters, and public health crises.

In selecting public policy examples to illustrate our points, we have been deliberately eclectic. Readers will find many examples from health care, environmental protection, education, homeland security, emergency relief, and other areas that receive prominent attention in the mass media. Readers will also find examples from child care, public utility regulation, transportation, and other activities that usually receive less public exposure. Despite the fact that we both teach in Washington, D.C., we cite numerous examples from state and local government agencies. We take federalism seriously, and we recognize that state agencies are important not only because they implement federal laws but also because they make policy in their own right.

A number of pedagogical tools help bring all of this into focus. We include at the beginning of each chapter a series of core questions to foster students' critical thinking about a particular aspect of the bureaucracy or a chapter's approach. At the end of each chapter we include a list of key terms for students to review. An appendix of annotated Web resources follows the last chapter so students can more easily pursue further study of the topics we raise. Most important, we feature throughout the book excerpts from interviews we conducted with four former cabinet secretaries. Insights from these interviews, featured conveniently as "Inside Bureaucracy" boxes within the text, bring bureaucratic decisions and disputes to life and illustrate how prominent practitioners view theoretical appraisals of themselves and their agencies. We would like to thank each of these distinguished public servants—James Baker III, Dan Glickman, Donna Shalala, and Richard Thornburgh—for taking the time to share their insights with us.

We would also like to thank many others for their help at various stages during the preparation of the second edition of the book. Steven Shull, Richard Ghere, Lorenda Naylor, and Scot Schraufnagel offered helpful comments on the first edition that guided us in our revisions. Donald Kettl and Jonathan Breul provided valuable advice on key questions. Joanna Mikulski, a graduate student at the Georgetown Public Policy Institute, provided skillful research assistance. At CQ Press, Charisse Kiino persuaded us to do a second edition and encouraged us to add a new chapter on disaster management. Mary Marik did an excellent job as copy editor. And Laura Henry and Allie McKay helped to convert our manuscript into a finished product.

We could not have undertaken either the first or the second edition without the considerable love, patience, and nurturing of our families. Bill would like to thank his wife, Rosie, for her stimulating ideas and warm support. He would also like to thank his daughter, Angela, for reminding him that no one wants to read a boring book. Steve would like to thank his parents, Steve and Carol, for their lifelong sacrifices and encouragement; his wife, Desi, for dutifully following National Park Service regulations as they pertain to the removal of rocks; and his children, Julie and Zoli, for having fun with Smokey Bear at the state fair (more fun than a bear should be allowed to have!).

# BUREAUCRACY AND DEMOCRACY

# 1 | Bureaucracies as Policymaking Organizations

For DECADES, POLICYMAKERS HAVE confronted three interrelated challenges in elementary and secondary education: (1) finding a way to render public schools more accountable to parents, taxpayers, and other vital constituencies; (2) determining how to improve the performance of public schools so that the confidence of a long-disillusioned citizenry is at last restored; and (3) determining how public schools can best help narrow the achievement gap between whites and minorities, the latter of whom depend especially heavily on the school system for advancement and success.

One potential solution that has generated considerable interest in recent years is student testing, sometimes in combination with organizational report cards and financial rewards and punishments. Today, virtually every state issues annual grades for schools and school districts. In many states, the law requires that such report cards be released to parents and the general public.[1] A related approach involves linking test scores to financial bonuses or penalties, an approach sometimes referred to as **high-stakes testing.** In South Carolina, for example, schools that experience larger than expected gains in reading and mathematics scores receive monetary awards as well as award flags for display. Schools that win an award two out of three years may also be granted greater flexibility in administering state regulations.[2]

These approaches are embodied in policy at the federal level as well. In 2002 President George W. Bush and a bipartisan coalition in Congress enacted landmark legislation aimed at enhancing educational accountability and performance through a combination of testing requirements and financial inducements. The **No Child Left Behind Act** included the following provisions:

- Every state must require annual tests in reading and mathematics for every public school child in grades three through eight, though states are free to design their own testing instruments.
- Public schools whose test scores fail to improve two years in a row are eligible for additional federal aid. However, schools whose scores continue to stagnate or decline must provide low-income students with a variety of educational options, such as money for tutoring and transportation to a higher-performing school. Personnel changes can be required if a school fails to improve for six years.
- Public schools must develop report cards showing how their test scores compare with those of other schools.
- Public schools must narrow the gap in test scores between white and minority students and between financially advantaged and disadvantaged students.
- Every state must participate in the National Assessment of Educational Progress, which periodically assesses the performance of a random sample of public school students in selected subjects.

Most observers agree that this law constitutes the most significant revision of the nation's education policy since the Elementary and Secondary Education Act of 1965. Philosophically, it is rooted in the premise that instruments such as high-stakes testing will promote accountability, which in turn will improve the performance of public schools. That premise has received support from research on state education accountability policies that existed prior to passage of the No Child Left Behind Act. States that established "consequential accountability systems" early experienced more rapid gains in student performance on standardized tests.[3] However, for a variety of reasons, it has not yet been possible to determine whether No Child Left Behind has improved student achievement or narrowed the achievement gap between whites and minorities.

Since its enactment, the No Child Left Behind Act has generated numerous disagreements between state and federal officials. States have complained that the federal government has failed to provide sufficient funds for the states to conduct tests, offer tutorial assistance, and facilitate student transfers to other schools, as required by federal law. States have argued that the federal government's rules for testing English language learners are inconsistent, unrealistic, or both. States have objected to requirements that all teachers be "highly qualified" in core teaching fields. For its part, the federal government has objected to the states' tardiness in meeting federal requirements. As Secretary of Education Margaret Spellings put it, "I'm enforcing the law—does that make me tough? Last year it was 'we're marching together toward the deadline,' but now it's time for 'Your homework is due.' "[4]

In a typical confrontation, Department of Education officials challenged the way eighteen states are testing English language learners. Under No Child Left Behind, immigrants must take the same grade-level reading tests as their native speaker peers, unless they have attended an American school for less than one year. Many school district officials believe this requirement is unrealistic because grade-level exams often include questions about similes, metaphors, and analogies that are hard to grasp if English is not your first language. Federal officials respond that it is important to test all students the same way in order to pinpoint problems and provide extra help where it is needed. Federal officials also note that some special accommodations are allowable, including use of a bilingual dictionary or more time to take the tests.[5] In early 2007, the Fairfax County, Virginia, school board defied the Department of Education by continuing to administer different tests to native speakers and English language learners.[6] The Fairfax County Board of Supervisors endorsed the school board's decision, accusing the Bush administration of having a "tin ear" with respect to the testing of non-English-speaking students.[7] Secretary Spellings reminded state and local officials that the "standards clause" of No Child Left Behind requires children with limited English to meet the same standards as other students.[8] In this high-stakes game of chicken, Fairfax County ran the risk of losing $17 million in federal education funding if the dispute was not resolved. After a two-month feud, Fairfax County acquiesced.[9] But the debate persists.

Although most of the disagreements over No Child Left Behind have focused on the implementation of the law's testing requirements and the adequacy of federal funding, some observers question the very wisdom of the law's unprecedented emphasis on accountability and performance in education. A persistent fear is that high-stakes testing will encourage teachers to **teach to the test** and pay scant attention to the fostering of creativity, problem solving, and other important abilities in their students. As Richard Rothstein has argued, standardized tests "are of little use in assessing creativity, insight, reasoning and the application of skills to unrehearsed situations—each an important part of what a high-quality school should be teaching."[10] A related fear is that teachers will feel so straitjacketed that they will abandon the quest for innovative teaching techniques and personalized instruction. In the worst-case scenario, they might abandon the teaching profession altogether.

A RAND Corporation study of teachers' responses to No Child Left Behind did find evidence of a decline in teachers' morale as standardized testing proliferated.[11] Also, the overwhelming majority of elementary and middle school teachers reported that the state's accountability system leaves little time to teach content not on the state tests.[12] These findings echo complaints that have been voiced by numerous teachers and their unions. However, the same study also reported changes for the better in teachers' general focus on student learning; students' learning of important skills and knowledge; the academic rigor of the curriculum; and the teachers' own teaching practices.[13] The overwhelming majority of teachers agreed with the following statement: "Because of pressure to meet the AYP (Adequate Yearly Progress) target, I am focusing more on improving student achievement at my school."[14]

Despite the concerns of teachers and others, the overall legacy of No Child Left Behind may turn out to be positive and important. By requiring annual testing, the law places a spotlight on schools and school districts whose students are not making adequate progress. By insisting on publicly disclosed test results for key subgroups of students—blacks, Hispanics, the poor, English language learners—the law encourages a reallocation of resources to students who need help the most. By keeping the focus on results, the law promotes creative strategies for success rather than creative explanations for failure. By enforcing key provisions of the law, the Department of Education helps to prevent shirking by state and local officials.

In this book, we evaluate the operation of public bureaucracies—such as schools, school districts, and education departments—as policymaking organizations in the American democratic system. In this opening chapter, we provide an introduction to the book's basic approach, which is to use several social scientific theories to guide an inquiry into accountability and performance, two key standards by which agencies are judged. This introduction is organized around three *core questions*:

- *WHY ARE ACCOUNTABILITY AND PERFORMANCE IMPORTANT IN UNIQUE WAYS IN PUBLIC BUREAUCRACIES?* Although accountability is vital in all sectors of society, it takes on distinct meanings when authority is exercised by teachers and other public servants. Such decision makers are empowered to serve not shareholders or boards of directors but families and the public.

- *WHAT ARE THE DIFFERENT FORMS OF ACCOUNTABILITY, AND HOW HAVE THEIR USE AND EFFICACY CHANGED OVER TIME?* In recent years, elected officials at all levels of government have sought to make school systems more accountable to political, as opposed to professional, concerns. The imposition of such external standards has important implications for teacher quality, satisfaction, and retention, all of which are in turn linked closely with student achievement.

- *WHY HAS PERFORMANCE BECOME SUCH AN IMPORTANT STANDARD BY WHICH TO EVALUATE PUBLIC BUREAUCRACIES?* Outputs, such as the amount of instructional time devoted to reading, and outcomes, such as student performance on standardized tests and high school graduation rates, have long been vital to education policy. But measuring these facets of performance is difficult, and it is even harder to demonstrate an unambiguous link between specific school activities and the growth and development of different types of children.

In addressing these questions, the chapter lays the foundation for a systematic inquiry into public bureaucracies, organizations where some of society's most fundamental decisions are made.

## The Contours of Public Bureaucracy

As the uncertainty surrounding the ultimate effects of No Child Left Behind so vividly demonstrates, many of the policy decisions that most deeply affect people's lives are made within public bureaucracies. A **public bureaucracy** is an organization within the executive branch of government, whether at the federal, state, or local level. Such organizations run the gamut from the Federal Energy Regulatory Commission to the South Dakota Department of Game, Fish and Parks to the Integrated Waste Management Department of Orange County, California.

As Figure 1.1 illustrates, the federal executive branch consists of dozens of public bureaucracies. Fifteen of these bureaucracies are **cabinet departments,** including the Department of Homeland Security, the first addition to the cabinet since 1989. Some noncabinet bureaucracies are referred to as **independent agencies** as they are structured to operate with relative autonomy from White House authority. The Federal Reserve System is a prominent example of such an organization. Despite their designation, however, not all independent agencies actually enjoy such autonomy. For example, presidents of

# Figure 1.1 The Government of the United States

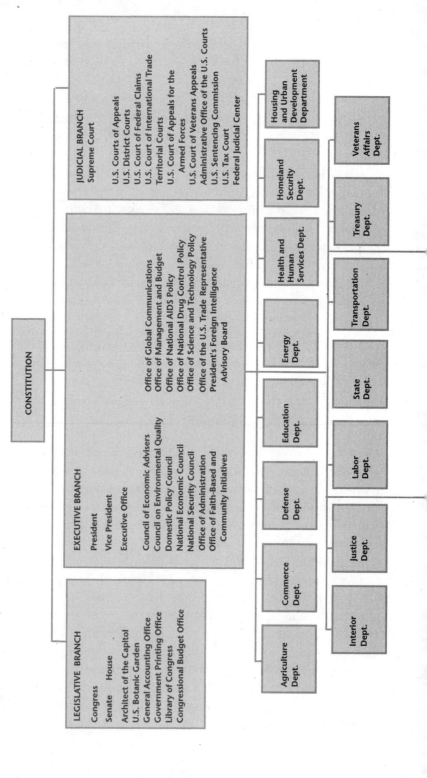

**CONSTITUTION**

**LEGISLATIVE BRANCH**

Congress

Senate    House

Architect of the Capitol
U.S. Botanic Garden
General Accounting Office
Government Printing Office
Library of Congress
Congressional Budget Office

**EXECUTIVE BRANCH**

President
Vice President
Executive Office

Council of Economic Advisers
Council on Environmental Quality
Domestic Policy Council
National Economic Council
National Security Council
Office of Administration
Office of Faith-Based and
  Community Initiatives
Office of Global Communications
Office of Management and Budget
Office of National AIDS Policy
Office of National Drug Control Policy
Office of Science and Technology Policy
Office of the U.S. Trade Representative
President's Foreign Intelligence
  Advisory Board

**JUDICIAL BRANCH**

Supreme Court

U.S. Courts of Appeals
U.S. District Courts
U.S. Court of Federal Claims
U.S. Court of International Trade
Territorial Courts
U.S. Court of Appeals for the
  Armed Forces
U.S. Court of Veterans Appeals
Administrative Office of the U.S. Courts
U.S. Sentencing Commission
U.S. Tax Court
Federal Judicial Center

Agriculture Dept.

Commerce Dept.

Defense Dept.

Education Dept.

Energy Dept.

Health and Human Services Dept.

Homeland Security Dept.

Housing and Urban Development Department

Interior Dept.

Justice Dept.

Labor Dept.

State Dept.

Transportation Dept.

Treasury Dept.

Veterans Affairs Dept.

## INDEPENDENT ESTABLISHMENTS AND GOVERNMENT CORPORATIONS

African Development Foundation
Central Intelligence Agency
Commodity Futures Trading Commission
Consumer Product Safety Commission
Corporation for National and
  Community Service
Defense Nuclear Facilities Safety Board
Environmental Protection Agency
Equal Employment Opportunity
  Commission
Export-Import Bank of the U.S.
Farm Credit Administration
Federal Communications Commission
Federal Deposit Insurance Corp.
Federal Election Commission
Federal Emergency Management Agency
Federal Housing Finance Board
Federal Labor Relations Authority
Federal Maritime Commission
Federal Mediation and Conciliation Service

Federal Mine Safety and Health
  Review Commission
Federal Reserve System
Federal Retirement Thrift Investment Board
Federal Trade Commission
General Services Administration
Inter-American Foundation
Merit Systems Protection Board
National Aeronautics and Space Administration
National Archives and Records Administration
National Capital Planning Commission
National Credit Union Administration
National Foundation on the Arts and
  the Humanities
National Labor Relations Board
National Mediation Board
National Railroad Passenger Corp. (Amtrak)
National Science Foundation
National Transportation Safety Board
Nuclear Regulatory Commission

Occupational Safety and Health Review
  Commission
Office of Government Ethics
Office of Personnel Management
Office of Special Counsel
Panama Canal Commission
Peace Corps
Pension Benefit Guaranty Corporation
Postal Rate Commission
Railroad Retirement Board
Securities and Exchange Commission
Selective Service System
Small Business Administration
Social Security Administration
Tennessee Valley Authority
Trade and Development Agency
U.S. Agency for International Development
U.S. Commission on Civil Rights
U.S. International Trade Commission
U.S. Postal Service

*Source: United States Government Manual, 2006–2007* (Washington, D.C.: Office of the Federal Register, Government Printing Office, June 1, 2006), 21.

all political stripes closely monitor and influence the priorities and decisions of the Environmental Protection Agency (EPA).

The Food and Drug Administration (FDA), created in 1906, is one of many important agencies located within the Department of Health and Human Services. The FDA's primary responsibility is to ensure the safety of the nation's food, drugs, and cosmetics. The FDA also inspects blood banks and biologics manufacturing firms. In addition, the agency monitors the safety of medical devices through its Bureau of Medical Devices. Figure 1.2 provides an overview of the FDA's organization. An administrator appointed by the president and confirmed by the Senate heads the FDA, overseeing a workforce of approximately 10,000 employees and a budget of about $2 billion.[15] Approximately 1,100 employees are investigators or inspectors who inspect about 15,000 facilities per year. The FDA's workforce is better educated than most, with more than 2,000 scientists on staff.

## Accountability and Performance in Public Bureaucracies

Because of the importance of their decisions, bureaucracies from the FDA to local school systems are accountable to a variety of individuals and organizations throughout government and society. These parties include political overseers, such as the president and city council members, as well as constituencies—parents, pharmaceutical users, and countless others—who are regulated or served by agencies.

Public bureaucracies are not unique in this regard. Business firms such as ExxonMobil and Home Depot must also answer to supervisors and clients, including their boards of directors and shareholders. Likewise, nonprofit organizations, such as the American Red Cross and Ford Foundation, are held accountable to their boards of directors and to the beneficiaries of their services. Unlike these other organizations, however, government agencies also bear the burden of being institutions of American democracy. In democratic institutions, **accountability** to the American public and its elected representatives is a vital and unique concern. It would be troubling, in other words, if policy were made by officials with little or no connection to the public.

Accountability in democratic policymaking is often viewed through the lens of **fairness.** According to this viewpoint, all parties desiring to participate in particular decision-making processes should be given the opportunity to make their preferences known.[16] This principle is embodied in the **Administrative Procedure Act,** the statute governing the process through which agencies formulate many of their most important policy decisions. This statute

# Figure 1.2 Organizational Chart of the Food and Drug Administration

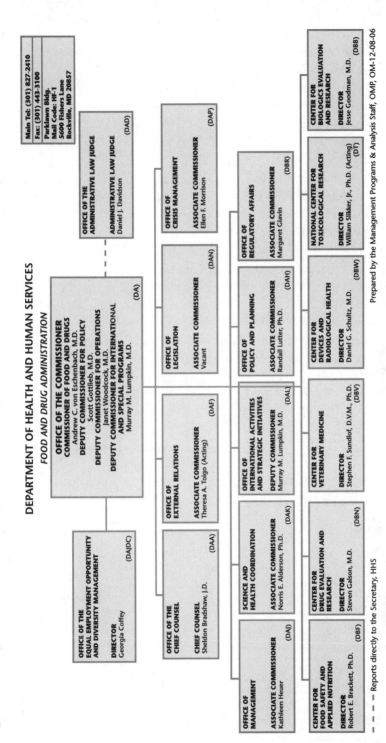

## DEPARTMENT OF HEALTH AND HUMAN SERVICES
### FOOD AND DRUG ADMINISTRATION

Main Tel: (301) 827-2410
Fax: (301) 443-3100
Parklawn Bldg.
Mail Code: HF-1
5600 Fishers Lane
Rockville, MD 20857

**OFFICE OF THE COMMISSIONER**
COMMISSIONER OF FOOD AND DRUGS
Andrew C. von Eschenbach, M.D.
DEPUTY COMMISSIONER FOR POLICY
Scott Gottlieb, M.D.
DEPUTY COMMISSIONER FOR OPERATIONS
Janet Woodcock, M.D.
DEPUTY COMMISSIONER FOR INTERNATIONAL
AND SPECIAL PROGRAMS
Murray M. Lumpkin, M.D. (DA)

**OFFICE OF THE ADMINISTRATIVE LAW JUDGE**
ADMINISTRATIVE LAW JUDGE
Daniel J. Davidson (DAD)

**OFFICE OF THE EQUAL EMPLOYMENT OPPORTUNITY AND DIVERSITY MANAGEMENT**
DIRECTOR
Georgia Coffey (DA|DC)

**OFFICE OF CRISIS MANAGEMENT**
ASSOCIATE COMMISSIONER
Ellen F. Morrison (DAP)

**OFFICE OF LEGISLATION**
ASSOCIATE COMMISSIONER
Vacant (DAN)

**OFFICE OF EXTERNAL RELATIONS**
ASSOCIATE COMMISSIONER
Theresa A. Toigo (Acting) (DAF)

**OFFICE OF THE CHIEF COUNSEL**
CHIEF COUNSEL
Sheldon Bradshaw, J.D. (DAA)

**OFFICE OF REGULATORY AFFAIRS**
ASSOCIATE COMMISSIONER
Margaret Glavin (DBR)

**OFFICE OF POLICY AND PLANNING**
ASSOCIATE COMMISSIONER
Randall Lutter, Ph.D. (DAH)

**OFFICE OF INTERNATIONAL ACTIVITIES AND STRATEGIC INITIATIVES**
DEPUTY COMMISSIONER
Murray M. Lumpkin, M.D. (DAL)

**SCIENCE AND HEALTH COORDINATION**
ASSOCIATE COMMISSIONER
Norris E. Alderson, Ph.D. (DAK)

**NATIONAL CENTER FOR TOXICOLOGICAL RESEARCH**
DIRECTOR
William Slikker, Jr., Ph.D. (Acting) (DT)

**CENTER FOR DEVICES AND RADIOLOGICAL HEALTH**
DIRECTOR
Daniel G. Schultz, M.D. (DBW)

**CENTER FOR VETERINARY MEDICINE**
DIRECTOR
Stephen F. Sundlof, D.V.M., Ph.D. (DBV)

**CENTER FOR DRUG EVALUATION AND RESEARCH**
DIRECTOR
Steven Galson, M.D. (DBN)

**OFFICE OF MANAGEMENT**
ASSOCIATE COMMISSIONER
Kathleen Heuer (DAJ)

**CENTER FOR FOOD SAFETY AND APPLIED NUTRITION**
DIRECTOR
Robert E. Brackett, Ph.D. (DBF)

**CENTER FOR BIOLOGICS EVALUATION AND RESEARCH**
DIRECTOR
Jesse Goodman, M.D. (DBB)

Prepared by the Management Programs & Analysis Staff, OMP, OM-12-08-06

– – – Reports directly to the Secretary, HHS

*Source:* Food and Drug Administration, www.fda.gov/oc/orgcharts/fda,pdf, February 15, 2007.

generally requires agencies to allow interested parties the opportunity to comment on proposed courses of action.

Like democracy itself, this approach to bureaucratic policymaking often proves cumbersome and untidy. Many agency proposals are highly controversial, take an exceedingly.long time to develop, and are ultimately met with vociferous opposition.[17] These difficulties raise a second fundamental standard that agencies are called upon to meet—performance.

As with accountability, performance in democratic institutions often means something very different from what it means in the context of other types of organizations. In the business world, performance is tracked through well-established indicators such as market shares and stock prices. Appropriate indicators also exist in the nonprofit sector, where the performances of foundations, hospitals, and colleges and universities are routinely measured and compared with those of similar institutions.

Yet such indicators are not always as useful as we would like them to be. As we have already highlighted, performance in education policy is difficult to assess, even with instruments such as report cards and standardized tests. Similar difficulties hold in other policy areas. How is the performance of the FDA to be judged? By the speed with which it approves new drug requests? But haste could be dangerous or even deadly. By the care with which it reviews new drug requests? But unwarranted delays could harm both pharmaceutical companies and consumers. The FDA, like many other bureaucracies, has competing goals that are sometimes difficult to reconcile.[18] These difficulties in turn make it hard for politicians and others to judge the agency's performance. Furthermore, even if one agreed on the relative importance of agency goals, many goals are notoriously difficult to measure. For example, it typically takes years to determine the safety of products on the market. At what point is evidence of product safety "hard" enough to be reliable? Also, some products reduce the risk of one ailment while elevating the risk of another. Is a product "safe" if it reduces health risks for one disease more often than it increases health risks for something else? These are among the many challenges of performance measurement.

Although it may be tough to judge accountability and performance in public bureaucracies, this task is crucial given the vital role agencies play in the policymaking process. Equally crucial is the need to carry out this evaluation in a systematic manner. With this in mind, we approach the bureaucracy from four distinct perspectives, which deal with the people who work inside executive branch agencies, the political actors who serve as the bureaucracy's supervisors, the clients whom agencies regulate and serve, and the conflict and cooperation that occur both within the bureaucracy and between agencies and other types of organizations. To better understand these facets of bureaucracy and their implications for accountability and performance, we draw on insights from four prominent social scientific frameworks—bounded rationality, principal-agent theory, interest group mobilization, and network theory. Before applying these frameworks to particular aspects of bureaucratic policymaking, we first lay out in greater detail what accountability and performance mean in the context of the executive branch so that the nature of the task at hand becomes fully apparent.

## Accountability and Its Many Faces

Accountability, like peace and motherhood, is one of those wonderful words that instantly evoke all sorts of positive images. But what exactly does it mean? In thinking about accountability within the executive branch, it is useful to distinguish between the source of control over agencies—internal or external—and the degree of control over agency actions—high or low.[19] As Figure 1.3 illustrates, there are four possibilities: **bureaucratic accountability,** where effective control emanates from within the executive branch; **legal accountability,** where control from the outside is effective; **professional accountability,** where internal structures and processes produce low levels of control; and **political accountability,** where control is external and limited. These distinctions can be summed up in this way:

> Under the bureaucratic system, expectations are managed through a hierarchical arrangement based on supervisory relationships; the legal accountability system manages agency expectations through a contractual relationship; the professional system relies on deference to expertise; while the political accountability system promotes responsiveness to constituents as the central means of managing the multiple expectations.[20]

In practice, these distinctions are not always borne out. For example, political control via instruments such as legislative oversight is not necessarily less potent than legal control through statutory requirements.[21] In the early 1990s, in a not uncommon chain of events, the Health Care Financing Administration (now the Centers for Medicare and Medicaid Services) made significant changes to its rules on Medicare physician payments after its administrator was dressed down at a congressional committee hearing.[22] It is also not always the case that professional norms and standards exert less

**Figure 1.3 Forms of Executive Branch Accountability**

### Source of Control over Agency

| | | Internal | External |
|---|---|---|---|
| **Degree of Control over Agency** | *High* | Bureaucratic accountability | Legal accountability |
| | *Low* | Professional accountability | Political accountability |

*Source:* Barbara Romzek and Melvin Dubnick, "Accountability in the Public Sector: Lessons from the Challenger Tragedy," *Public Administration Review* 47 (May/June 1987): 227–238. Used with permission.

influence over agency behavior than hierarchical supervision within the bureaucracy.[23] Over the past several decades, the influx of economists into the federal workforce has had a dramatic effect on how agencies assess the impact of their regulations, socially as well as economically.

Because of such complications, policymakers must think very carefully when promoting a particular form of accountability. A decision to emphasize one form of accountability over another can have significant consequences. At times it can even spell the difference between life and death. On January 28, 1986, the National Aeronautics and Space Administration (NASA) defied the views of engineers who warned that the Space Shuttle *Challenger* was not fit to be launched that day. Despite concerns that O-rings, or seals, would fail to function properly if temperatures were too low, the agency succumbed to political pressure to launch the vehicle more or less on schedule. The *Challenger* exploded not long after takeoff, and its seven-member crew, including schoolteacher Christa McAuliffe, perished in the accident. By substituting political accountability for professional accountability in a situation in which technical judgments were absolutely crucial, the agency made a fatal mistake.[24]

## The Evolution of Accountability

During the latter half of the twentieth century, accountability emerged as a dominant concern among both policymakers and those outside government. Some bureaucracies, such as the now-defunct Interstate Commerce Commission, were viewed as runaway agencies, beyond the control of elected officials and ordinary citizens. In 1966, in response to such concerns, Congress passed the **Freedom of Information Act,** aimed at making the government's information more readily available to the public. Ten years later the **Government in the Sunshine Act** specified that most federal commission meetings must be open to interested parties from outside government. Congress did not stop there. It also created inspectors general in most cabinet departments to serve as internal watchdogs over agency officials and passed "whistle-blower" legislation to protect federal employees who expose illegal or inappropriate behavior by others in the bureaucracy. While all of this was going on, congressional oversight of the executive branch was becoming more frequent and more intense.[25]

At the state level, similar developments were under way.[26] Many states passed their own freedom of information acts and sunshine laws. Across the country, states enacted legislation requiring the appointment of a public or consumer representative to occupational licensing boards. Most states created offices of consumer counsel to act as advocates for ratepayers in public utility commission proceedings. The overwhelming majority of states established a nursing home ombudsman's office to represent residents before governmental and nongovernmental organizations. Furthermore, many states enacted legislative veto provisions that facilitated political oversight of administrative rules and sunset laws that terminated relatively small agencies on a fixed date unless the legislature intervened.

The overall thrust of these reforms was to make the executive branch more accountable to politicians and to citizens or their surrogates. These reforms, in other words, emphasized external sources of control over bureaucratic and professional approaches. Whereas the Progressives had sought to insulate the bureaucracy from politics during the early days of the twentieth century, reformers in the 1960s, 1970s, and 1980s saw insulation as the problem to be solved. To put it differently, these three decades saw an era of "watchful eye" reforms aimed at curbing the bureaucracy.[27] Other reform movements, such as scientific management in the early twentieth century and liberation management in the 1990s, placed greater faith in bureaucratic discretion and internal sources of control.

## The Limits of Accountability

Just as the quest for particular forms of accountability has ebbed and flowed over the years, it has also varied across agencies, depending especially on the complexity of the issues the agency must resolve. For agencies dealing with highly complex issues, both politicians and judges have been more willing to delegate authority and defer to the agency's technical expertise.[28] For instance, financial regulatory agencies, such as the Securities and Exchange Commission, often enjoy more autonomy than most agencies in part because of the arcane nature of their jurisdictions.

Such independence enables skilled, creative leaders to manage their agencies more effectively than would otherwise be possible. For example, during the 1990s, Alan Greenspan, then chairman of the Federal Reserve Board, was widely credited with using his extraordinary influence over the nation's monetary policy to help propel the economy into one of its most robust periods of growth ever.[29] Although Greenspan's effectiveness was derived in no small part from his personal credibility and experience,[30] his agency's independence from Congress and the president enabled him to pursue his vision of sound monetary policy without interference and distraction.

Complexity alone does not account for the enormous power vested in some agencies. Political factors play a central role as well. The interests regulated by the Securities and Exchange Commission—brokerage firms, investment banks, mutual funds, and stock exchanges, to name a few—are quite diverse and generally at odds with one another.[31] Given this conflict, members of Congress find it desirable to empower the agency and, in the process, avoid the inevitable wrath of those parties that come out on the losing end of securities policy. If the agency's political environment were less contentious, then Congress might insist on a greater measure of political or legal, as opposed to professional, accountability.

A final factor to consider is the tradeoff between accountability today and accountability in the future.[32] In democratic politics, the majority is never more than an election away from being banished to minority status. When such a shift occurs, the bureaucracy naturally falls under the domain of a new majority. Fearful that this shift will bring about a fundamental change in the political pressure exerted on the executive branch, the existing majority has an incentive to insulate agencies from outside sources of control. This incentive is especially strong when the existing majority has only a tenuous grip on the reins of power. During such times, great emphasis is placed on bureaucratic and professional accountability, and agencies are loaded with cumbersome structures and procedures. For example, some agencies are given restrictive mandates and are located within the executive branch in places relatively impervious to external influence. In the end, the lack of political and legal accountability decried by officials from across the ideological spectrum owes its existence not only to factors internal to the bureaucracy but to the dictates of electoral politics as well.

## The Push for Performance

In the 1990s the concept of **performance** came to rival accountability as a standard for evaluating executive branch agencies. On its own merits, performance is important in democratic institutions, as the public is well served by government organizations that operate effectively and produce generally acceptable results. Performance is also of concern because it is intimately connected with accountability. To take one example, agencies subjected to particularly strict forms of political accountability may find it difficult to take sufficient advantage of their expertise and specialization. In recent years, scores of teachers have expressed deep dissatisfaction with an ongoing erosion of their classroom autonomy, arguing that this erosion stifles not only their instructional efforts but also the learning possibilities of many of their students.

Like accountability, performance can be defined and measured in a variety of ways. One approach is to focus on the activities, or **outputs,** over which agencies exert direct control. For an organization such as the EPA, outputs include the number of inspections conducted and the amount of monetary fines imposed. Another approach is to pay attention to the results, or **outcomes,** that agencies seek to bring about. Examples include cleaner air, lower poverty, safer workplaces, less disease, and more employment. A third approach is to focus on the effects of agency outputs on societal outcomes, controlling for other factors—economic growth, to name one—that play an important role in shaping such outcomes.

Managing for results is not an entirely new idea. The Wizard of Oz, for example, was an early believer in this managerial strategy. When Dorothy, the Scarecrow, the Tin Man, and the Cowardly Lion came to the Emerald City and submitted some very specific requests, the Wizard had some choices. He could have simply acceded to their requests on the spot, which would not have challenged these highly resourceful individuals to do their very best. Or he could have told them to compile statistics on how many miles they had traveled along the Yellow Brick Road. But instead he told them, "Bring me the broomstick of the Wicked Witch of the West!" In other words: Produce results, and I will grant your requests! Which they did, and which he did too.

Just as accountability is multidimensional, so too is performance. Consider, by way of example, the distinction between routine performance and behavior during a crisis. A given agency may do well when handling routine tasks but may stumble when called upon to confront a novel challenge or situation. Most observers acknowledge that the U.S. Postal Service is a remarkably efficient and productive organization.[33] In part, the agency's success derives from the nature of its fundamental task, which is unambiguous and easy for all to see. When it comes to delivering the mail under normal, relatively favorable conditions, then, letter carriers and clerks perform well.

But what about when the agency suddenly found itself confronting mail contaminated by potentially deadly anthrax spores? On October 15, 2001, a letter that had passed through a District of Columbia postal processing facility, on its way to the office of Sen. Tom Daschle, D-S.D., tested positive for anthrax. When postal workers expressed concern and asked whether they should take antibiotics, their supervisors told them antibiotics would not be necessary.[34] At a press conference, Postmaster General John Potter offered reassurances that the contaminated letter posed little, if any, threat to postal or congressional employees. Tragically, however, two postal workers died within a week, and many others found themselves potentially at risk.[35] In fairness to the postmaster general, he got much of his advice from the Centers for Disease Control and Prevention, whose scientists drew inappropriate conclusions from the limited evidence available to them. Regardless, the decision not to administer antibiotics proved to be a fatal error in a time of crisis for a normally effective organization.

A related distinction exists between **policymaking** and **implementation.** An agency such as the Social Security Administration (SSA) may perform well because its central task is routine—distributing checks to retirees and other program recipients. When performing roles such as this one, agencies implement policies established elsewhere in government. An agency can, without too much difficulty, develop procedures for effectively delivering resources to beneficiaries. If Congress specifies social security legislation in sufficient detail, then the SSA need not fret about bigger, more difficult policy concerns.

Other agencies make policy all the time, a much harder task to perform well. For example, the EPA takes many important actions each year. In fiscal year 2006 alone the agency issued forty-two rules considered particularly significant.[36] These rules, which have the full force of law, ultimately determine the cleanliness of air, ground, and water, as well as who bears the costs of providing these public goods. Although the agency's enforcement practices have their own difficulties, it is generally easier to conduct an inspection or even to organize a cluster of inspections than to develop a rule from scratch.

Distinguishing between **efficiency** and **equity** as operational manifestations of performance is also important. For decades, state welfare agencies were free to set benefit levels but were not free to deny services to eligible clients. With the passage of the Personal Responsibility and Work Opportunity Reconciliation Act of 1996, these agencies were, for the first time, granted the discretion to decide who gets services and who does not. Such judgments, which determine how equitable welfare policies will be, require agency officials to make the tough decisions previously made by state legislators and other elected politicians. To further complicate matters, equity can be defined in many different ways. The distinction between equality of opportunity and equality in outcomes is just one dimension that must be considered. The end result of all of this is that it is tougher to measure equity than to gauge efficiency, and it is exceedingly difficult to reconcile competing views of how resources should be allocated across society. As this discussion implies, performance cannot be meaningfully separated from the values that make up the core of American democracy.

## The Government Performance and Results Act

Given the centrality of performance in democratic policymaking, the federal government has for some time experimented with management reforms aimed at rationalizing the allocation of scarce resources. These experiments—with names such as "management by objectives" and "zero-base budgeting"—have been roundly criticized as fads long on symbolism and short on substance.[37] Despite these reforms, critics have contended, federal budgeting continues to be incremental in nature, with powerful interests blocking any significant departure from the status quo.

The enactment of the **Government Performance and Results Act** (GPRA) in 1993 struck some observers as a more promising development. Unlike other management reforms, put forth by the executive branch alone, GPRA was a law with bipartisan support from both the legislative and executive branches. GPRA also differed from previous reform efforts in that it allowed agencies several years to develop and implement strategic plans and performance measures and reports. After the initial incubation period, these documents were to be used by the executive and legislative branches in making budgetary decisions. According to one interpretation, agencies that performed poorly would get less, while agencies that performed well would get more. According to another interpretation, performance measures and reports would help policymakers redesign failing programs and learn from successful ones.

In implementing GPRA's early requirements, most agencies were successful in meeting congressional deadlines for producing various documents, but few were successful in actually measuring results. For example, the Department of Housing and Urban Development collected and reported data on uncollected rents but not on housing quality, thus severely limiting its ability to measure the performance of its public housing program. Other agencies, such as the Forest Service, struggled with conflicting goals (producing timber versus sustaining wildlife, for example), which made it difficult to measure overall success. Four years after GPRA's enactment, the **Government Accountability Office** (GAO) characterized the law's implementation as "uneven."[38]

Two years after this characterization, in 1999, the GAO concluded that "moderate" improvements had been made but that "key weaknesses" remained.[39] A few agencies, such as the Department of Transportation, Department of Education, and Department of Justice, had assembled credible performance information. But most agencies still struggled with conceptual and methodological issues. Despite GPRA's emphasis on shifting from outputs to outcomes, many agencies continued to measure outputs (for example, the number of clients enrolled in a program) rather than outcomes (the impact of enrollment on health, employment, or some other desired result). For example, the Medicaid program's goals for the Department of Health and Human Services include process measures (assisting states in conducting payment accuracy studies, participating with the states in the Performance Measurement Partnership Project, improving the quality of nursing home surveys) and output measures (increases in child immunization rates, increases in State Children's Health Insurance Program enrollment rates, reducing the use of restraints in nursing homes) but only one outcome measure (reducing pressure ulcers in nursing homes).[40]

Some of the biggest challenges confront agencies with significant intergovernmental relationships. This is because intergovernmental grant programs tend to be more flexible with respect to data gathering and outcome measurement than other government programs.[41] This flexibility makes it more difficult for the federal government to assess success. The EPA, for example, depends on states to implement numerous programs aimed at reducing water pollution. Because states measure water quality in many different ways, it is difficult for the agency to know how much progress has been made over time and across different areas of the country. Even within the same region, states use different sampling methods to determine water quality. Within New England, Rhode Island samples all of its waters every two years, while New Hampshire focuses its efforts on problematic waters. Other states sample one-fifth of all their waters annually.

Similarly, the Department of Health and Human Services relies upon states to measure progress in areas such as welfare reform, child support enforcement, and access to health care services. For such programs, the data the agency supplies to Congress are only as good as the data generated by the states. Definitional variations present problems here as well. For example, the Centers for Medicare and Medicaid Services allows states to define what constitutes "full immunization" for a two-year-old child when reporting such data to the federal government. Again, in New England, states differ from each other in how many shots each requires before children are considered fully immunized. As Table 1.1 illustrates, Vermont does not require two-year-olds to receive the hepatitis B vaccine, while Massachusetts, New Hampshire, and Rhode Island call for three such immunizations.

Although the GAO has criticized the executive branch for implementing GPRA in a poor and uneven fashion, the truth is that Congress deserves at least some of the blame. With few exceptions, legislators have ignored performance data, even from agencies that have produced relatively useful and complete information. In the end, congressional appropriators continue to pay little or no attention to GPRA reports when making resource allocations.

## The Program Assessment Rating Tool

More than most presidents, George W. Bush has exhibited a keen interest in linking performance measures to budgetary decisions. His most important contribution to performance management within the federal government has been the creation of the **Program Assessment Rating Tool** (PART), administered by the **Office of Management and Budget** (OMB), which helps the president oversee the preparation of the federal budget and the making of executive branch regulations. Beginning in fiscal year 2003, OMB has annually

## Table 1.1 "Full Immunization" of Two-Year-Old Children, New England States

| | Diphtheria, Tetanus, and Pertussis | Injectable or Oral Polio Vaccine | Mumps, Measles, and Rubella | Hemophilus Influenza Type B | Hepatitis B Vaccine | Varicella Zoster Vaccine |
|---|---|---|---|---|---|---|
| Connecticut | 4 | 3 | 1 | 3 | 2 | 0 |
| Maine | 4 | 3 | 1 | 1 | 2 | 0 |
| Massachusetts | 4 | 3 | 1 | 1 | 3 | 0 |
| New Hampshire | 4 | 3 | 1 | 3 | 3 | 0 |
| Rhode Island | 4 | 3 | 1 | 4 | 3 | 0 |
| Vermont | 4 | 3 | 1 | 4 | 0 | 0 |

*Source:* Centers for Medicare and Medicaid Services, "Government Performance and Results Act: Immunization of Medicaid Two-Year-Old Children" (Baltimore, Md.: CMS, July 2002). Also Karen Halverson, Vermont Department of Health, e-mail communication with Gormley, July 23, 2002.

*Note:* The numbers indicate how many shots or other forms of immunization are required for two-year-olds to satisfy the state's definition of what constitutes "full immunization."

rated federal programs as effective, moderately effective, adequate, ineffective, or "results not yet demonstrated." In putting together these ratings, OMB has sought to explicitly incorporate performance measures into its budgetary decision making.[42]

Through PART, OMB examiners have been able to encourage program managers to develop better measures of program success. In contrast with GPRA, there is much more emphasis on adopting authentic outcome measures.[43] Also in contrast with GPRA, there is a stronger commitment to a link between program assessments and budget decisions. Departments with a substantial proportion of programs rated "results not yet demonstrated" have been told that their budgets might be reduced—a powerful incentive to develop appropriate measures of program success! As a result, the proportion of programs rated "results not yet demonstrated" has declined over the years.[44] Of graded programs, grades have increased more often than they have decreased.[45]

According to John Gilmour and David Lewis, PART scores have had an impact on OMB's budget decisions. Specifically, programs with higher PART scores receive larger budget increases. The impact seems to be greater for small and medium-sized programs than for large programs.[46] However, the "results" component of PART contributes less to budget decisions than other elements of the total PART score. Also, some evidence suggests that PART scores matter more for "traditionally Democratic departments" than for other departments.[47] If so, it would seem that PART has been politicized to some degree. In short, PART has enabled the executive branch of the federal government to link program assessments to budget decisions, but that link still needs improvement.

## Agency Reputations in the Real World

Although the quest for systematic measures of performance has developed considerable momentum in recent years, perceptions of bureaucratic performance still depend in large part on soft judgments rather than hard data, on intuitions rather than indicators. To put it differently, a revolution in data generation does not guarantee a revolution in data utilization. Sometimes a vivid story matters more than a well-designed chart or graph. Sometimes a clever phrase or a lovable mascot proves more effective than a thick document chock full of statistics.

In a world where bureaucratic reputations are at times only loosely linked to actual performance, several points should be made about how agencies are perceived. First, perceptions vary dramatically. Those who must pay taxes have a rather different view of the Internal Revenue Service (IRS) than those who prepare tax returns for a living. Among the latter, 61 percent believe the IRS does a good or excellent job. Among the former, only 40 percent give the IRS such a rating. To cite another example, 68 percent of environmental advocates believe the EPA does a good or excellent job. In contrast, only 41 percent of business managers give the agency such a rating.[48]

Second, perceptions change, sometimes very quickly. As Frank Sinatra sang, you can be "riding high in April, shot down in May." Consider the case of the Securities and Exchange Commission (SEC), once regarded as the crème de la crème of federal regulatory agencies.[49] In 2002, following accounting scandals at Enron and other corporations, some observers accused the SEC of being "asleep at the wheel."[50] They singled out its chairman, Harvey Pitt, for meeting with corporate executives whose firms were being investigated for securities fraud and for requesting that the SEC be elevated to cabinet status. Congress rejected, and even President Bush disavowed, this request, which would have boosted Pitt's salary by nearly $30,000.[51] Not long after these episodes, Pitt stepped down as SEC chairman under great pressure from an administration embarrassed by his missteps and bent on shoring up perceptions of its ability to manage the economy effectively.

Bureaucratic reputations can also change for the better. In 2003 NASA was widely seen as an agency in disarray. Early that year, the Space Shuttle *Columbia* disintegrated during reentry, claiming the lives of all seven crew members and leaving the future of manned space exploration in doubt. Two years later, though, the agency's reputation began to turn around with the appointment of Michael D. Griffin as NASA administrator. One of Griffin's first moves was to replace the majority of NASA's top civil servants, a move that prompted one observer to state: "It's a rare moment when you get a housecleaning like this. It could presage a strong turnaround for an agency that's been adrift for years if not decades."[52] These internal changes were quickly followed by external evidence of success, most notably the return to flight of the shuttle fleet in the summer of 2005. In a broader sense, Griffin's "messianic vision" has rekindled confidence in some quarters that NASA has the ability to spearhead human exploration of the moon, Mars, and the solar system beyond.[53]

Third, perceptions can be manipulated. Many agencies have their own publicity machines and work hard at generating both diffuse and specific support. A century ago, the Forest Service was particularly successful at generating political support. By mailing out more than 9 million circulars annually, the Forest Service created a highly favorable image for itself in the public's mind.[54] The agency then helped sustain this image by conjuring up a marvelous "spokesman"—the legendary Smokey Bear, who is depicted in action in Figure 1.4. In similar fashion, state health agencies have recently generated popular support for the Children's Health Insurance Program by linking their programs to popular local symbols, such as the badger (Wisconsin) or the husky (Connecticut).

Fourth, perceptions matter. By winning the support of most Progressive magazines and newspapers, the Postal Service was able to convince Congress to establish a postal savings system in 1910.[55] For years the Federal Bureau of Investigation enjoyed a reputation for no-nonsense, vigorous law enforcement that enabled the agency to augment its budget and staff. Movies and television shows celebrating G-men and their crusade against gangsters such as Al Capone enabled the agency to fare well on Capitol Hill, even when times were tight. For example, J. Edgar Hoover received congressional authorization to establish a Division of Identification and Information in 1930, right in the heart of the Great Depression.[56] More recently, a positive image helped the FDA win passage of user fee legislation, which requires pharmaceutical and biotechnology companies to pay the agency to review new drug applications.[57] As this example illustrates, perceptions are not wholly separate from actual

**Figure 1.4  1956 Poster of Smokey Bear**

*Source:* Forest Service, USDA. The name and character of Smokey Bear are the property of the United States, as provided by 16 U.S.C. 580p-1 and 18 U.S.C. 711, and are used with the permission of the Forest Service, U.S. Department of Agriculture.

performance, as the user fees collected by the FDA played a key role in helping the agency cut its average approval time nearly in half during the mid-1990s.

## Accountability and Performance: Theories and Applications

Thus far the discussion has emphasized that accountability and performance are multifaceted concepts of fundamental importance when it comes to evaluating the place of executive branch bureaucracies in the American democratic system. A number of questions remain, however: How are accountability and performance best judged, given their significance and complexity? Are there theories of politics and organizations that might provide particular insight into various aspects of accountability and performance? In the end, what general lessons can be learned about the determinants of both bureaucratic successes and failures? These questions motivate the chapters that follow.

Our basic orientation is to evaluate accountability and performance not through impressions and anecdotes, however telling these may sometimes be, but through systematic analysis. As summarized in Table 1.2 (and noted earlier in the chapter), we consider the bureaucracy from four different perspectives, in each instance drawing on a well-known social scientific theory especially well equipped to shed light on at least one facet of accountability and performance. We then apply the lessons learned from this exercise to case studies of particular agencies and issues to bring the implications of the disparate frameworks together in the context of actual agency experiences. We conclude by offering some general rules of thumb about the prospects for bureaucratic accountability and performance in light of the unique place occupied by administrative agencies in American democracy.

Chapter 2 focuses on the bureaucracy's people, from the secretaries who head cabinet departments to the teachers and other public servants with whom citizens have direct, sometimes daily, contact. We approach the behavior of these officials through the lens of **bounded rationality**. The basic premise holds that although individuals in organizations are rational, they do not comprehensively assess the benefits and costs of all, or even most, of their possible courses of action. Rather, decision makers seek to **satisfice**—that is, to arrive at outcomes that, while not necessarily ideal, are nonetheless quite satisfactory. Bounded rationality draws our attention to shortcuts, such as problem disaggregation and standard operating procedures, which are routinely a part of bureaucratic decision making.

Chapter 3 turns our attention to the bureaucracy's bosses, from the president all the way down to local officials. All of these actors routinely delegate

**Table 1.2  Evaluating Bureaucratic Accountability and Performance**

| | Theoretical framework | | | |
| --- | --- | --- | --- | --- |
| | *Bounded Rationality* | *Principal-agent theory* | *Interest group mobilization* | *Network theory* |
| Aspect of bureaucratic accountability and Performance | The bureaucracy's people | Bureaucratic supervisors | Agency clients | Conflict and cooperation |
| Form of accountability emphasized | Bureaucratic and professional | Political and legal | Political | Bureaucratic |
| Key performance value | Problem solving | Policymaking and implementation | Responsiveness to constituents | Coordination and influence across organizations |
| Some important structures and processes | Specialization, standard operating procedures, authority, socialization | Institutional design, oversight, appropriations, appointments | Direct lobbying, grassroots, legislative support | Grants-in-aid, public-private partnerships, interagency meetings |
| Social science roots | Psychology, public administration | Economics, political science | Political science | Sociology, public administration |

policymaking authority to the bureaucracy. Delegation is essential given the scope and complexity of contemporary government, yet it also raises the possibility that the agencies charged with making and implementing public decisions may serve their own interests rather than those of the citizenry and its elected representatives. According to **principal-agent theory,** the key for the bureaucracy's bosses is to design agencies wisely and to carefully monitor the behavior of executive branch actors. Although there are a variety of ways in which these tasks can be accomplished, no particular strategy is foolproof in limiting agency freedom.

Chapter 4 also focuses on actors external to the bureaucracy—the individuals and organizations that agencies regulate and protect. For these clients, the consequences of bureaucratic policymaking vary over time and across issues. Importantly, the distribution of benefits and costs affects the mobilization of interest groups and the general public. At times, benefits accrue to small segments of society, such as specific businesses and industries, while costs are spread widely across the population. In these situations, organized interests, but not broad societal forces, are compelled to bring their influence to bear on government agencies through **interest group mobilization.** Although it is widely thought that the prevalence of such situations has declined in recent decades, interest groups certainly continue to play a central role in shaping public policy.

In Chapter 5 we return to the bureaucracy itself and consider how agencies interact with one another, and with other organizations, through a variety of **networks.** These networks include intergovernmental partnerships in areas such as environmental protection, collaborations between agencies and nongovernmental organizations, and interagency structures such as the president's cabinet. By linking network theory to what is sometimes known as the tools approach, we gain an understanding of how networks actually operate. In general, the use and efficacy of networks are topics of emerging importance for understanding accountability and performance in the executive branch.

Chapter 6 assesses the utility of the four theoretical perspectives by applying each of them to the management of three types of disasters—an unprecedented disaster (the September 11, 2001, terrorist attacks); a disaster with ample precedent (Hurricane Katrina); and a disaster that has not yet taken place (an avian flu pandemic). Because these high-stakes cases are extremely challenging, both conceptually and logistically, they run the risk of portraying the bureaucracy in an unfavorable light. Nevertheless, these cases are undeniably important in evaluating bureaucratic accountability and performance. If the theoretical perspectives are useful, they ought to help us understand and analyze what went wrong, what went right, and (most important) why. They may also help us to do a better job of preparing for future disasters.

Finally, in Chapter 7 we consider the factors, including accountability, that account for variations in executive branch performance. In doing so, we rely on evaluations of dozens of federal agencies that have been carried out in recent years. These ratings are then used to support a series of general propositions regarding the root causes of bureaucratic successes and failures.

As we view bureaucratic accountability and performance from all of these perspectives, it will become apparent that the executive branch is a dynamic collection of organizations that perform, in some instances better than others, innumerable vital functions in the American political system. Along the way we will hear directly from four well-known public servants—James Baker III, Dan Glickman, Donna Shalala, and Dick Thornburgh—who have run federal agencies under several presidential administrations. Through their stories, the bureaucracy will be brought to life in a way that complements our effort to think systematically about the internal and external workings of executive branch organizations.

## Key Terms

Accountability, 8
Administrative Procedure Act, 8
Bounded rationality, 24
Bureaucratic accountability, 11
Cabinet departments, 5
Efficiency, 17
Equity, 17
Fairness, 8
Freedom of Information Act, 13
Government Accountability
   Office, 18
Government in the Sunshine
   Act, 13
Government Performance and
   Results Act, 17
High-stakes testing, 1
Implementation, 16
Independent agencies, 5

Interest group mobilization, 26
Legal accountability, 11
Networks, 26
No Child Left Behind Act, 1
Office of Management and
   Budget, 19
Outcomes, 15
Outputs, 15
Performance, 15
Policymaking, 16
Political accountability, 11
Principal-agent theory, 26
Professional accountability, 11
Program Assessment Rating
   Tool, 19
Public bureaucracy, 5
Satisfice, 24
Teach to the test, 3

# 2 | Bureaucratic Reasoning

WHEN A STATE CHILD CARE INSPECTOR visits a day care center and finds some routine problems, it is relatively easy to know what to do. Consider, for example, the following hypothetical scenario presented to state child care inspectors in Colorado, North Carolina, Oklahoma, and Pennsylvania:

> You visit the Little Flower Day Care Center for a renewal visit and discover that one of the toilets is overflowing onto the bathroom floor. The center director is already aware of the situation and has called a plumber. Before you leave, the plumber has arrived and fixed the problem.

A majority of child care inspectors in each of the four states would talk with the director; a majority in three of the four states would place a record in the center's file.[1] For this particular problem, there is a strong consensus on how to proceed. Child care regulators in all four states have developed similar **standard operating procedures** to follow when they encounter an isolated code violation that does not pose a serious threat to the health and safety of children.

Many other kinds of agencies have also developed standard operating procedures for dealing in a consistent way with situations regularly encountered. One goal in the use of such procedures is equitable treatment. In Detroit, Michigan, for instance, the Environmental Enforcement Division, which deals with problems of debris and overgrowth and closely follows a set of bureaucratic rules, has a policy of responding to every citizen contact referred to the agency. The Sanitation Division is also organized around an egalitarian principle—"pick up garbage from each residence once a week, every week."[2]

The resulting patterns of service delivery are relatively apolitical and relatively predictable.

But standard operating procedures, helpful in routine circumstances, may be of limited use when bureaucrats encounter unusual circumstances. Consider, for example, the following hypothetical scenario, also presented to child care inspectors in the same four states:

> You visit the Little Bow Peep Day Care Center after receiving a complaint that a staff member required an entire class of preschoolers to stuff a sock in their mouths for two minutes as a disciplinary measure. Your investigation reveals that the incident did occur, that two children vomited afterwards, and that the director refused to fire the responsible staff member despite parental complaints. Your investigation further reveals sloppy record keeping, occasional lunches without vegetables, and no field trips in recent memory. Although matters have worsened since the center's last license renewal, the center has had some serious problems in the past, including inadequate supervision of children, infrequent washing of children's hands, and a malfunctioning hot-water heater.[3]

Unlike in the previous example, child care inspectors would respond in strikingly different ways to these provocations. Some inspectors would issue a monetary fine, while others would not. Some inspectors would issue a provisional or probationary license, while others would not. The percentage of inspectors who would revoke the center's license (the ultimate sanction) ranged from 12 percent in Oklahoma to 32 percent in Colorado to 60 percent in Pennsylvania to 64 percent in North Carolina.[4] Standard operating procedures, which proved so helpful when inspectors encountered a minor code violation, were of little use when inspectors considered a truly egregious day care center.

Standard operating procedures may also fail when personnel deal with unprecedented situations. Consider the terrorist attacks of September 11, 2001. Responding to the news that the World Trade Center had been hit by an airplane (later, two airplanes), New York City's police officers and firefighters converged on the scene. Despite the chaos, they did their best to follow standard operating procedures, encouraging an orderly evacuation of the imperiled buildings. Unfortunately, there were no manuals to guide the heroic civil servants in those specific circumstances, to warn them about the imminent danger of collapse and the need for speed.

Together these examples illustrate important differences between the handling of routine problems and the handling of crisis situations. With routine problems, the reliance on standard operating procedures usually serves both bureaucrats and the citizenry reasonably well. When a crisis occurs, the use of standard operating procedures, while it may still prove very helpful, may not be enough to avoid disaster.

These cases also illustrate another important point: bureaucratic decisions are a function of both the task environment (in this case, the provocation or threat) and the decision maker (in this case, civil servants). In the first child care and Detroit examples, the task environments were simple, familiar, and determinative; in the second child care and September 11, 2001, examples, the task environments were much more complex and unusual. The World Trade Center crisis also reveals how decision makers may affect the outcome of events.

Reports have suggested that there was a difference between how the police departments and how the fire departments responded to the crisis. Police officers, equipped with high-tech radios and trained in their use, received the highly useful information that the North Tower was glowing red. This helped them save others and themselves through a swift evacuation. Although 37 New York Port Authority police and 23 New York City Police Department officers did lose their lives, casualties could have been much worse. In contrast, the New York City Fire Department, which had purchased such radios, had not trained its firefighters to use them. Cut off from vital intelligence, 343 firefighters perished in the disaster. The decisions made about training were thus significant.[5]

Communication matters, especially in a crisis; bureaucrats need to be in touch with other bureaucrats and with their superiors. A full analysis of decision making requires that one pay attention to both the problem to be solved and the persons who have been asked to solve it. This critical insight can be traced to the writings of Herbert Simon, an important figure in political science, economics, and cognitive psychology and a Nobel Prize winner.[6]

In this chapter, we try to understand how individual bureaucrats reason and how they behave within an organizational setting. The *core questions* we will explore are:

- *HOW DO BUREAUCRATS MAKE DECISIONS?* We consider some strategies for simplifying problems and note how these strategies differ from those employed in what is known as a rational choice model.

- *Do bureaucrats manage to approximate rational behavior?* We argue that they do, and we highlight the concept of satisficing as a key explanation for the notion of bounded rationality.

- *What motivates bureaucrats?* We discuss empathy and commitment and attitudes toward risk. We do not denigrate bureaucrats as purely self-interested, but neither do we romanticize them as wholly public spirited.

- *How do organizations promote cohesion?* Here we consider the roles of training, information, and professionalism.

More broadly, we consider the consequences of bounded rationality for organizational performance.

## The Bounded Rationality Model

**Herbert Simon,** a leading figure of public administration, helped to explain bureaucratic decisions by developing a model of **bounded rationality.**[7] According to Simon, individuals who work within organizations, such as bureaucrats, face at least three difficulties. First, their knowledge of the consequences of possible choices is fragmentary. Given time constraints and the limits of the human mind, knowing all the consequences that will flow from a given choice is impossible. For example, if you close a day care center, some children may be relocated to a better center, but others may be placed with relatives who really would prefer to be doing something else. Thus the quality of care the children receive may not improve. Second, values can be only imperfectly anticipated because the experience of a value differs from the anticipation of that same value. By this Simon means that when we experience something (a vacation, a dessert, a public policy), the actual experience may cause us to rethink how valuable the goal was in the first place. If parents pay 20 percent more for a better day care center, they may or may not conclude that the additional expense was worthwhile. Third, only a few alternatives can be considered. In the case of a bad day care center, a child care inspector might have the option of pursuing literally dozens of options. In practice, however, inspectors tend to zero in on only a handful of options.

Simon's perspective distinguishes him from Charles Lindblom, another prominent decision theorist. According to Lindblom, typical individuals and organizations rely on **incrementalism** as a decision-making tool.[8] Instead of beginning with a range of choices, as Simon posits, most decision makers begin with the status quo, Lindblom believes. Decision makers then deviate from the status quo cautiously, yielding policies that differ only incrementally from previous policies. Incrementalism as an outcome is entirely possible under Simon's model of bounded rationality, but it is not preordained because incrementalism as a procedure is not the only way for decision makers to cope with limited time and information. As studies have shown, incrementalism is not always the best way to describe the policymaking process.[9] Nor is it always the best way to describe bureaucratic decision making.

Simon's model of bounded rationality also stands in sharp contrast to the **rational choice model.** In its purest form, this model assumes that individuals making decisions know their preferences, are able to consider all possible alternatives, and can anticipate the full set of consequences that will flow from each alternative. In short, decision makers **optimize,** that is, they make the best decision. Some versions of the rational choice model do not go quite so far. For example, economists routinely note the absence of complete and perfect information and how that affects decisions.[10]

In any case, the rational choice model assumes much greater rationality than Simon believes to be possible. According to him, real bureaucrats make decisions through the use of **shortcuts** that help them to function effectively despite cognitive and situational limits. He refers to this process as **satisficing.** In effect, satisficing means that a bureaucrat, or another decision maker, considers options only until finding one that seems acceptable given the personal values of the bureaucrat and the probable consequences of that option. In

Simon's words: "Because administrators satisfice rather than maximize, they can choose without first examining all possible behavior alternatives and without ascertaining that these are in fact all the alternatives."[11] Although satisficing sometimes leads to bad decisions, it is remarkably quick and productive. Think of it this way: Would you rather devote an entire week to getting one decision exactly right or, instead, get one hundred decisions approximately right? The latter outcome might well be worth the risk of getting a few decisions wrong.

Whatever model might be employed by decision makers in an ideal world, satisficing seems to be the one most of them use in the real world. For example, when urban planners in the San Francisco Bay area contemplated mass transit options in the 1950s and the 1960s, they considered a relatively narrow range of options. Planners for the five-county Bay Area Rapid Transit (BART) system considered only rail options, ignoring buses and automobiles as means of transportation. In nearby Oakland, planners for the two-county Alameda–Contra Costa Transit Authority (AC) gave initial consideration to a wider range of options, but only because they inherited a multimodal system. Following a decision by the California Public Utilities Commission to allow the use of buses instead of trains, AC gave serious consideration to bus options only. The systems ultimately developed by these two sets of planners reflected these circumscribed alternatives: BART evolved as a rail system, while AC evolved as a bus system.[12]

The U.S. Customs and Border Protection's response to the problem of "port running" also illustrates satisficing behavior. Port running is a particularly bold form of smuggling in which the driver of a vehicle carrying illegal contraband proceeds brazenly to an inspection booth. If challenged by the inspector, the driver attempts to escape with little regard for life or property. When port running between Mexico and the United States became a serious problem in the mid-1990s, the Customs Service (as it was then known) actively considered approximately five solutions.[13] Eventually, the agency chose to arrange concrete barriers in a zigzag pattern just behind the inspection booths. Drivers leaving the inspection booth had to maneuver slowly through the barriers before they could drive away. If they tried to run, they could be stopped without putting other people at great risk. There is no way of knowing whether this was the best possible solution. For the Customs Service, it was sufficient that this policy seemed to reduce the number of port-running incidents and contributed to a substantial increase in the black-market price of running an illegal load (a good sign that smugglers regarded the new policy as an effective one!).

## Simplified Problem Solving

Over the years, bureaucracies have developed several familiar techniques to help solve difficult problems. These include problem disaggregation, the use of standard operating procedures, attention to sunk costs, and the use of simulations and tests. The purpose of these techniques is to simplify problems and the search for solutions. If these techniques work, bureaucracies can save time and money and make some progress toward important goals. In short, bureaucratic performance improves.

### Problem Disaggregation

Most problems are multifaceted or multidimensional. By breaking such problems down into their component parts—**problem disaggregation**—bureaucrats can transform a daunting megaproblem into an assortment of soluble miniproblems.

Consider, for example, the problem of pollution. In 1970 the newly created Environmental Protection Agency (EPA) attacked the problem by breaking it down in several ways. First, the agency distinguished pollution by medium—air versus water versus land. Second, it distinguished between pollution from point sources (such as power plants) and pollution from nonpoint sources (such as runoff from farms). Third, the EPA distinguished between pollution in attainment areas (relatively good environmental quality) and pollution in nonattainment areas (relatively poor environmental quality).

With these distinctions in mind, and with considerable guidance from Congress and the federal courts, the EPA was able to zero in on problems based on several factors—severity, visibility, and tractability. Initially, the agency tackled air pollution from point sources, especially in nonattainment areas. Next, it focused on water pollution from point sources. Eventually, it would make considerable progress in both areas. For example, the amount of lead in the atmosphere declined sharply (see Table 2.1),[14] and several major waterways became fishable and swimmable again. Other pollution problems, such as hazardous waste disposal, nonpoint pollution, and global climate change, proved more vexing and initially received little attention. But over time they, too, would receive more attention. Had the EPA attempted to address all these problems at once, the outcome would probably have been much frenetic activity with few positive results.

### Table 2.1  Changes in Air Quality and Emissions, 1986–1995

| Pollutant | Air Quality Change | Emissions Change |
|---|---|---|
| Carbon Monoxide | −37% | −16% |
| Lead | −78% | −32% |
| Nitrogen Dioxide | −14% | −3% |
| Ozone | −6% | −9% |
| Particulate Matter | −22% | −17% |
| Sulfur Dioxide | −37% | −18% |

*Source:* Clarence Davies and Jan Mazurek, *Pollution Control in the United States* (Washington, D.C.: Resources for the Future, 1998), 60.

Efforts to solve the drug problem have also yielded some progress, following critical decisions on how to disaggregate the problem and how to allocate scarce resources. The Department of Justice, for example, has distinguished between domestic and international cases, between major and minor cases, and between arrests (which generate favorable statistics in the short run) and breaking up drug cartels (arguably more important in the long run).

## Standard Operating Procedures

Habits and routines are excellent devices for coping with familiar problems. In Simon's words: "Habits and routines may not only serve their purposes effectively, but also conserve scarce and costly decision-making time and attention."[15] Within the bureaucracy, the routines are often called standard operating procedures, norms designed to suit specific circumstances, available to organization members when situations resembling those circumstances occur. Standard operating procedures arise from many sources. When environmental agency officials prepare an environmental impact statement before approving a major project, it is because they are required by law to do so. When welfare caseworkers insist on receiving a Social Security number before endorsing a welfare application, it is because they are required by law to do so. Many standard operating procedures originate with the political executives who run the bureaucracy. And some procedures originate with bureaucrats on the front lines—**street-level bureaucrats,** as Michael Lipsky calls them.[16]

A particularly interesting standard operating procedure emerged within the military during World War I. Much of the warfare in France and Belgium occurred in or near trenches, where opponents were pinned down in close proximity to one another. After a pitched battle, sentries patrolled each side's perimeter, placing themselves and their enemy counterparts at great risk. Remarkably, an unspoken agreement emerged over time that neither side would shoot at the other, giving everyone a breather from the stresses and strains of warfare. This live-and-let-live system evolved without the approval of higher authorities and persisted despite efforts to control it.[17] It is a good example of a standard operating procedure developed by street-level bureaucrats.

Though standard operating procedures do tend to persist over time, they can be changed. For instance, a common approach to child care regulation is to visit all day care centers once a year, to make sure they are complying with state rules and regulations. This approach seems fair in that it treats all day care centers alike, but it is inefficient (and ultimately unfair) because it leaves insufficient time to address serious problems at really bad day care centers.

**Table 2.2 Workers' Compensation Claims, Maine**

| Year | Workers' Compensation Claims (Injuries with 1 Lost Workday or More) | Incidence Rates (Lost Workday Cases per 100 Full-Time Workers) |
|------|------|------|
| 1991 | 8,923 | 49.43 |
| 1992 | 7,090 | 43.39 |
| 1993 | 5,808 | 37.43 |
| 1994 | 4,695 | 37.48 |

*Source:* Maine Area OSHA Office, "Annual Report on the Maine Top 200 Program, 1995." Data supplied by Dr. John Mendeloff, Graduate School of Public and International Affairs, University of Pittsburgh.

For this reason, some state child care agencies have opted for **differential monitoring,** linking the frequency of inspections to past performance, giving more attention to the worse facilities, less to the better ones.[18]

Similar changes have occurred in child protection agencies. For example, Missouri's child protective services agency used to treat serious and nonserious cases alike. As a result of legislation passed in 1994, the agency developed a differential response system calibrating the agency's response to fit the severity of the provocation: more serious cases continued to trigger an investigation by child protection personnel and police; less serious cases were referred to family assessment personnel, who provided assistance rather than punishment.[19] Other states followed Missouri's lead. As of 2003, eleven states had established statewide differential monitoring systems for child protective services, while nine had pilot or local programs.[20] A random-assignment evaluation of Minnesota's differential monitoring plan found that families randomly assigned to an alternative response track (counseling plus social services) were less likely to have a repeat report than families randomly assigned to the traditional investigative track.[21]

Occupational safety and health agencies have also embraced differential monitoring. In Maine, the regional office of the Occupational Safety and Health Administration (OSHA) discovered that 200 firms were responsible for approximately 44 percent of the state's workplace injuries, illnesses, and deaths. OSHA gave each of the 200 firms a choice: conduct a comprehensive hazard assessment, correct all hazards identified, and develop an improvement plan for the future or face a comprehensive inspection. An overwhelming majority of the firms opted for the former, and worker compensation claims dropped dramatically thereafter (see Table 2.2).[22]

Some cities, led by Baltimore, have tried to alter standard operating procedures across multiple agencies, through the use of **performance measures** on city agencies. When Martin O'Malley took over as mayor of Baltimore in 1999, he established CitiStat, which requires agency officials to meet with the mayor and his team every two weeks in sessions that highlight worrisome trends. Although CitiStat encountered some bureaucratic resistance at first, it has helped to turn some agencies around and improve living conditions. For example, thanks to CitiStat, the mayor's office was able to reduce overtime payments at the Department of Public Works and at city fire stations. Thanks to CitiStat, the mayor's office was also able to reduce lead violations by 25 percent and increase the number of children tested for lead by 51 percent.[23] Other cities, such as Atlanta, Chattanooga, Providence, and San Francisco, have emulated Baltimore's CitiStat program.[24] O'Malley, who became governor of Maryland in January 2007, has vowed to replicate Baltimore's successes at the state level.[25]

Baltimore's performance management system and its counterparts elsewhere are not without their risks. By rewarding "good numbers" and punishing "bad numbers," city officials can encourage a preoccupation with statistics at the expense of problem solving. In season 3 of *The Wire*, a gritty television drama based in Baltimore, the police commissioner and his deputy publicly berate police majors whose numbers fail to measure up. In desperation, Major Colvin legalizes drugs in one corner of west Baltimore, which becomes known as "Hamsterdam." The experiment yields a noticeable decline in crime, which impresses Colvin's bosses until they learn that he has legalized drug trafficking without their authorization. The moral of the story is debatable. Should we care more about drug sales or the corresponding crimes that accompany them? Once performance goals have been set by politicians, should bureaucrats be free to pursue them through any means necessary? Fortunately, it is possible to improve performance, as measured by statistical indicators, without violating the law. Nevertheless, this fictional case illustrates some real-world dilemmas that will arise with greater frequency as performance management catches on.

### Sunk Costs

Although procedural changes do occur, bureaucrats become invested in a certain way of doing things because any new procedure or strategy requires upfront costs that may turn out to be considerable. In Simon's words: "Activity very often results in 'sunk costs' of one sort or another that make persistence in the same direction advantageous."[26] In effect, **sunk costs** refer to the investment already made in a particular strategy that renders the pursuit of other strategies less attractive.

The phenomenon of sunk costs helps explain why it is so difficult to create a new agency or cabinet-level department. To bureaucrats, the status quo means established cubicles in familiar buildings at convenient subway stops, established relationships with familiar personnel whose quirks and foibles are well understood, and an established mission that flows from a familiar statute whose nuances are well known. Occasionally, the sunk-costs argument can be overcome. But it takes national emergencies (such as those that led to the Department of Energy and the Department of Homeland Security) or strong constituencies (such as those involving the Department of Education and the Department of Veterans Affairs) to do so.

## Simulations and Tests

When familiar problems arise, bureaucrats can rely on standard operating procedures. But what are they to do when unfamiliar problems arise? The question has become even more pressing in recent times because new technological developments have accelerated the generation of new problems. For example, in the late 1990s government officials began to fret that massive computer failures would occur when the year 2000 arrived because computers had been programmed with two-digit codes for year (00–99), making them ill equipped to cope with the transition from 1999 to 2000. From a human point of view, the transition was a logical progression from one year to the next; from a computer's point of view, however, it was a backward shift of ninety-nine years. To a computer, 00 meant 1900, not 2000. Without appropriate corrections, this reading could result in enormous calculation errors, malfunctions, and shutdowns. Imagine, for instance, how someone's Social Security check might be deflated in keeping with a retroactive cost-of-living adjustment of nearly a century!

To anticipate the transition to the year 2000 (or Y2K), companies, agencies, and others ran **simulations,** or tests, to discover what might happen. The Chrysler Corporation, for instance, turned all of its clocks to December 31, 1999, at its Sterling Heights automobile assembly plant. The security system shut down and would not let anybody out! A Florence, Arizona, prison conducted a similar test and got the opposite result: the security system opened all its doors.[27] Not a good outcome for a prison! Fortunately, it was a test. Such simulations can be very helpful to bureaucrats (and to private employers) as a way of confirming that real problems do exist. Eventually, government agencies (and private employers) were able to correct the computer problems. When Y2K arrived, few problems developed. A serious crisis was thus averted.

## Implications for Policy Analysis

An important development in the history of bureaucratic decision making has been the creation of policy analysis bureaus within administrative agencies. The purpose of such bureaus is to provide a cabinet secretary or other agency head with valuable information on the probable consequences of choices under active consideration. In Simon's words, such bureaus recognize important limits to individual and organizational rationality and seek to overcome them.

If Simon is correct, policy analysis within the bureaucracy differs from the rational choice model of neoclassical economics, which assumes a world of complete and perfect information and unlimited time and cognition. According to one version of the rational choice model, the decision maker specifies some values or goals, considers a wide range of alternatives, gathers evidence on the expected consequence of each alternative, and chooses the one that best maximizes the values of overriding importance.[28] Simon assures us that decision making in the real world cannot be so comprehensive.

At the same time, Simon believes that bureaucrats are *trying* to be rational. In a brief discussion of firefighting, for example, the problem is not that some neighborhoods are whiter than others or more affluent than others or represented by a more powerful alderman than others but rather that bureaucrats cannot know the likelihood that a fire will break out in one section of the city rather than another.[29]

If Simon sees less rationality in policy analysis than some economists, he sees more rationality than some political scientists. Deborah Stone, for example, argues that policy analysis is inherently political.[30] Instead of trying to clarify their values, decision makers try to disguise them. For example, Alan Greenspan, the former head of the powerful Federal Reserve Board, was known for his cryptic utterances. He once said before the Senate Banking Committee, "If I say something which you understand fully in this regard, I probably made a mistake."[31] The search for alternatives may also be less public spirited than Simon suggests. Instead of a good-faith search for interesting alternatives, we sometimes see a deliberate effort to keep threatening alternatives off the agenda.

From yet another perspective, policy analysis within the bureaucracy tends to be inconsistent with both economic rationality and bounded rationality. Based on research at the Department of Energy (DOE), Martha Feldman contends that policy analysis is usually not intended for a specific decision, that it rarely addresses a well-specified problem, and that it seldom is completed in time to have an impact. For example, she notes that of twelve policy papers prepared by DOE policy analysts within a three-month period, only one could be clearly linked to a pending decision. According to Feldman, policy analysts do not help to solve problems, as Simon suggests; rather, they produce interpretations of issues that help policymakers gain a better understanding of the world around them.[32]

Despite these objections, some forms of policy analysis conducted by bureaucrats are strikingly consistent with bounded rationality. One is **cost-benefit analysis.** Rooted in microeconomics, cost-benefit analysis attempts to place a monetary value on both the costs and the benefits of proposed policy alternatives. To the extent that it is successful, this type of analysis helps to render bureaucratic decision making more rational by supplying decision makers with benefit-cost ratios that facilitate easy comparisons across policy options. Thus if a dam in Mississippi has a benefit-cost ratio of 6/1, while a dredging project in Louisiana has a benefit-cost ratio of 2/1, the Army Corps of Engineers ought to prefer the dam.

At first, it might appear that cost-benefit analysis is more consistent with pure rationality than with bounded rationality. After all, the basic idea is to monetize all costs and benefits and to produce a single number comparing the two. In the real world, however, cost-benefit analysis always suffers from incomplete and imperfect information. Benefits are notoriously difficult to measure, and discount rates, which convert future costs into current dollars, are controversial. Though animated by a vision of pure rationality, cost-benefit analysis resembles bounded rationality in practice.

## Motivation

In a pure rational choice model, self-interest motivates bureaucrats. In advancing their self-interest, bureaucrats seek to maximize utility. A number of scholars have questioned whether this perspective adequately characterizes bureaucrats, politicians, and voters.[33] These scholars would agree with Peter Clark and James Q. Wilson, who argue that **purposive incentives** (such as the

## Table 2.3 Types of Bureaucrats

*Climbers* consider power, income, and prestige as nearly all-important in their value structures.

*Conservers* consider convenience and security as nearly all-important. In contrast to climbers, conservers seek merely to retain the amount of power, income, and prestige they already have, rather than to maximize it.

*Zealots* are loyal to relatively narrow policies or concepts, such as the development of nuclear submarines. They seek power both for its own sake and to effect the policies to which they are loyal. We shall call these their sacred policies.

*Advocates* are loyal to a broader set of functions or to a broader organization than zealots. They also seek power because they want to have a significant influence upon policies and actions concerning those functions or organizations.

*Statesmen* are loyal to society as a whole, and they desire to obtain the power necessary to have a significant influence upon national policies and actions. They are altruistic to an important degree because their loyalty is to the "general welfare" as they see it. Therefore statesmen closely resemble the theoretical bureaucrats of public administration textbooks.

*Source:* Adapted from Anthony Downs, *Inside Bureaucracy* (originally published by Little, Brown & Co., Boston, Mass., 1967, p. 88). Copyright ©1967 RAND Corporation, Santa Monica, Calif. Reprinted with permission.

pursuit of the public interest) and **solidary incentives** (such as the respect of one's peers) are powerful motivating forces for some bureaucrats.[34] After analyzing survey data from federal bureaucrats, John Brehm and Scott Gates concluded that material incentives (good pay, job security) help to explain why individuals join the civil service and remain there. However, they also found that solidary and purposive incentives were highly important.[35] Even some economists acknowledge that many bureaucrats have "mixed motives," combining self-interest and altruistic support for certain values. Anthony Downs, for instance, asserts that **zealots, advocates,** and **statesmen,** not just **climbers** and **conservers,** populate the bureaucracy (see Table 2.3).[36] It is difficult to reduce the behavior of zealots, advocates, and statesmen to self-interest alone.

### Empathy and Commitment

Empathy represents one departure from pure self-interest. Certain bureaucrats identify with disadvantaged constituents, such as the poor or the disabled. Other bureaucrats identify with regulated firms, perhaps because they interact so often with the firms' representatives. Still other bureaucrats, who belong to a particular ethnic group, identify with members of that group. Gender is another source of empathic bonds.

Technically, empathy and self-interest can be reconciled. If a bureaucrat's concern for others directly affects that bureaucrat's own welfare as well, then one can argue that this is just a subtle manifestation of self-interest. As Amartya Sen notes, however, some people "commit" themselves to a principle that clashes with self-interest.[37] When a bureaucrat fights for a principle or cause that puts at risk that bureaucrat's personal career, such commitment suggests that purposive incentives are at work. When a white bureaucrat fights prejudice against blacks in a school or firm, the underlying motivation may well be commitment rather than empathy.

A study of bureaucratic motivation during the Reagan administration found considerable evidence of self-interested behavior, where bureaucrats complied with questionable directives from above for fear of losing their jobs. This proved especially true at the National Highway Traffic Safety Administration and Food and Nutrition Service. In contrast, bureaucrats at the Civil Rights Division of the Department of Justice and the EPA were more willing to place their jobs at risk. A strong sense of professionalism motivated some rebellious bureaucrats; ideological aversion to President Reagan's policies motivated others.[38]

## Representative Bureaucracy

Many bureaucrats empathize more with some groups than with others. Bureaucrats often identify with groups to which they belong. Race and gender are among the more powerful sources of group identification. Although many whites are fully capable of empathizing with blacks and Hispanics, studies of what is known as **representative bureaucracy** show that race and ethnicity can shape bureaucratic attitudes and behavior. For example, one study found that school districts with a higher percentage of black teachers are less likely to penalize or stigmatize black students by suspending them from school, assigning them to "educable mentally retarded" classes, or assigning them to special education classes.[39] Another study found that teachers are more likely to perceive a student as disruptive or inattentive if the teacher does not share the student's racial or ethnic identification.[40] This phenomenon appears to be much more pronounced in the South than elsewhere in the country.

Gender also matters, though more in some contexts than others. A study of child care inspectors found no gender differences in the propensity to be tough with child care providers who have violated state rules and regulations.[41] On the other hand, a study of local police forces found that rapes were more likely to be reported in jurisdictions with a higher percentage of females on the force. Of course, this might be a function of rape victims' perceptions that female officers would be more responsive or more sensitive than male officers rather than the actual attitudes or behavior of police officers. However, arrests for rape are also more likely in jurisdictions with a higher percentage of females on the force (after controlling for the number of rape reports), which suggests that female police officers are more proactive in pursuing rapists.[42]

## Attitudes toward Risk

Observers often assert that bureaucrats are **risk averse.** In fact, most people are risk averse most of the time. Most of us wear seatbelts when we drive, don't smoke, stay home during a bad snowstorm, and avoid crime-ridden neighborhoods after dark. Once the dangers of Pinto fuel tanks were exposed, consumers switched to other cars; once the dangers of Firestone tires were exposed, consumers switched to other tires. Our collective investment in homeland security after September 11, 2001, suggests a collective aversion to risk. Thus the question is not whether bureaucrats are risk averse but whether they are more risk averse than the rest of us.

Foreign Service officers, within the State Department, are sometimes depicted as unusually risk averse. Specifically, some observers claim the officers are more cautious and timid than the political appointees who run the department. Chester Bowles, who believed this, argued that Foreign Service officers, being less prepared to take risks and less likely to think creatively, made poor candidates for top positions at State.[43]

Not everyone would agree. Charles Bohlen, who served as U.S. ambassador to the Soviet Union during the 1950s, argued that Foreign Service officers "were just as willing, in fact more so, to stick their neck out than were political appointees."[44] More broadly, it appears that while attitudinal differences between bureaucrats and politicians do exist, they are less striking in the United States than in other countries.[45]

In thinking about risk, bureaucrats and politicians alike seem to be guided by what cognitive psychologists call the **availability heuristic.** Rather than considering all existing examples of some phenomenon and then reaching a conclusion, people tend to judge a situation based on the most readily available case, oftentimes the most recent case.[46] In the wake of an accident or a disaster, we become more cautious, more risk averse because that accident or disaster is more readily available to us, more easily called to mind. This helps to explain why bureaucrats and politicians reacted with strong rhetoric and tough policies to the Three Mile Island accident of 1979, which threatened the possibility of a meltdown of a nuclear power plant reactor core. Although this kind of bounded rationality might seem perverse, it has its advantages. In addition to saving time and effort, it takes into account the psychological costs of certain choices. In Charles Perrow's words, the availability heuristic recognizes that "the public's fears must be treated with respect, and a way found to bring them into policy considerations."[47]

## Organizational Advancement

For many bureaucrats, the welfare of the bureaucracy itself comes to rival the individual bureaucrat's welfare in importance. Bureaucracy's defenders and critics alike have observed a striking tendency for bureaucrats to identify with their organizations and the organizations' goals. As Herbert Simon put it,

<table>
<tr><td align="right">Inside<br>Bureaucracy<br>with</td><td>James Baker III<br>Secretary of the Treasury (1985–1988)<br>Secretary of State (1989–1992)</td></tr>
</table>

"You have in the Foreign Service a higher degree of career employees than at other bureaucracies. They come from a very prestigious source: the Foreign Service exam. It's different in that respect from other bureaucracies. Sometimes it affects them beneficially and sometimes negatively. As with anybody else, you've got good apples and bad apples.

"Some people think that cabinet secretaries are here today, gone tomorrow. I'm not saying that all Foreign Service officers are that way. More than anything else, they want to be players. When I took office, I said I was going to be the White House's man at the State Department instead of the State Department's man at the White House. There were mumblings and grumblings, but that all went away when it became clear that the State Department was going to be the main agency implementing George Herbert Walker Bush's foreign policy. Bureaucrats relate warmly and well to strong secretaries. And I was one because I was a close friend of the president. Nobody was going to get between me and the president. I think the same thing happened in the Kissinger years at State."

"The common claim that economic self-interest is the only important human motivation in the workings of a society is simply false, for it is an easily observable fact that, within organizations, organizational identification requires at least equal billing with self interest."[48]

A key advantage of **organizational identification** is that it enables the bureaucracy to socialize its members to pursue organizational goals that have been duly authorized by elected officials. In this sense, organizational identification promotes legal accountability. By ensuring that civil servants and political executives promote the same organizational goals, it also promotes bureaucratic accountability. But what if political executives or politicians sacrifice organizational goals for political self-promotion? A potential disadvantage of organizational identification is that bureaucrats who simply do what their bosses tell them may lose sight of the broader goals the organization is supposed to promote. If the bureaucracy veers substantially from its legitimate goals, individual bureaucrats may veer with it, rather than challenging the organization from within (what Albert Hirschman would call **voice**) or resigning in public protest (what Hirschman would call **exit**).[49]

## Promoting Organizational Cohesion

How do bureaucracies and their political appointees promote the kind of **organizational cohesion** Simon and others have noticed and applauded? One strategy is to train bureaucrats so they know exactly what is expected of them. When a new recruit arrives, it is customary to have a probationary period, during which the new arrival learns the ropes from a mentor or a cluster of mentors. At some agencies, the probationary period is relatively long and the training process relatively rigorous. Police departments, for example, rely on police academies to ensure the learning of proper techniques.

A second strategy is to ensure that information flows up and down the organization. Regular meetings offer one opportunity for superiors and subordinates to exchange information and ideas. Organizers hope that by the meeting's end, all personnel will be on the same wavelength. Memos are also important tools for feedback from below and guidance from above.

A third strategy is to rely upon professions to socialize individuals and to certify both skills and values. By hiring members of a profession whose tenets and norms match its own, a bureaucracy can save itself a good deal of time and effort. In his classic study of the Forest Service, Herbert Kaufman noted how bureaucrats used this technique to counter centrifugal tendencies inherent in

"By and large I found the Forest Service personnel to have an esprit de corps. I used to call it my little Marine Corps. They were out there. They were pretty much on their own. They felt they had this historic sense of mission. They wear uniforms. There's hierarchy. They directly interface the public. The Food and Nutrition Service is just a totally different animal, much more of a classic regulatory operation. Some of them are out there interfacing the public but not a lot. Most of them are designing regulations. They would be much more as classic government employees or bureaucrats."

an agency whose employees work, for the most part, in remote locations and with limited supervision. By hiring professional foresters for numerous jobs, including personnel management, administrative management, and budgeting positions that actually could have been filled by persons with different credentials, the Forest Service helped to ensure a common outlook that lessened the need for close supervision.[50] By rotating these professionals on a regular basis, the Forest Service also helped to ensure that tendencies toward **capture** and **localism** would be overcome. Capture occurs when regulatory agencies adopt the thinking of the interests they are supposed to be regulating; localism occurs when clientele agencies adopt the thinking of local clients.

Although some agencies rely heavily on one profession, as the Forest Service does, most recruit individuals with diverse professional backgrounds. Such practices help agencies to perform varied and complex tasks by taking advantage of people with different professional norms and skills. For better and for worse, these professionals are like the tiger whose stripes remain well after being placed in a zoo.

Consider, for example, the Federal Trade Commission (FTC), which has recruited both lawyers and economists to handle antitrust matters. The lawyers, with a relatively short time frame and a penchant for litigation, prefer to pursue lots of antitrust cases, including small ones, at once. The economists, with a longer time frame and a preference for restructuring industries, would rather wait for a blockbuster case to come along.[51] While conflicts between economists and lawyers who work for the same agency may require managers to spend some time arbitrating disputes, those conflicts between the two professions can also be constructive. For example, the FTC pursues a good mix of difficult and easy cases, thanks to the combined input of economists and lawyers.

## Consequences of Bounded Rationality

Is bounded rationality a virtue, a vice, or a necessary evil? Simon's perspective is clear. Although bounded rationality underscores the limits of organizational decision making, Simon was not pessimistic about either individual or organizational behavior. Rather, he believed that individuals have the ability to adapt to formidable challenges through satisficing and other shortcuts. Furthermore, he believed that organizations can help ensure that individuals make decisions roughly consistent not only with their personal preferences but also with their organizations' most important goals. In Simon's words: "The rational individual is, and must be, an organized and institutionalized individual. If the severe limits imposed by human psychology are to be relaxed, the individual must in his decisions be subject to the influence of the organizational group in which he participates."[52] In short, Simon was optimistic about bounded rationality.

Is such optimism justified? To answer that question, it is useful to reconsider some of the essential elements of bounded rationality: a narrow search, problem disaggregation, approximations, and standard operating procedures.

### A Narrow Search

A hallmark of bounded rationality is its explicit willingness to limit the decision-making process to a relatively narrow range of options. We saw that planners for the BART system limited their choices to rail initiatives, while planners for the nearby AC system limited their choices to bus routes. One can easily imagine that these pragmatic decisions, understandable in the short run, might prove disastrous in the long run. Yet a careful analysis reveals quite the opposite. Thanks to a circumscribed range of options, the two mass transit systems developed independently as **parallel systems,** or organizations with similar goals but with very different strengths and weaknesses. When strikes afflicted one of the systems, the other could absorb a sudden spike in demand. When bad management plagued one of the systems, the other could keep running smoothly. When technical breakdowns undermined one of the systems, the other could help out. The result, though serendipitous, was far better than two blended systems would have been. As Jonathan Bendor concluded, "Taken together, AC and BART form a more flexible response to long-term problems than does either one taken separately."[53] Chalk one up for satisficing.

## Problem Disaggregation

In an essay Anne Lamott describes a childhood scene etched in her memory: her brother, a procrastinator, had put off writing a lengthy report on birds until the night before it was due. Frustration led to fear, then to panic. How could he possibly finish the assignment on time? Their father, calm and reassuring, put his arm around his son's shoulder and shared one of the secrets of writing (and problem solving): "Bird by bird, buddy. Just take it bird by bird."[54]

Like Lamott's brother, bureaucratic decision makers have learned that they need to break big problems down into digestible chunks. That is how NASA managed to put a man on the moon. That is how Robert Moses transformed the landscape of New York City. That is how Jaime Escalante enabled disadvantaged students from a Los Angeles barrio to excel in mathematics and pass the Advanced Placement calculus exam. And that is how environmental bureaucrats have combated pollution.

Yet the bird-by-bird approach has a down side. In the case of environmental protection, the EPA's decision to tackle pollution medium by medium has been reinforced by structural arrangements that mimic this approach. Thus the EPA has an Air and Radiation Division, a Water Division, and a Solid Waste and Emergency Response Division (see Figure 2.1). Unfortunately, the Air and Radiation Division focuses so single-mindedly on air that it pays limited attention to water and land impacts; the Water Division focuses so single-mindedly on water that it pays limited attention to air and waste impacts. Because most pollution transcends a single medium, a **stovepipe mentality,** in which problems are disaggregated and compartmentalized, may inhibit a more **holistic perspective.** Although some state environmental agencies have attempted to take crossmedia transfers into account—for example, through streamlined permitting systems—this remains a serious problem, at both the state and federal levels.[55]

## Approximations

Another feature of bounded rationality is its willingness to settle for approximately correct answers rather than precise answers. Perhaps it is this sort of

**Figure 2.1 EPA Organizational Structure**

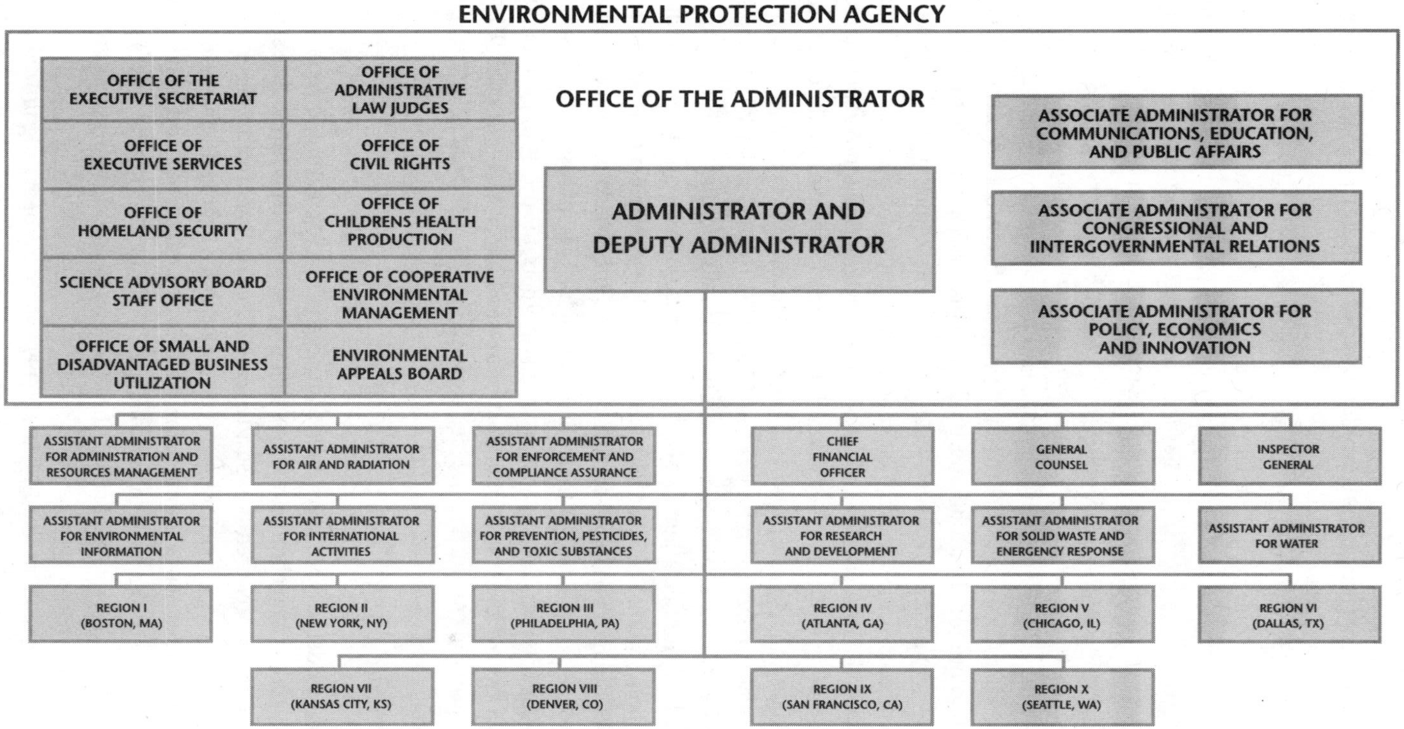

## ENVIRONMENTAL PROTECTION AGENCY

### OFFICE OF THE ADMINISTRATOR

ASSOCIATE ADMINISTRATOR FOR COMMUNICATIONS, EDUCATION, AND PUBLIC AFFAIRS

ASSOCIATE ADMINISTRATOR FOR CONGRESSIONAL AND IINTERGOVERNMENTAL RELATIONS

ASSOCIATE ADMINISTRATOR FOR POLICY, ECONOMICS AND INNOVATION

**ADMINISTRATOR AND DEPUTY ADMINISTRATOR**

OFFICE OF THE EXECUTIVE SECRETARIAT

OFFICE OF ADMINISTRATIVE LAW JUDGES

OFFICE OF EXECUTIVE SERVICES

OFFICE OF CIVIL RIGHTS

OFFICE OF HOMELAND SECURITY

OFFICE OF CHILDRENS HEALTH PRODUCTION

SCIENCE ADVISORY BOARD STAFF OFFICE

OFFICE OF COOPERATIVE ENVIRONMENTAL MANAGEMENT

OFFICE OF SMALL AND DISADVANTAGED BUSINESS UTILIZATION

ENVIRONMENTAL APPEALS BOARD

INSPECTOR GENERAL

GENERAL COUNSEL

CHIEF FINANCIAL OFFICER

ASSISTANT ADMINISTRATOR FOR ENFORCEMENT AND COMPLIANCE ASSURANCE

ASSISTANT ADMINISTRATOR FOR AIR AND RADIATION

ASSISTANT ADMINISTRATOR FOR ADMINISTRATION AND RESOURCES MANAGEMENT

ASSISTANT ADMINISTRATOR FOR WATER

ASSISTANT ADMINISTRATOR FOR SOLID WASTE AND ENERGENCY RESPONSE

ASSISTANT ADMINISTRATOR FOR RESEARCH AND DEVELOPMENT

ASSISTANT ADMINISTRATOR FOR PREVENTION, PESTICIDES, AND TOXIC SUBSTANCES

ASSISTANT ADMINISTRATOR FOR INTERNATIONAL ACTIVITIES

ASSISTANT ADMINISTRATOR FOR ENVIRONMENTAL INFORMATION

REGION VI (DALLAS, TX)

REGION V (CHICAGO, IL)

REGION X (SEATTLE, WA)

REGION IV (ATLANTA, GA)

REGION IX (SAN FRANCISCO, CA)

REGION III (PHILADELPHIA, PA)

REGION VIII (DENVER, CO)

REGION II (NEW YORK, NY)

REGION VII (KANSAS CITY, KS)

REGION I (BOSTON, MA)

*Source: U.S. Government Manual, 2006–2007, p. 379.*

thinking that gave us the Leaning Tower of Pisa! But in most instances, approximations serve us rather well.

Consider the problem of tips earned by waiters and waitresses at restaurants and similar establishments. Because these are often cash transactions, some employees underreport their earnings, thus failing to meet their tax obligations and imposing a burden on the rest of us. Instead of counting tips at every restaurant in the United States—a herculean task—the Internal Revenue Service (IRS) decided in 1994 to calculate probable tip revenue based on business volume. By the end of 1996 the IRS had introduced this system at more than 22,000 establishments, and reported tip income had increased by more than $2 billion.[56] Estimates of tip revenue were sufficiently conservative that no one, or almost no one, paid more than was actually owed.

For the reasons discussed earlier, cost-benefit analysis, which seeks considerable precision, nevertheless falls short much of the time. In some instances, the imperfections of cost-benefit analysis result in bad decisions. For example, in evaluating the Dickey-Lincoln School hydroelectric power project in Maine, the Army Corps of Engineers estimated the benefit-cost ratio to be 2/1, when in fact the ratio was more like 0.8/1 or 0.9/1.[57] Luckily, the mistake was discovered, and Congress terminated funding for the project. More often, cost-benefit calculations fall well beyond the boundary of 1.0, thus reducing the policy implications of calculation error. For example, a cost-benefit analysis of the EPA's proposal to reduce the amount of lead in gasoline yielded a benefit-cost ratio higher than 10/1, although it was impossible to measure all the benefits.[58] In this instance, as in many others, the policy implications were clear. Even if the true benefit-cost ratio was 11/1 or 12/1—or even 9/1—the EPA was fully justified in proceeding with its lead reduction plan.

## Standard Operating Procedures

In a wonderful set of mysteries featuring park ranger Anna Pigeon, Nevada Barr has written about situations that may require departures from standard operating procedures. In case after case, Anna deviates from well-established rules and norms in order to gain evidence, catch criminals, and save lives. In *Blind Descent*, for example, Anna returns to a dangerous and fragile cave in order to rescue an abandoned colleague, without securing her boss's permission.[59] Anna, a pragmatist, justifies this by arguing that you shouldn't go by the book when lives are at stake.[60]

It is possible to identify cases where standard operating procedures, designed to rationalize bureaucratic decision making, produce questionable results. Regulatory inspectors who always go by the book sometimes behave unreasonably.[61] Policy analysts who become preoccupied with routines sometimes waste time and lose sight of broader goals.[62] Adherence to standard operating procedures does not always prevent accidents from occurring.[63] Standard operating procedures may be useless in a novel situation.

Nevertheless, standard operating procedures help street-level bureaucrats to process cases and resolve routine problems quickly. These procedures also help managers to control those street-level bureaucrats. In addition, standard operating procedures help to prevent police officers from abusing suspects, inspectors from playing favorites, and IRS auditors from targeting individuals for political reasons. Furthermore, they help bureaucracies to devote more resources to novel problems because bureaucrats need not reinvent the wheel when a familiar problem appears.

One of the simplest, but most compelling, examples of a standard operating procedure that works well is the emergency response calling system. Over time, most adults and even some young children have learned that in an emergency they should dial 911. This arrangement has helped to save an untold number lives. It is particularly interesting because it involves a standard operating procedure for nonroutine situations. Even in the middle of a crisis, standard operating procedures can be extremely helpful.

## Conclusion

Bounded rationality is a useful starting point for an in-depth discussion of bureaucratic politics because it is much more realistic than a rational choice or incremental perspective. With limited information, limited alternatives, and limited time, real bureaucrats make decisions as best they can without necessarily being constrained by the status quo. They learn from experience, relying on standard operating procedures to make their tasks more manageable. They simplify problems by disaggregating them, or breaking them into bite-size chunks. In Simon's words, they satisfice because they cannot optimize.

Despite its strengths, bounded rationality is not the only useful way to think about bureaucratic decision making. In a sense, the world described by Simon resembles a planet populated by *Star Trek*'s Vulcans, beings such as Spock, known for his iron logic, his capacity for independent thought, and his incorruptibility. What is missing from Spock, and from Simon's bureaucrats, is not just emotion but politics. In the real world, pressure from legislators, chief executives, judges, interest groups, journalists, and citizens constrains bureaucratic decision making. These actors do not appear in Simon's account.

In our next chapter, we focus on some of these actors—the politicians and the judges authorized to tell bureaucrats what to do. We introduce an alternative theoretical perspective, known as principal-agent theory, which pays much closer attention to the bureaucracy's sovereigns. Bureaucrats do not make decisions in a vacuum, as Simon sometimes implies. Yet, as we shall see, the bureaucracy's principals experience many of the same limitations that bureaucrats do. As they seek to control the bureaucracy, politicians and judges are constrained by limited information, limited options, and limited time.

## Key Terms

Advocates, 42

Availability heuristic, 45

Bounded rationality, 31

Capture, 48

Climbers, 42

Conservers, 42

Cost-benefit analysis, 41

Differential monitoring, 37

Exit, 46

Herbert Simon, 31

Holistic perspective, 50

Incrementalism, 32

Localism, 48

Organizational identification, 46

Organizational cohesion, 47

Optimize, 32

Parallel systems, 49

Performance measures, 38

Problem disaggregation, 34

Purposive incentives, 41

Rational choice model, 32

Representative bureaucracy, 44

Risk averse, 44

Satisficing, 32

Shortcuts, 32

Simulations, 39

Solidary incentives, 42

Standard operating procedures, 28

Statesmen, 42

Stovepipe mentality, 50

Street-level bureaucrats, 35

Sunk costs, 39

Voice, 46

Zealots, 42

# 3 | The Bureaucracy's Bosses

In THE WANING DAYS OF THE Clinton presidency, the Occupational Safety and Health Administration (OSHA) issued a rule designed to protect workers against injuries caused by repetitive motion. This rule was a major policy action in that hundreds of thousands of Americans, in settings as diverse as corporate offices, meat-cutting plants, and medical facilities, miss work each year because of "ergonomics-related" injuries. The rule was also highly controversial. Analysts projected that collectively businesses would incur costs in the billions of dollars to comply with OSHA's requirements, which included reviewing employee complaints, redesigning problematic workstations, and providing compensation for disabilities.

Shortly after George W. Bush assumed the presidency, the controversy surrounding the **ergonomics rule** erupted on Capitol Hill. Most Republican legislators, as well as some Democrats, vehemently opposed the rule, preferring either a less expansive approach or no regulation at all. Seeking to overturn OSHA's action, these lawmakers resorted to an obscure parliamentary maneuver. Under the **Congressional Review Act** of 1996, agency rules can be nullified if both chambers of Congress enact a **resolution of disapproval.** Because it is relatively difficult to subject such resolutions to committee hearings, extensive debate, and other standard features of the lawmaking process, they are easier to pass than normal legislation. On March 21, 2001, barely two months after it took effect, the ergonomics rule became the only agency action ever to have been repealed in this way when President Bush signed into law a resolution disapproving the standards established by OSHA.[1]

The ergonomics controversy illustrates the power that policymakers outside the bureaucracy can wield over an agency. They usually exercise this power more subtly, however. Efforts by legislators to influence bureaucracies often take, for example, the form of informal staff communications and re-quirements that agencies give advance notice of their intended actions.

Despite the ubiquity of such efforts, bureaucracies retain considerable autonomy over policymaking, even in the face of open hostility from else-where in government. In the aftermath of the September 11, 2001, terrorist attacks, Congress with great fanfare enacted an aviation and transportation security law. This law gave the Department of Transportation (DOT) sixty days to devise a system for screening all checked baggage for explosives. Not only did the agency publicly resist this deadline, it also simultaneously estab-lished a policy—moving passengers through security checkpoints in ten min-utes or less—that many observers decried as contrary to the law's primary aim of making air travel safer.[2]

Episodes such as these are commonplace in the American political sys-tem. They are also vitally important. The interactions of agencies with their external political environments determine which public decisions will be made in bureaucracies and which will be made in other institutions of gov-ernment. Put differently, the outcomes of these interactions establish the very boundaries of bureaucratic authority.[3]

As illustrated by the ergonomics and explosives examples, these bound-aries are sometimes, but not always, set with an eye to democratic principles such as accountability and performance. Congress and the president took away OSHA's authority to make ergonomics policy not long after control of the White House shifted from one political party to the other, a particularly blunt imposition of political accountability. In the case of DOT, it is not clear that outputs such as screening baggage and moving passengers quickly are effective in bringing about the outcomes—safety and convenience in air travel—desired by policymakers and their constituents. In the end, the boundaries of bureaucratic authority are best understood as manifestations of the ongoing contest between government agencies and their political su-pervisors for control over the policymaking process.

With these issues in mind, this chapter provides a detailed examination of the relationship between agencies and the outside political world. It is organized around the following *core questions:*

- **UNDER WHAT CONDITIONS IS POLICYMAKING RESPONSIBILITY DELEGATED TO THE BUREAUCRACY?** For years elected officials en-trusted OSHA with the authority to make ergonomics policy, only to severely limit this authority when the political environ-ment was transformed.

- *IN WHAT WAYS DO OTHER GOVERNMENT ACTORS SEEK TO INFLU-
  ENCE THE MANNER IN WHICH AGENCIES EXERCISE THEIR RESPON-
  SIBILITIES?* The Aviation and Transportation Security Act of 2001
  not only gave DOT the authority to screen baggage but also
  attached a strict timetable to this authority, thereby limiting the
  agency's flexibility in making and implementing policy in this
  area.

- *TO WHAT EXTENT ARE EFFORTS AT POLITICAL CONTROL SUCCESS-
  FUL, IN LIGHT OF THE FACT THAT AGENCIES CAN, AND DO, TAKE
  STEPS TO PRESERVE AND EXTEND THEIR AUTHORITY?* Facing stiff
  resistance from DOT and a variety of other sources, Congress
  ultimately extended the baggage screening deadline, allowing airports a significant amount of additional time to get explosives
  detection systems up and running.

The chapter approaches these core questions primarily from the perspective of principal-agent theory, an approach widely used to understand
the origins and implications of delegated authority. It is particularly appropriate in that it places bureaucratic policymaking in its broader context.
Agencies do not operate in a vacuum, but rather in an environment where
public decisions can be, and often are, made in alternative venues. As will become apparent, this environmental reality has fundamental consequences for
both bureaucratic accountability and performance.

## Delegation, Adverse Selection, and Moral Hazard

**Delegation** is a common feature of modern life. Clients grant attorneys the
authority to provide legal representation, patients rely on doctors to treat illnesses, and employers hire workers to perform tasks of all sorts. These types
of relationships share fundamental characteristics. Clients, patients, and employers all face difficulties in choosing and monitoring those to whom they
delegate authority. Principal-agent theory is an approach to understanding
the causes and consequences of these difficulties.[4]

A **principal** is an actor who enters into a contractual relationship with
another actor, an **agent.** The agent is entrusted to take actions that lead to
outcomes specified by the principal. For example, doctors act as agents when
they prescribe medicines and perform procedures to enhance the duration
and quality of the lives of their patients (that is, principals), and lawyers act as

agents for persons accused of a crime. These arrangements arise when principals lack the ability to achieve their goals by themselves. Self-representation is not advisable, in most cases, for defendants seeking to minimize the likelihood of a guilty verdict!

A key assumption of principal-agent theory is that self-interest primarily motivates both principals and agents. These actors, in other words, are considered to be rational decision makers. In general, principals and agents face divergent incentives, and this divergence means that purely self-interested behavior on the part of agents may not produce the outcomes desired by principals. For instance, the owners of business firms are concerned first and foremost with maximizing profits. Although rank-and-file employees certainly share a stake in company performance, their subordinate status shapes their actions in important ways. The workers on assembly lines may have little reason to work at top speed if the benefits of their efforts accrue solely to corporate executives and shareholders.

Principals face two specific difficulties when dealing with agents. The first is known as **adverse selection.** This difficulty arises when principals cannot directly observe important characteristics of agents but must rely on rough indicators. Defendants cannot easily discern the true motivations and skills of attorneys and therefore must select legal representation on the basis of factors such as reputations and caseloads. Although such proxies may have merit, they are not foolproof. In the end, principals run the risk of hiring agents not ideally suited for the task at hand.

The second difficulty is known as **moral hazard.** This difficulty stems from the fact that agents, once selected, cannot be readily evaluated in their work environments. As a result, principals must make inferences about the degree to which agents are effectively securing the outcomes they were hired to bring about. Potential patients often judge doctors who perform laser eye surgeries by their success rates. Such measures, however, prove to be far from perfect. It may be hard to discern the individual performance of a doctor who works as part of a team of laser eye surgeons. To further complicate matters, the outcomes of surgeries are affected not only by the doctors' actions but also by the patients' presurgery eyesight conditions (such as how nearsighted or farsighted they were). Because of these uncertainties, agents may find it possible to shirk their duties, or even to undermine the goals sought by principals, without being detected.

Can principals overcome the difficulties caused by adverse selection and moral hazard? One of the main lessons of principal-agent theory is that delegation almost invariably leads to **agency loss.** Agency loss occurs when the behavior of agents leaves principals unable to achieve their goals in an efficient manner or realize them at all. Agency loss, however, can be limited under the right circumstances. For principals, then, the key task is to take steps that help bring such circumstances about.[5]

Perhaps the most common way to mitigate the agency loss associated with adverse selection is the use of **screening mechanisms.** Basically, principals induce agents to reveal their motivations and skills before hiring them. For example, employers routinely judge the qualifications of applicants through apprenticeships and examinations. The problem of moral hazard can be ameliorated in two distinct ways. The first is **institutional design.** Here, principals place agents in situations in which they find it in their self-interest to work toward outcomes favored by their principals. Corporations, for instance, commonly provide workers with a financial stake in company performance through devices such as stock options. The second approach is **oversight** of agent actions. By monitoring agents at work, principals aim to identify and redirect behavior inconsistent with their objectives. Principals can also use oversight as a deterrent. The mere possibility of being monitored may compel agents to forgo activities that do not serve principals well.

Principal-agent theory can readily be applied to policymaking in the bureaucracy. Administrative agencies are agents to whom policymaking authority is delegated. This authority originates with principals such as chief executives, legislatures, and judiciaries. The act of delegation brings each of these principals face-to-face with particular manifestations of adverse selection and moral hazard. For example, legislators have relatively little influence over the selection of agency officials, as personnel matters fall largely under the domain of the chief executive and the civil service system. Given such difficulties, why do principals empower agencies in the first place? Put differently, what are the benefits of policymaking in the bureaucracy?

## Why Bureaucracy?

One obvious rationale for bureaucracy is the scope of modern government. Early in its history, the federal government performed only a handful of functions, such as setting duties on foreign goods. Figure 3.1 illustrates that as the government's reach extended, the size of the bureaucracy grew as well. During the New Deal, perhaps the most ambitious expansion of government power in American history, the number of civilian employees in the executive

### Figure 3.1 The Size of the Federal Bureaucracy, 1821–2005

Number of Civilian Employees (in thousands)

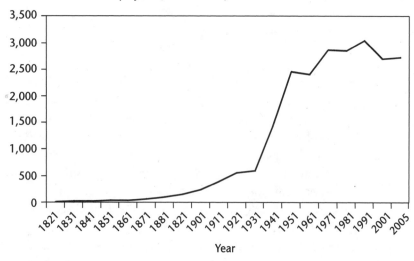

Year

Sources: U.S. Bureau of the Census, *Historical Statistics of the United States, Colonial Times to 1970,* bicentennial ed., part 1 (Washington, D.C.: Government Printing Office, 1975). U.S. Census Bureau, *Statistical Abstract of the United States: 2000,* 120th ed. (Washington, D.C.: Government Printing Office, 2000). U.S. Bureau of the Census, *Federal Government Employment and Payroll Data,* www.census.gov/govs/www/apesfed.html, February 13, 2007.

branch nearly tripled, from about half a million to close to 1.5 million. Another indication of bureaucracy's growth is the number of pages the *Federal Register* (the executive branch's official daily publication) consumes. The documents published in the *Federal Register* include agency regulations and proposed rules, as well as executive orders and other presidential materials. As indicated in Table 3.1, the size of the *Federal Register* has grown more than fivefold since 1960.

Contemporary government addresses issues not only wide ranging but often quite complex as well. In formulating the ergonomics rule, OSHA had to synthesize knowledge from fields as diverse as economics, engineering, medicine, and management. Policymaking efforts such as this one are simply beyond the existing capabilities of other government institutions. Congress, even with hundreds of members and thousands of staffers, possesses a mere fraction of the specialized expertise found in the bureaucracy.

**Table 3.1  Number of Pages in the *Federal Register,* 1960–2006**

| Year | Number of Pages |
|------|-----------------|
| 1960 | 14,479 |
| 1965 | 17,206 |
| 1970 | 20,036 |
| 1975 | 60,221 |
| 1980 | 73,258 |
| 1985 | 50,502 |
| 1990 | 49,795 |
| 1995 | 62,645 |
| 1996 | 64,591 |
| 1997 | 64,549 |
| 1998 | 68,571 |
| 1999 | 71,161 |
| 2000 | 74,258 |
| 2001 | 64,438 |
| 2002 | 75,606 |
| 2003 | 71,269 |
| 2004 | 75,675 |
| 2005 | 73,870 |
| 2006 | 74,937 |

*Source:* Office of the *Federal Register,* National Archives and Records Administration.

Bureaucracies are also valuable to government actors pursuing specific, self-interested goals. Legislators build their cases for reelection in part by helping constituents overcome bureaucratic "red tape." [6] An example of such **casework** is the assistance commonly offered to retirees whose Social Security checks have been lost in the mail. On a broader scale, elected officials can use agencies to avoid the blame that comes with controversial or difficult decisions.[7] By placing responsibility for explosives detection in the hands of DOT, Congress distanced itself from culpability in the event of a catastrophic breakdown in the screening system.

Importantly, the motivation behind the delegation of authority to the bureaucracy cannot be meaningfully separated from agency effectiveness. For example, agencies called upon to perform contradictory tasks may find it particularly difficult to succeed. Despite the emphasis on aviation security, Congress still expects DOT to look after the financial stability of air carriers and other traditional concerns that may be jeopardized by antiterrorism measures. In a similar vein, OSHA's mission—to save lives, prevent injuries, and protect workers' health—does not mention consideration of the costs imposed on businesses, even though it is central to the agency's often contentious decision-making processes. In general, the efficacy of agencies as institutions of democratic policymaking is in part a product of the politics surrounding the bureaucracy's supervisors.

## Why Delegation Varies

Although delegation to the bureaucracy is widespread, it nevertheless varies considerably across issue areas, as laid out in Figure 3.2. When issues are low in **salience,** politicians are more likely to delegate authority to the bureaucracy. Occupational licensing and child care regulation usually fall into this category. When issues are high in salience, as in the case of civil rights disputes and environmental policy, delegation is less viable because citizens and organized interests expect elected officials to act decisively.[8] **Complexity** also matters, especially for highly salient issues. When issues are high in salience and low in complexity, politicians often seek to control the bureaucracy by specifying the substance of policy in great detail. Antidiscrimination edicts exemplify this approach. When issues are high in both salience and complexity, elected officials are more likely to exert leverage over policymaking

## Figure 3.2 Explaining Variation in Delegation

|  | Complexity | |
|---|---|---|
|  | **Low** | **High** |
| **Salience** | | |
| **Low** | Delegation | Delegation |
| **High** | Substantive controls | Procedural controls |

*Source:* William Gormley Jr., "Regulatory Issue Networks in a Federal System," *Polity* 18 (Summer 1986): 607.

through procedural instruments, such as the requirement that agencies conduct environmental impact assessments before adopting rules likely to have major ecological effects.[9]

For similar reasons, delegation also varies within issue areas. It is thought that congressional control of the Environmental Protection Agency (EPA) is greatest when both legislative preferences and capabilities are strong, as when issues are high in salience and low in complexity. Among the key provisions of the Clean Air Act Amendments of 1990, those pertaining to acid rain best fit this description. The acid rain portion of the law has a much higher concentration of detailed substantive provisions than the sections addressing air toxins, mobile sources, and chlorofluorocarbons.[10] Here is one example of this type of provision:

> The Administrator shall not allocate annual allowances to emit sulfur dioxide pursuant to section 405 in such an amount as would result in total annual emissions of sulfur dioxide from utility units in excess of 8.90 million tons.[11]

When congressional preferences and capabilities are not as well developed, Congress is less apt to provide such precise instructions.

Issue characteristics alone do not determine whether delegation occurs and what form it takes. Characteristics of the delegating body are also significant determinants of bureaucratic authority. Consider the capacity of state legislatures. Some legislatures, such as in California, Michigan, and New York, closely resemble Congress in their professionalism. These legislatures meet for many days throughout the year, employ thousands of staff members, and compensate their elected representatives handsomely.[12] In contrast, the legislature in Mississippi is in session for three months at best, has a permanent staff of 150, and pays its legislators a base salary of $10,000.

As one might expect, **legislative professionalism** is closely linked to delegation. As capacity increases, legislators who might like to limit bureaucratic power are in fact more inclined to craft detailed statutes that delegate little policymaking authority.[13] During the 1990s, states all across the country sought to create managed care programs as a way of containing the skyrocketing costs of Medicaid, which provides health care to low-income and other needy residents. However, individual states approached this task in different ways. In crafting its Medicaid managed care statute, the Texas legislature spelled out specific details regarding numerous aspects of the program, including eligibility requirements, continuity of care, and competition among public and private providers.[14] By contrast, the Medicaid managed care statute enacted in Idaho reads in its entirety:

> The Department of Health and Welfare is hereby directed to develop
> and implement, as soon as possible, a new health care delivery system
> for those clients on Medicaid, utilizing a managed care concept.[15]

The Idaho legislature—comprising " 'citizen' legislators, not career politicians"—delegated significantly more authority to the bureaucracy in the area of Medicaid managed care policy than did its more professional Texas counterpart.[16]

Partisan control of the legislative and executive branches affects delegation as well. When **divided government** exists—one party controls at least one chamber in the legislature and the other the office of chief executive—delegation becomes less likely.[17] Understandably, Democratic legislators are less trusting of bureaucracies headed by Republicans, and Republican legislators less trusting of bureaucracies run by Democrats. The history of major trade legislation illustrates these tendencies quite vividly. In the postwar period, it has been a virtual certainty for Congress to increase bureaucratic discretion over tariff rates in times of unified government and decrease this discretion when divided government is in place.[18]

In the end, political principals evaluate policymaking in the bureaucracy against its alternatives. The critical question is: Would these principals be better served by making policy themselves or by delegating authority to bureaucratic agents? As we have seen, principals sometimes eschew delegation altogether. The benefits of delegation, however, often prove too irresistible to pass up. For principals, then, the trick is to capture these benefits without being unduly harmed by the actions of self-interested agents.

## Implementing Child Care Legislation

To more fully appreciate the politics of the delegation decision and the boundaries of bureaucratic authority, consider the implementation of a pair of federal child care laws passed in 1990 and 1996. In both instances, Congress approved child care subsidies to be distributed by state governments to families with relatively low incomes. The first law created the Child Care and Development Block Grant, while the second consolidated a number of different funding streams, including the block grant, under the rubric of the Child Care and Development Fund.

As Table 3.2 indicates, the 1990 legislation, sometimes known as the ABC bill, delegated considerable discretion to the Department of Health and Human Services. In addition to appropriating a certain amount of money for the program, thereby placing a ceiling on how much could be spent, Congress stressed the importance of parental choice, indicating that it wanted children to be enrolled with the provider preferred by parents "to the maximum extent practicable." In interpreting this provision, the agency specified that a state could not exclude certain categories of care (such as family child care), certain types of providers (such as church-based centers), or "significant numbers of providers" in any category or type of care. As for payment rates, Congress specified that the agency must take the costs of different settings and age groups into account and that there should be separate rates for children with special needs. But Congress left it up to the agency to determine whether states should be free to pay providers more for delivering higher-quality services. After wrestling with this issue, the agency decided to allow such differentials but to limit these differences to 10 percent. In effect, Congress established basic guidelines for administration of the block grant but left a lot of the specific operational decisions to the agency.

When revisiting the program in 1996, Congress decided to reiterate its strong commitment to parental choice and payment rates that would promote equal access. For its part, however, the agency decided to lift the 10 percent

**Table 3.2 Implementation of the 1990 Child Care Law**

| Issue | Provision of the Law | Agency Implementation |
|---|---|---|
| Parental choice | The child will be enrolled with the eligible provider selected by the parent "to the maximum extent practicable." | State and local rules cannot have the effect of excluding certain categories of care, certain types of providers, or "significant numbers of providers" in any category or type of care. |
| Payment rates | Payment rates must take into account variations in the costs of providing child care in different settings, for different age groups, and for children with special needs. | States may distinguish between higher-quality and lower-quality providers within a category of care in setting payment rates, but such rate differentials may not exceed 10 percent. |
| Administrative expenses | States must spend 75 percent of their child care allotments to improve the quality and availability of child care, and a "preponderance" of the 75 percent must be spent on child care services. | For the first two years at least 85 percent of the 75 percent share must be spent on child care services, as opposed to administrative expenses. |

*Source:* Adapted from House Ways and Means Committee, Subcommittee on Human Resources, *Regulations Issued by the Department of Health and Human Services on Child Care Programs Authorized by Public Law 101-508* (Washington, D.C.: Government Printing Office, September 13, 1991).

ceiling on rate differences within a category of care. In addition, for the first time the agency decided to recommend that states imposing a copayment requirement on parents restrict that copayment to 10 percent of the total fee. Table 3.3 provides a summary of these new provisions.

A comparison of these decisions helps clarify both the constraints that legislation imposes on the bureaucracy and the discretion that agencies can use to promote their own policy preferences. The Department of Health and Human Services (HHS) under President George H. W. Bush, headed by Louis Sullivan, imposed limits on state child care agencies to promote parental

## Table 3.3 Implementation of the 1996 Child Care Law

| Issue | Provision of the Law | Agency Implementation |
|---|---|---|
| Copayments | Rates should be designed in a way that facilitates parental choice. | It is recommended that no state require a copayment greater than 10 percent; copayments, if required, can be waived for children in protective services or for families with incomes at or below the poverty level. |
| Payment rates | Rates should be designed in a way that promotes equal access. | States should be free to set differential payment levels within categories of care, to reward providers who offer higher quality; a prior limit of 10 percent for differential payment levels within a category is rescinded. |
| Market rate survey | Payment rates established by states should be comparable to those paid by families who are not eligible for subsidies. | States must conduct a biennial market rate survey to ensure that payment rates reflect changing market conditions. |

*Source:* Adapted from U.S. Department of Health and Human Services, Administration for Children and Families, "Child Care and Development Fund; Final Rule," *Federal Register,* July 24, 1998, 39935–39998.

choice and keep costs down. In contrast, the HHS under President Clinton, headed by Donna Shalala, sought to foster improvements in child care quality and limit the financial contributions parents would have to pay. Together these episodes demonstrate that the preferences of elected officials fundamentally shape bureaucratic decisions and that the influence of these political principals is invariably limited when policymaking authority is delegated.

## Managing Delegation

Given the persistence of agency loss, political principals not only make delegation decisions with an eye to strategic considerations but also think carefully about managing the authority vested in agencies. Principals differ in the tools they can call upon as they set about this exceedingly difficult task. Some principals find themselves better equipped to cope with adverse selection issues than with moral hazard concerns, while others find the reverse to be true.

## Presidential Power

When cataloging the efforts of principals to limit agency loss, a logical place to start is with the president, the formal head of the federal bureaucracy. The presidency is a unique institution in American politics. Only the president has a national constituency and a strong desire to build a legacy that will be remembered fondly in history. For these reasons, the president, more so than others in government, has an incentive to bring the bureaucracy under **coordinated control.**[19] A bureaucracy that functions well as a unit, rather than as an uncoordinated batch of agencies, would be a valuable asset for a president seeking grand policy achievements. But does the president possess the capabilities necessary to bring such coordination about?

*UNILATERAL ACTIONS.* The ambiguity of Article II of the Constitution is widely viewed as important in determining the president's ability to command the bureaucracy. Historically, the relative dearth of enumerated powers has been taken as a sign of presidential weakness. With little formal authority, presidents must generally rely on their interpersonal skills to persuade other policymakers to go along with White House initiatives.[20] This lack of authority holds even within the executive branch, where the president is "chief" in name only.[21]

Recently, Article II's ambiguity has come to be seen by some analysts in a fundamentally different light.[22] Throughout history, presidents have taken **unilateral actions** not explicitly permitted by the Constitution. Famous examples include the Louisiana Purchase, the Emancipation Proclamation, and the creation of the EPA. Such actions are unilateral in that they are not subject to congressional or judicial approval. In fact, it is difficult for Congress and the courts to stand in the way of presidential unilateralism, even when such behavior expands and consolidates the power of the White House. The ability of the president to control the nation's policymaking apparatus, including the federal bureaucracy, has therefore accumulated over time and continues to accumulate to this day.

Two examples, one each from the Clinton administration and the presidency of George W. Bush, illuminate the potency of unilateral action as well as the boundaries of this approach to policymaking. Facing a Republican Congress hostile to his agenda, President Clinton turned to **executive orders** as a means of steering the bureaucracy and influencing public policy. Executive orders are declarations issued by the president that carry the full force of law without requiring the assent of Congress. President Clinton made good use of this unilateral authority by signing a number of executive orders that instituted significant, and sometimes controversial, policy changes such as revising the food labeling system and banning discrimination against homosexuals in federal hiring practices.[23] As Paul Begala, one of the president's advisers put it, "Stroke of the pen, law of the land. Kind of cool."[24]

Although President Clinton projected far-reaching authority through executive orders, his power of unilateral action was not without limitation. The administration's executive order barring federal contractors from hiring permanent striker replacements was struck down in court. In addition, strident opposition from the nation's governors compelled the administration to suspend an executive order on federalism it had issued just three months earlier.[25]

President George W. Bush has also experienced both the utility and constraints of unilateral action as a means of steering the bureaucracy. Shortly after the September 11, 2001, terrorist attacks, the Bush administration instituted a program of monitoring, without first obtaining warrants, the international communications of individuals inside the United States when either the individual or the interlocutor was suspected of having ties to al-Qaida or other terrorist organizations.[26] This program placed surveillance authority in the hands of the National Security Agency (NSA), an organization that has traditionally focused on foreign communications, not domestic ones.

For four years, the program operated without any public disclosure. Knowledge of the program was limited to a handful of key policymakers.[27] Although some of these insiders, including Sen. John D. Rockefeller IV, D-W.Va., privately expressed concerns about the legality and constitutionality of eavesdropping inside the United States without a warrant, the program was never abandoned or modified in a substantial way.[28] The Bush administration's actions were a stark manifestation of the use of unilateral power as a tool for managing policymaking in the bureaucracy.

Even in this instance, however, the limitations of unilateral action were ultimately put on display. In 2006, after the *New York Times* exposed the program, both Congress and the courts took steps to limit the NSA's discretion. Committees in both the House and Senate held hearings on the program and heard testimony from administration officials such as Attorney General Alberto R. Gonzales.[29] Legislation to modify the program, either at the margins or more fundamentally, was introduced but never enacted into law.[30]

In the meantime, organizations such as the American Civil Liberties Union filed lawsuits against the program in federal courts throughout the country. In Detroit, a federal district judge ruled the program unconstitutional.[31] Perhaps in response to these accumulated efforts as well as to the midterm elections that delivered to Democrats control of Congress, the Bush administration agreed, in January 2007, to subject the program to court supervision, a move it had publicly resisted for more than a year.[32] In the end, unilateral actions that do not clearly derive from formal presidential authority provide presidents with opportunities to exert powerful influence over the bureaucracy. That said, other policymaking institutions can check these opportunities when the conditions are "right," as they eventually were in the area of terrorism communications and surveillance.

**APPOINTMENTS.** In terms of formal authority, the president is relatively well equipped to address the problem of adverse selection. Presidents have the power to appoint cabinet secretaries, regulatory commissioners, administrators of independent agencies, and a host of subordinates to these top-ranking officials. All in all, political appointees fill approximately three thousand positions in the executive branch bureaucracy.[33]

What factors do administrations consider when filling agency vacancies? Each presidency is somewhat distinctive, with the Reagan administration, for example, valuing loyalty to the conservative movement and the administration of George H. W. Bush putting a premium on individuals who had served in previous positions with the president.[34] Although observers generally agree that substantive knowledge and administrative competence are attributes that would serve any appointee well, there is no escaping the centrality of politics in the nomination process.[35]

One reason for this emphasis on politics is the fact that executive branch appointments normally require **Senate confirmation** before they can take effect. At first glance, the Senate—which approves almost every nominee offered by the president—does not act as much of a hurdle, but, as one expert has stated, "that is the wrong conclusion drawn from the wrong evidence."[36] Presidents strategically anticipate Senate reactions to their nominees and routinely put forth individuals likely to pass muster at confirmation. In addition, the Senate flexes its constitutional muscles in ways other than outright rejection, through tactics such as delay in considering and voting on nominations. In recent administrations, nominees to top positions in the executive branch have waited on average more than eight months to be confirmed.[37] Delay is particularly prevalent during periods of divided government and ideological polarization in the Senate, suggesting that even the most well qualified individuals can run into trouble if the nomination is ill-timed.[38]

The politics of confirmation point out that appointments can be powerful instruments for influencing the scope and content of bureaucratic policymaking. For example, outputs in agencies ranging from the Food and Drug Administration (FDA) to the Equal Employment Opportunity Commission have shifted noticeably as a direct response to changes in leadership. Product seizures by the FDA declined by more than 50 percent after the Reagan White House tapped Arthur Hull Hayes—a champion of regulatory relief for business—to lead the agency.[39]

Despite such successes, appointees face a variety of constraints when seeking to shape bureaucratic decisions. The tenure of the average agency head is less than three years.[40] With such a short time horizon, appointees must move quickly if they want to leave a significant mark on their organization. The fact that most appointees are not personal associates of the president and therefore do not enjoy open access to the White House and its resources makes this task all the more difficult. Hence, appointees are largely left to their own devices in dealing with their subordinates, the vast majority of whom were at the agency long before the current administration came to power and will continue in their positions well after the presidency has again changed hands. In this difficult environment, it is not uncommon for appointees to **go native.**[41] Rather than act as advocates for the administration, such appointees seek to advance the positions of civil servants inside the bureaucracy, those professionals with whom they interact regularly. The utility of appointments as a way of managing delegated authority is best viewed as highly variable across administrations, agencies, and appointees themselves.

What separates effective leaders from appointees who run into difficulties in dealing with their agencies and the administration? Instructive is the case of Paul O'Neill, President George W. Bush's first secretary of the treasury. Less than two years into his tenure, O'Neill became the first cabinet member to leave the administration. Several months of criticism about his handling of an economy in the midst of a prolonged slump preceded O'Neill's departure.

Despite his experience as chairman and chief executive officer of aluminum giant Alcoa, O'Neill did not enjoy the confidence of Wall Street, an absolutely critical constituency for any treasury secretary. In addition, O'Neill did not demonstrate the flair for publicity that successful appointees so often bring to their positions. Even on a made-for-TV trip to Africa, alongside rock star Bono, O'Neill came off as a wooden leader who did not fully understand and appreciate the plight of debt-ridden countries in the developing world.[42] In the end, O'Neill did not possess the combination of personal and professional skills necessary to be an effective appointee for President Bush.

By contrast, Tommy Thompson compiled a commendable, though certainly not flawless, record as secretary of health and human services during President Bush's first term. For starters, Thompson enjoyed regular access to the White House, having campaigned long and hard for Bush's candidacy and having played a central role at the 2000 Republican National Convention.[43] Thompson was also a skilled administrator who managed to get HHS's geographically dispersed and independent agencies—including the Centers for Disease Control and Prevention in Atlanta and the National Institutes of Health in Bethesda, Maryland—to communicate and coordinate with each other more effectively.[44] Finally, Thompson, as a former governor, was well versed in generating publicity on behalf of his favored policy initiatives, as when he famously lost fifteen pounds as part of an effort to attract attention to the nation's ever increasing, and costly, obesity problem.[45] To be sure, Thompson had his share of difficult moments, particularly early in his tenure. During the anthrax crisis in the fall of 2001, for example, Thompson wrongly speculated that the first victim might have contracted the illness not through contaminated mail but by drinking water out of a stream. Such missteps aside, Thompson performed credibly in a job that has been called the "consummate management challenge in the federal government."[46]

FIRINGS. Although the most common transitions from office for political appointees are either voluntary resignations or departures by mutual consent, some appointees are fired outright, especially when they become embroiled in controversy. This occurred when it came to light that recovering Iraq war veterans were receiving substandard medical care at the Walter Reed Army Medical Center in Washington, D.C. As congressional and public protests escalated, three top officials lost their jobs, including Secretary of the Army Francis Harvey, Maj. Gen. George Weightman (commander of Walter Reed), and Lt. Gen. Kevin Kiley (surgeon general of the army).[47] These dismissals helped the White House and Defense Department assert that those responsible for the problem were being held accountable.

The president enjoys considerable—but not boundless—authority to fire political appointees. A relatively small number of independent commissioners cannot be dismissed without cause.[48] Also, even when the president has the authority to fire appointees, dismissals for political reasons sometimes draw critical attention. When Attorney General Alberto Gonzales fired eight U.S. attorneys in December 2006, presumably with the blessing of the White House, he appeared to have been responding in part to pressure from Republican members of Congress. News accounts revealed that two Republican members of Congress from New Mexico contacted one of the fired U.S. attorneys a few months earlier in an apparent effort to accelerate a corruption investigation against a Democratic officeholder.[49] Other disclosures revealed that high-ranking Justice Department officials had proposed firing U.S. attorneys who were "underperforming" or who were not "loyal Bushies."[50] Gonzales's failure to speak candidly about the political factors underlying these eight dismissals led to calls for his own dismissal.

CIVIL SERVICE REFORM. Through much of the nation's history, presidents have sought to enhance their control over the bureaucracy by reforming the rules that govern civil servants, those executive branch officials not subject to presidential appointment and Senate confirmation. In 1905 President Theodore Roosevelt formed the **Keep Committee** to investigate ways of improving the organization and effectiveness of the federal government.[51] Franklin Roosevelt oversaw passage of the **Reorganization Act** of 1939, establishing the **Executive Office of the President,** which provides the White

House with an apparatus for directing and coordinating policy in areas particularly central to the president's agenda. The Council of Economic Advisers and the National Security Council have both been a part of the Executive Office for many years. Under President George W. Bush, the White House also includes a handful of newly established entities such as the President's Homeland Security Advisory Council and Office of Faith-Based and Community Initiatives.

In 1978 the **Civil Service Reform Act** brought significant changes to the personnel system of the executive branch. For example, the act established the **Senior Executive Service,** a group of top-level civil servants with less job security than their colleagues but more of an opportunity to earn bonuses based on productivity and other performance measures. The idea behind this reform was to create a senior management system under the president that could meaningfully compete with the private sector in recruiting and retaining individuals of exceptional talent. In terms of enhancing the president's capacity to influence decision making inside executive branch agencies, the act and similar reform efforts have garnered mixed reviews.

At first glance, career bureaucrats—who number in the millions—would seem unlikely to be very responsive to presidents and politics more generally.[52] Consider, however, that rather than remain loyal to supervisors in the face of changing presidents and administrative tasks, thousands of senior executives instead exited the federal bureaucracy altogether in the years following passage of the Civil Service Reform Act.[53] From the early 1970s to the early 1990s—a period during which Republicans controlled the White House for all but four years—top-level civil servants became increasingly conservative and Republican as a group.[54] In 1970 President Nixon faced a civil service leadership that favored Democrats by a three-to-one margin. By the first Bush administration, Republicans enjoyed an 11 percent edge among these officials.

The potency of personnel management is illustrated by the debate over the creation of the Department of Homeland Security.[55] In 2002 President Bush proposed merging twenty-two agencies and 170,000 employees into a single organization aimed at protecting the American homeland from terrorist threats. The president's proposal ran into difficulty in the Senate, then under Democratic control. The key stumbling block was presidential prerogatives in managing the department's civil servants. President Bush requested the authority to hire, demote, and transfer employees for national security reasons. A majority of senators opposed this request on the grounds that it

represented too significant an erosion in the collective bargaining rights usually held by federal employees. Not until Republicans gained control of the
Senate following the November 2002 elections did the administration muster
the congressional support necessary to secure a personnel system with the
flexibility and control President Bush sought.

The implementation of this system proved challenging for the Bush administration. In early 2005, four labor unions filed suit to block the Department of Homeland Security from adopting its rules, several years in the
making, for strengthening the link between employee pay and performance on
the job.[56] A series of court decisions upheld the unions' complaint, compelling
the agency to redraft its rules, a cumbersome and time-consuming process.[57]

REGULATORY REVIEW. As the scope and complexity of bureaucratic policymaking have grown, presidents have taken steps to enhance their ability to
observe and evaluate agency decisions. One way in which recent presidents
have coped with the problem of moral hazard is by systematically reviewing
agency regulations. Established in 1981 by President Reagan in **Executive
Order 12291, regulatory review** is widely considered one of the most important developments in the executive branch during the past several decades.[58]
Under regulatory review, agencies are required to submit drafts of prospective actions to the **Office of Information and Regulatory Affairs** (OIRA), an
organization located in the White House's **Office of Management and Budget** (OMB). Only after OMB clears an agency submission can the rule be published in the *Federal Register* and become law. OIRA, a bureaucracy in itself,
serves as a kind of **counterbureaucracy,** overseeing executive branch agencies to ensure that regulations will not be unnecessarily costly or deviate too
significantly from presidential priorities.[59]

From its inception, regulatory review has been controversial. Supporters
of review argue that White House clearance promotes consistency and overarching standards in an otherwise uncoordinated regulatory system;[60] thus
bureaucratic decision making is strengthened by passing through an array of
economic, scientific, and technical checkpoints and by possessing the political and constitutional legitimacy of presidential approval. Critics claim that
centralized clearance provides industry interests and ideological opponents
of regulation with a way of undermining efforts to protect health, safety, and
the environment. OMB review, according to this perspective, is grounded in
ideas, such as cost effectiveness, that are inherently antiregulatory in their
orientation.[61]

Information presented in Table 3.4 leaves no doubt that regulatory review has had a profound effect on the work of the bureaucracy. Although OIRA rarely rejects agency rules altogether, it alters the content of hundreds of actions each year. During the Reagan administration, OIRA grew increasingly tough on agencies. In 1981 OIRA required modifications in only 4.87 percent of the rules it reviewed. By 1988, this percentage had grown nearly fivefold, to 21.99 percent.

President Clinton brought important changes to regulatory review shortly after taking office. **Executive Order 12866,** issued on September 30, 1993, limited OIRA's jurisdiction to rules designated as significant and with an annual impact on the economy of at least $100 million. Because of this limitation the number of rules reviewed by OMB dropped noticeably from 1994 forward. With this smaller portfolio, OIRA now requires agencies to alter well over half their submissions before granting approval.

How effective is regulatory review as a way for presidents to mitigate the agency loss that follows from moral hazard? OIRA is charged with not only pursuing presidential priorities but also increasing the role of economic analysis in the regulatory process. At times, these dual missions point OIRA in the same direction. But what about when political imperatives and economic considerations are at odds? Here, the evidence suggests that accountability to the president trumps fealty to analytical ideals.[62]

During the entire Clinton administration, the only ostensibly proregulation presidency since the beginning of OMB review, only sixteen rules were

## Table 3.4 Review of Agency Regulations by Office of Management and Budget, 1981–2006

| Year | Rules reviewed No. | Rules rejected No. | Percent | Rules altered No. | Percent |
|------|------|------|---------|------|---------|
| 1981 | 2,790 | 45 | 1.61 | 136 | 4.87 |
| 1982 | 2,637 | 56 | 2.12 | 271 | 10.27 |
| 1983 | 2,483 | 32 | 1.28 | 314 | 12.64 |
| 1984 | 2,112 | 58 | 2.74 | 321 | 15.19 |
| 1985 | 2,213 | 34 | .72 | 510 | 23.04 |
| 1986 | 2,010 | 29 | 1.44 | 461 | 22.93 |
| 1987 | 2,315 | 10 | .43 | 547 | 23.62 |
| 1988 | 2,360 | 29 | 1.22 | 519 | 21.99 |
| 1989 | 2,220 | 29 | 1.30 | 431 | 19.41 |
| 1990 | 2,137 | 21 | .98 | 412 | 19.27 |
| 1991 | 2,523 | 28 | 1.10 | 685 | 27.15 |
| 1992 | 2,286 | 9 | .39 | 593 | 25.94 |
| 1993 | 2,167 | 9 | .41 | 509 | 23.48 |
| 1994 | 831 | 0 | — | 310 | 37.30 |
| 1995 | 620 | 3 | .48 | 242 | 39.03 |
| 1996 | 507 | 0 | — | 261 | 51.47 |
| 1997 | 505 | 4 | .79 | 283 | 56.03 |
| 1998 | 487 | 0 | — | 289 | 59.34 |
| 1999 | 587 | 0 | — | 365 | 62.18 |
| 2000 | 583 | 0 | — | 352 | 60.37 |
| 2001 | 700 | 18 | 2.57 | 319 | 45.57 |
| 2002 | 669 | 5 | .74 | 363 | 54.26 |
| 2003 | 715 | 2 | .27 | 431 | 60.27 |
| 2004 | 627 | 1 | .15 | 393 | 62.67 |
| 2005 | 611 | 1 | .16 | 400 | 65.46 |
| 2006 | 600 | 0 | — | 415 | 69.16 |

*Source:* Data gathered by authors from Web site produced by the Office of Management and Budget and General Services Administration, www.reginfo.gov/public/.

*Note:* The numbers in the cells represent the number of rules reviewed, rejected, and altered by the Office of Information and Regulatory Affairs (OIRA) in a given year. For example, in 1981 OIRA reviewed 2,790 rules, rejecting 45 (1.61 percent) and altering 136 (4.87 percent).

prevented from taking effect. During the administration of George W. Bush, who has emphasized a strong response to the threat of terrorism, OIRA has not rejected a single rule addressing homeland security even though such regulations often have ill-defined benefits and high costs.[63] OMB review apparently has provided the president with an institutionalized mechanism for competing with other principals who seek to influence the content of bureaucratic decisions.

## Congressional Control of the Bureaucracy

Owing to its orientation as a lawmaking and investigatory body, Congress is naturally equipped to manage the bureaucracy through institutional design and oversight. Congress enacts, usually with presidential approval, the statutes that create and assign tasks to executive branch agencies. These statutes provide legislators with opportunities to place structural and procedural constraints on bureaucratic policymaking. When Congress established the Consumer Product Safety Commission in 1972, for example, it allowed the agency to issue regulations but limited this authority to standards that had been offered by industry interests, representatives of the general public, and other parties from outside government.[64]

Congress also bears responsibility for keeping a watchful eye on the policies and programs formulated and operated within the executive branch. It carries out these responsibilities through channels such as **oversight hearings** and investigations into allegations of waste, fraud, and abuse. Many of these monitoring activities are routine and attract little outside attention, but occasionally oversight becomes front-page news and transforms bureaucratic organizations, as happened in the late 1990s when Senate hearings exposed wide-spread mistreatment of taxpayers by officials in the Internal Revenue Service.[65]

Toward what ends do legislators usually make use of instruments of institutional design and oversight? Although hundreds of different constituencies are enfranchised in the Senate and House of Representatives, congressional control of the bureaucracy is fundamentally uncoordinated in its orientation.[66] Specific committees and subcommittees may influence what goes on in particular agencies, but the bureaucracy as a whole does not operate under the direction of Congress as an institution. In the end, no matter how potent Congress and its members may be, the control exercised by the legislative branch is particularistic rather than aimed at furthering general societal and political interests.

**POLITICS OF BUREAUCRATIC STRUCTURE.** At times, agencies seem designed to fail, or at least to operate in ways not even their most ardent supporters can appreciate and understand. Consider again the Consumer Product Safety Commission (CPSC). The CPSC is an independent regulatory body charged with reducing the risk of injury and death associated with consumer products. Reluctant to champion the burgeoning consumer movement, the Nixon administration originally proposed placing the CPSC within the Department of Health, Education, and Welfare, where it would have had relatively little power and could have been easily monitored by the White House.[67] Congress, however, rejected this proposal and structured the CPSC so it would be well insulated from presidential control. Importantly, this insulation was not complete because the commission was forced to rely on the Justice Department to carry out most legal actions against violators of safety standards. Over time such requirements have served to weigh the CPSC down and inhibit its ability to carry out its mission effectively.

Why do legislators structure agencies in ways that all too often undermine bureaucratic accountability and performance? Two features of the democratic process are particularly salient when considering these structural choices.[68] The first is **political uncertainty.** Thanks to periodic elections, powerful politicians and their favored constituencies cannot count on controlling the institutions of government into the indefinite future. Inevitably, opposing ideological and partisan forces will take over the reins of power. This uncertainty has important implications for bureaucratic design as agency benefactors have incentives to protect their creations from meddling by unkind political authorities. In the case of the CPSC, such protection came through the appointment of commissioners to fixed, staggered, seven-year terms, which effectively distanced the commission from presidential control, even administrations with consumerist sentiments. In the end, political uncertainty leads agency supporters to "purposely create structures that even they cannot control."[69]

The second key feature of the democratic process is **political compromise.** Under the separation of powers system, opponents of legislative action are usually granted concessions. At times, these concessions prove to be of great consequence, severely limiting the ability of legislative advocates to achieve their objectives. The creation of the CPSC was not a total loss for business interests. In addition to the **offeror process** and Justice Department enforcement, these interests secured the right to judicial review of CPSC decisions and a guarantee that the agency would come up for reauthorization in the short span of three years. In other words, Congress gave business and other CPSC foes the leverage necessary to immediately set about the task of undermining the agency and abolishing it completely before it became too entrenched in the executive branch. In general, the dictates of political compromise imply that agencies are designed "in no small measure by participants who explicitly want them to fail."[70] The lessons of political uncertainty and political compromise, taken together, reveal that if Congress has difficulty managing delegated authority, this difficulty springs not only from bureaucratic behavior but also from the nature of the legislative process.

***ADMINISTRATIVE PROCEDURES.*** Within the constraints imposed by bureaucratic structure, Congress can influence what the executive branch does by manipulating the **administrative procedures** under which agencies operate. Administrative procedures specify the steps agencies must follow when making decisions and formulating policies. These steps typically include gathering certain types of information and consulting with stakeholders in particular ways. The **National Environmental Policy Act** requires agencies to prepare environmental impact statements for rules with potentially significant ecological consequences, as when the Federal Energy Regulatory Commission considers whether to approve the construction of a hydroelectric facility.[71] Such assessments lay out the likely effects of the rule—harm to a fishery, for example—and the steps the agency will take to minimize prospective environmental damage.[72]

Administrative procedures sometimes target specific agencies or decisions. For example, a statute requires the Federal Railroad Administration (FRA) to hold public hearings during all of its rulemakings.[73] These hearings provide interested parties with opportunities to address agency officials in person, often without having to leave their communities. When seeking to modify its regulations on the power braking systems used in non-passenger trains, the FRA convened hearings not only in Washington, D.C. but also Chicago, Sacramento, and Newark.[74]

In what ways do administrative procedures potentially enhance congressional control over the bureaucracy? Administrative procedures can create bureaucratic environments that mirror the politics that occurred in Congress when it delegated authority to the agency.[75] In 1996 Congress amended the Safe Drinking Water Act. While working on the amendments, legislators heard from three distinct types of stakeholders—utilities and other water producer interests, state and local regulators, and environmental and consumer organizations.[76] The amendments delegated great authority to the EPA to set standards for contaminants, such as arsenic, that pose a threat to drinking water. The amendments also specified very carefully the composition of the National Drinking Water Advisory Council, a stakeholder organization with which the agency consults when crafting drinking water regulations. Specifically, the advisory council must be composed of an equal number of water producers, state and local government officials, and representatives of the general public. This membership requirement means that the agency can expect to hear from the interests that participated in the congressional debate over the amendments. In other words, the pattern of participation in drinking water rulemakings is likely to resemble closely the participatory environment that had characterized the lawmaking process.

Administrative procedures can also stack the deck in favor of particular constituencies. Over time, the National Environmental Policy Act has brought ecological considerations more to the fore than they would otherwise have been in agency proceedings. For example, environmentalists have used the act to stop construction projects initially endorsed by the Army Corps of Engineers. These successes have led to a noticeable change in the types of projects the corps is willing to propose.[77] Similarly, the Federal Energy Regulatory Commission became substantially more inclined to render proenvironment licensing decisions in the years following passage of the act.[78]

Finally, administrative procedures can place bureaucratic policymaking on autopilot. In other words, as the preferences of enfranchised constituencies change, agency decisions change correspondingly. During the 1970s the cable television industry emerged as a powerful political force in Congress. Shortly thereafter, the industry became the beneficiary of a major deregulation effort by the Federal Communications Commission. This deregulation occurred without any direct congressional intervention but via changes in the set of interests represented in commission proceedings.[79] In general, well-designed administrative procedures obviate the need for constant legislative attention to agency behavior.

Administrative procedures, it is important to recognize, vary in the leverage they give members of Congress over the management of delegated authority. Some administrative procedures, such as the requirement that the FRA hold public hearings, serve to place hurdles in front of agencies.[80] These hurdles increase the costs to agencies of doing their day-to-day business. The FRA for years deferred acting on power braking systems as a result of hostile and contradictory testimony delivered at its rulemaking hearings.[81] Other administrative procedures, by contrast, increase the costs of taking particular courses of action. The National Environmental Policy Act makes it difficult for agencies to give short shrift to the environment in cases where the ecological stakes are relatively pronounced. With this variation in mind, it is difficult to make blanket claims about the efficacy of administrative procedures in promoting congressional control of the bureaucracy.

**OVERSIGHT.** Legislators possess the ability to reduce their moral hazard problem through oversight of the bureaucracy. Oversight occurs in a variety of forms, including committee hearings and scandal-induced investigations.[82] For a long time, observers maintained that members of Congress tend to neglect oversight in favor of other functions, such as bringing federal projects and other forms of "bacon" home to their constituents.[83] Thus, in practice oversight has not been viewed as an especially important tool of congressional control.

This assessment has come under critical scrutiny in recent years as evidence suggests a significant increase in the volume of oversight activity in the 1970s and 1980s.[84] On average, congressional committees collectively spent fewer than 200 days per year conducting oversight during the decade of the 1960s. By 1983, this level of activity had grown substantially, to 587 days. In relative terms, oversight as a percentage of total committee activity increased from 9.1 percent in 1971 to 25.2 percent in 1983. Oversight, then, emerged as an integral part of the surveillance system used by members of Congress to monitor the bureaucracy's exercise of delegated authority.

Why did legislators become more interested during these years in actively overseeing executive branch agencies? Internally, the congressional reforms of the early 1970s, such as the proliferation of subcommittees and staff resources, enhanced the ease with which most members could carry out meaningful oversight. Externally, increases in the size and complexity of government made bureaucratic accountability and performance more valuable commodities than in previous eras of policymaking.[85] Together with divided government, these internal and external changes made it exceedingly difficult to create new legislation and therefore put a premium on influencing policy by overseeing already existing programs.

High, sustained levels of oversight are still not a given, even under the favorable environmental conditions of the postreform Congress. It is well established that the business of governance, including oversight, was not a strong suit of congressional Republicans when, in 1995, they returned to a bicameral majority for the first time in four decades.[86] Democrats promised—and delivered—a revival of oversight when they regained full control of Congress in 2007. Within two months after assuming control of Congress, Democratic legislators conducted a total of 81 hearings on the Iraq war.[87] Congressional Democrats also held high-profile hearings on security leaks (the outing of Central Intelligence Agency undercover employee Valerie Plame), the quality of medical care at Walter Reed Army Medical Center, and other subjects.

When engaging in oversight of the executive branch, members of Congress can pursue one of two basic strategies. The first is **police patrol oversight.** In police patrols, legislators search for bureaucratic actions that fail to conform to congressional expectations, much in the way that officers on the beat seek to ferret out criminal activity. In contrast, **fire alarm oversight** places much of the burden of monitoring the bureaucracy on citizens and organized interests, through instruments such as the Freedom of Information Act and Government in the Sunshine Act. Like firefighters, legislators swing into action after an alarm is sounded, using their policymaking apparatus to bring recalcitrant agencies under control. Given that police patrols require a relatively significant investment of congressional time and resources, it is widely presumed that the fire alarm approach dominates oversight.[88]

This presumption is not necessarily accurate, however. By some accounts, committee hearings more often than not prove to be police patrol in their orientation.[89] In 1995, for example, 86.1 percent of the House Judiciary Committee's hearings consisted of routine, ongoing legislative activities, not reactions to crises and other types of galvanizing events. These activities included consideration of the reauthorization of the **Administrative Conference of the United States,** an organization charged with studying agency processes and making recommendations to Congress regarding how to improve these processes. Several months after this hearing, Congress voted to terminate the agency's funding. All of this occurred with very little outside involvement or even awareness. Rather, Congress's oversight of the Administrative Conference took place within the context of the agency's regularly scheduled reauthorization process.

In all forms, oversight is inherently limited in its ability to constrain agency behavior. Once they identify transgressions, legislators must have the incentive and capacity to sanction and redirect agencies. Each set of tools that might be used for such purposes—appointments, budgets, and legislative actions—is problematic in important respects.[90] Congress, with its dispersion of authority across chambers and committees, has difficulty passing legislation of any kind. Even if Congress enacts legislation targeting an agency, there is no guarantee that the new law will succeed where previous efforts failed in bringing about compliant behavior. Although oversight occasionally produces dramatic results, more often than not it is most useful as a way of deterring agencies from running too far afoul of legislators and their preferred policies.

## Judicial Review

The judicial system, like the presidency and Congress, is appropriately viewed as a principal to the bureaucracy's agents. Judges routinely oversee and review the work of executive branch agencies. In this vein, one of the most common judicial tasks is verifying that bureaucrats act in accordance with the law. A somewhat less common task is ensuring that bureaucratic actions are consistent with the Constitution. If an agency takes steps deemed illegal or unconstitutional, then its work can be overturned in the judiciary. When this happens, the court in question will often remand the action to the bureaucracy, with specific instructions as to how the agency's legal or constitutional mistakes might be rectified. How, then, do the courts go about dealing with their moral hazard difficulties?

*JUDGES V. POLITICIANS.* **Judicial review** has several characteristics that distinguish it from instruments of presidential and congressional control. First, whereas politicians can engage in either police patrol or fire alarm oversight, the latter alone is available to judges. Courts can only hear cases brought to their doorsteps by plaintiffs. Put differently, judges must wait for individuals or organizations to pull a fire alarm indicating that they have been injured or aggrieved by some agency action. Thus, in its basic orientation toward the bureaucracy the judiciary is more passive than either the executive or legislative branch.

Second, judges place greater emphasis than politicians on procedural fairness and irregularities. One of the hallmarks of judicial review is an acute awareness of the requirements the Administrative Procedure Act and other relevant laws impose on agencies. The courts sometimes overturn bureaucratic actions because agencies have failed to provide adequate notice of a proposed rulemaking. Likewise, an agency that fails to provide interested parties with an adequate opportunity to comment on a proposed rule or fails to adequately explain the reasoning behind a final rule may find itself prohibited from completing or implementing the action at hand.

Third, because the judiciary is subject to numerous legal and operational constraints, interactions between judges and agencies tend to be more formal and less frequent than those between politicians and agencies. The nature of these interactions can lead to both negative and positive results. On the one hand, formal, infrequent interactions discourage flexible problem solving by agencies and stifle negotiations between judges and bureaucrats. On the other hand, these arrangements make it somewhat more difficult for agencies to shirk judicial orders. Unlike politicians, who express themselves through laws, hearings, executive orders, informal meetings, telephone conversations, and other mechanisms, judges essentially express themselves only through official decisions and decrees. Agencies can at times deflect pressure from one politician by contending that demands from elsewhere impose obligations to the contrary. Pressure from judges is far more visible, much easier to document, and ultimately more difficult to resist.

These characteristics can be observed in the reactions of federal agencies to Supreme Court decisions that reversed or remanded executive branch actions. From 1953 to 1990 there were 229 such decisions. Although uncommon relative to the total number of cases handled in that time, these decisions provoked a significant response on the part of the bureaucracy. Major policy change occurred after 72.7 percent of the decisions, while moderate and minor alterations followed 14.1 and 5.9 percent of them, respectively. Only 7.3 percent resulted in a complete absence of policy change.[91] As these episodes indicate, the coercive power of the Supreme Court and other judicial bodies is rather potent on those occasions when it is imposed. What remains an open question is whether this coercion serves to enhance bureaucratic performance as well as accountability.

CIRCUIT COURTS AND ADMINISTRATIVE LAW. Within the federal judi-ciary, most lawsuits challenging agency decisions originate in district or trial courts. By law, however, some agency decisions may be appealed directly to a circuit court of appeals. Regardless of where a case originates, circuit courts of appeals are particularly important in the field of administrative law. Prominent among them is the U.S. Court of Appeals for the District of Co-lumbia—or the **D.C. Circuit**—because a disproportionate number of ap-peals are filed in the city, where most agencies are headquartered. Indeed, legal analysts sometimes refer to the D.C. Circuit as the second most impor-tant court in the land, behind only the Supreme Court.[92] Whether or not that assessment is true, it is indisputable that the D.C. Circuit "enjoys an un-matched reputation as a leader in determining the substance and content of administrative law."[93]

As a general rule, circuit courts of appeals affirm decisions made by ex-ecutive branch agencies. During the 1970s circuit courts affirmed, on average, more than 60 percent of all agency decisions subjected to challenges. During the 1980s this affirmation rate rose to more than 70 percent. The D.C. Circuit, however, has been consistently less deferential than other circuit courts. During the 1970s and 1980s the D.C. Circuit sustained agencies only 57 and 56 percent of the time, respectively.[94]

The greater judicial activism of the D.C. Circuit can be traced back to the 1970s, especially to the thinking of Judge Harold Leventhal. In *Greater Boston Television Corp. v. Federal Communications Commission,* Leventhal first articulated the **hard look doctrine** of judicial review, which called for judges to take their supervisory responsibilities seriously. In that decision, Leventhal wrote that a court must intervene if it "becomes aware, especially from a combination of danger signals, that the agency has not really taken a 'hard look' at the salient problems, and has not genuinely engaged in reasoned decision-making."[95] In a series of subsequent decisions, Leventhal and other judges on the D.C. Circuit struck down a variety of major bureaucratic actions after tough scrutiny of the agencies' substantive reasoning in complex cases. For example, in *International Harvester Co. v. Ruckelshaus,* the D.C. Circuit invalidated the EPA's emission standards under the Clean Air Act by challenging the agency's underlying methodology.[96]

Another prominent D.C. Circuit judge, David Bazelon, supported Leventhal's call for tough scrutiny but preferred strong procedural review over strong substantive review. In the *International Harvester* case, for example, Bazelon argued that the agency's refusal to grant a one-year suspension of its 1975 emission standards was procedurally flawed because the agency had not allowed the petitioners a general right of cross-examination during the rule-making proceedings.[97] Ultimately, in the *Vermont Yankee* case in 1978 the Supreme Court curbed the D.C. Circuit's penchant for strong procedural review when it held that a federal court may not impose procedural requirements on an agency above and beyond those specified in the Administrative Procedure Act.[98] Importantly, this decision left strong substantive review untouched and may have even encouraged it.[99]

Although the D.C. Circuit enjoys considerable prestige, the Supreme Court does not automatically defer to it or any other court. The *Vermont Yankee* decision aptly illustrates this point. In 2001 the Supreme Court overruled a 1999 decision by the D.C. Circuit that had overturned a soot and smog rule adopted by the EPA. In *American Trucking Associations v. EPA,* the D.C. Circuit had reversed the agency's rule by reviving a moribund tenet of administrative law known as the **nondelegation doctrine.** This doctrine states that Congress may not delegate legislative authority to the executive branch of the government. In effect, the doctrine implies that congressional standards must have some teeth, some specificity. In *American Trucking,* the Supreme Court unanimously upheld the agency's authority to set new and tougher clean air standards without first considering the potential economic impact of these standards on the trucking industry. The Supreme Court also explicitly declined to invoke the nondelegation doctrine, thus repudiating the D.C. Circuit.[100]

In perhaps the most important case in modern administrative law, *Chevron v. Natural Resources Defense Council,* the Supreme Court constrained judicial review by articulating the doctrine of **administrative deference.**[101] In short, the justices upheld the authority of the EPA to define sources of air pollution under the Clean Air Act of 1977. More generally, this ruling means that judges must defer to agency interpretations of executive branch authority when the statute granting this authority is ambiguous and the agency's interpretation of the underlying ambiguity is reasonable.

**SUPREME COURT.** In light of these decisions and doctrines, it is not surprising that, like circuit courts of appeal, the Supreme Court is more likely to defer to agencies than overturn them.[102] While the outcome of any Supreme Court case depends on many factors—the legal merits of the case, the skills of the attorneys, and so forth—political ideology also plays a role in the Court's decision making. The more liberal Warren Court (1953–1969) supported liberal agency decisions 85.7 percent of the time, while the more conservative Burger Court (1969–1986) supported liberal agency decisions only 69.1 percent of the time. Similarly, the Warren Court supported conservative agency decisions 63.4 percent of the time, a rate nearly 20 percent lower than that of the Burger Court. Although the Supreme Court, and courts more generally, often hesitate to rule against agencies, this does not mean judicial review is ineffectual. Agencies undoubtedly craft decisions with an eye to the possibility that their procedures and substantive reasoning may at some point be subjected to judicial scrutiny.

## Principal-Agent Theory and the Bureaucracy's Clients

Consistent with principal-agent theory, chief executives, legislatures, and judiciaries all find themselves in positions where they can limit the loss associated with the delegation of policymaking authority to the bureaucracy. None of these political principals, however, can completely eliminate the problems raised by adverse selection and moral hazard. When setting about the task of managing delegation, each principal faces unique difficulties, from the judiciary's inherently reactive nature to the president's ambitious desire for coordinated control of a sprawling bureaucracy.

An approach common to all of these principals is enlisting the help of third parties in the use of screening mechanisms, institutional design, and oversight. For many years the White House has relied on organized interests to put forth and evaluate presidential appointees. In fact, President George W. Bush stoked a mild controversy when he broke from precedent by declining to consider the recommendations of the American Bar Association in filling federal judgeship vacancies. In Congress, the essence of fire alarm oversight is the empowerment of citizens and groups to keep a watchful eye on agency proceedings and decisions. To keep their dockets full, the courts rely on litigants to press claims about the illegality and unconstitutionality of bureaucratic actions.

All of this raises the question of whether principal-agent theory can provide insight into the role and influence of agency clients in bureaucratic policymaking. Strictly speaking, clients are not bureaucratic principals as they are neither the hierarchical supervisors of agencies nor the wellsprings of delegated authority. As a result, clients are only as potent as the public officials whose backing they enjoy.

For such backing to materialize, clients must possess attributes of significant value to political principals. For example, members of Congress have a never-ending need for information about the views of their constituents, the predispositions of their colleagues on pending legislation, and the outcomes likely to follow from their policy choices.[103] Clients who can meet these information needs are naturally advantaged in the lawmaking process. These advantages carry over into the bureaucracy when legislators structure agencies, design administrative procedures, and conduct oversight in ways targeted to ensure that policymaking in the executive branch does not stray too far from deals struck in Congress.

Who then are the clients best positioned to serve as powerful third parties in the principal-agent hierarchy? The key consideration here is mobilization. For some time it has been clear that not all parties with a stake in government activity organize in pursuit of their policy preferences.[104] Likewise, the extensiveness of client mobilization varies greatly across the issues that fall under the domain of the executive branch. In the end, principal-agent theory points not only to the unique position of clients in the policymaking hierarchy but also to the need for a close examination of the factors affecting the mobilization of both the beneficiaries and targets of agency actions.

## Principals and Principles

As this chapter has demonstrated, the bureaucracy has no shortage of bosses. At times these bosses exercise extraordinary influence over what agencies can and cannot do. With one vote Congress nullified OSHA's ergonomics rule, a major policy action years in the making. Such highly visible cases aside, the bureaucracy's bosses usually exercise their authority, if at all, in much subtler and more conditional ways. A year after Congress ordered that all checked baggage be screened for explosives, DOT had not yet completed the task. When the agency pressed for a year's extension, Congress granted it.[105]

If the power of those who serve as the bureaucracy's principals is conditional, then what specific conditions determine the contours of agency discretion? Part of this story deals with the tools principals possess, and do not possess, to combat adverse selection and moral hazard. Although the Constitution provides the presidency with few formal advantages vis-à-vis the bureaucracy, presidents are powerful in ways difficult to measure. When the president puts the full authority and prestige of the White House behind an initiative, as George W. Bush did with the creation of the Department of Homeland Security, it is often difficult for other policymakers, including bureaucrats, to resist. Yet from the perspective of these policymakers, presidential agendas are usually rather limited in scope. As a result the president exercises power on only an occasional basis.

The judiciary is also a potent principal that gets involved in agency decision making under a limited set of circumstances. For most agencies most of the time, judicial review undoubtedly represents an unpleasant prospect, but one they experience only occasionally. The same cannot be said when it comes to legislative principals. Legislators have their hands on everything from agency design to oversight of the bureaucracy. Although these instruments give Congress and other such principals strong leverage over the problem of moral hazard, this leverage by no means eradicates agency loss, as the following example illustrates.

The Resource Conservation and Recovery Act of 1976 empowers the EPA to issue standards for the treatment, storage, and disposal of hazardous wastes.[106] The act requires the agency to adhere to a variety of analytical, disclosure, and participation procedures when setting these standards. Importantly, the agency has found a way to get around these requirements when it so desires. In cases where it wishes to evade congressional scrutiny, the EPA eschews the issuance of formal rules and makes policy instead through **guidance**

**documents.** Although guidance documents (statements agencies produce to flesh out their stances on particular issues) lack the full force of law, regulated firms routinely comply with them. Thus, despite Congress's efforts, hazardous waste policy is often made beyond the reach of the tools legislators normally use to limit bureaucratic discretion.

To put it differently, part of the story of the boundaries of bureaucratic authority concerns the willingness of agency officials to respond to their bosses' cues. In the broadest sense, the bureaucracy's bosses include not only chief executives, legislatures, and judiciaries but the public—the very society within which agencies operate—as well. With this in mind, many bureaucrats try to represent the public interest as best they can determine it. When viewed in this way, agencies appear to be populated for the most part with officials who are **principled agents.**[107] That is, agency officials are hard workers who are highly professional, devoted to the mission of their organizations, and only rarely driven to shirk or sabotage the policy aims of their bosses. In the end, control of the bureaucracy emanates not only from political principals but also from other sources inside and outside of agencies.

## Key Terms

Administrative Conference of the United States, 84
Administrative deference, 89
Administrative procedures, 81
Adverse selection, 58
Agency loss, 59
Agent, 57
Casework, 61
Civil Service Reform Act, 74
Complexity, 62
Congressional Review Act, 55
Coordinated control, 68
Counterbureaucracy, 75
D.C. Circuit, 87
Delegation, 57
Divided government, 64
Ergonomics rule, 55
Executive Office of the President, 73

Executive Order 12291, 75
Executive Order 12866, 76
Executive orders, 69
*Federal Register,* 60
Fire alarm oversight, 84
Go native, 71
Guidance documents, 91
Hard look doctrine, 88
Institutional design, 59
Judicial review, 86
Keep Committee, 73
Legislative professionalism, 64
Moral hazard, 58
National Environmental Policy Act, 81
Nondelegation doctrine, 88
Offeror process, 80
Office of Information and Regulatory Affairs, 75

Office of Management
  and Budget, 75
Oversight, 59
Oversight hearings, 78
Police patrol oversight, 84
Political compromise, 80
Political uncertainty, 79
Principal, 57
Principled agents, 92

Regulatory review, 75
Reorganization Act, 73
Resolution of disapproval, 55
Salience, 62
Screening mechanisms, 59
Senate confirmation, 70
Senior Executive Service, 74
Unilateral actions, 68

# 4 | The Bureaucracy's Clients

IN THE SUMMER OF 2000 wildfires of historic proportions raged across the American West. One of the most devastated areas was Montana's Bitterroot National Forest, where more than 355,000 acres of ponderosa pines burned. From one of these trees state wildlife officials dramatically rescued a malnourished, orphaned black bear cub. The cuddly cub, with his singed paws wrapped in bandages, enthralled the nation and came to epitomize nature's resiliency in the face of horrific destruction.[1]

A year and a half later, resiliency of a different sort sparked a political firestorm. On December 18, 2001, the Forest Service announced a plan to make more than 46,000 acres of burned timber available for logging. According to the agency, the removal of this charred lumber would promote the forest's revitalization by reducing the fire threat posed by thousands of dead and dying trees. The agency's plan was heartily endorsed by the logging industry and other local economic interests, all of which stood to benefit greatly from the harvest. Environmentalists staunchly opposed the recovery operation on two ecological grounds: one, it would interfere with the decomposition that naturally occurs after forest fires; two, it might produce runoff harmful to bull trout and other fish already threatened by abnormally high sediment levels.[2]

The controversy surrounding Bitterroot's revitalization put the Forest Service in a difficult, yet not uncommon, position. By law, the agency must pursue "sustainable multiple-use management" of the land under its domain.[3] This mission means that the agency must serve the interests of both environmentalists seeking to conserve natural resources and parties seeking to foster rural economic development.

The two constituencies flexed their political muscles during the debate over Bitterroot. Groups such as the Montana Wood Products Association pressured the agency not only to open the forest up to timber removal but also to act without delay. Within two years burned trees dry and crack, losing their commercial value. Responding to this concern, the Forest Service waived the public appeals process that usually takes place before the agency finalizes logging decisions.

On the day the recovery operation was announced, two environmental groups—the Wilderness Society and American Wildlands—went to court to block the Forest Service's action. Within hours a federal judge issued an order prohibiting the agency from moving ahead with the harvest. The order castigated the agency for failing to provide the public with an opportunity to contest the logging plan, vividly noting that "trees cannot be returned to their stumps."[4]

Several weeks later, with time for a profitable and environmentally sound harvest running short, the same judge ordered the Forest Service, logging interests, and environmentalists to work out a compromise. Within days environmental groups agreed to drop their appeal and let the recovery operation begin immediately. In return the agency and the timber industry promised not to harvest trees located in the most environmentally sensitive, roadless areas of Bitterroot. Under the terms of this settlement, the industry ultimately removed a little less than 15,000 acres of charred lumber from the forest, not quite a third of the acreage it had originally hoped to log.[5]

The court's intervention in the dispute over Bitterroot's future illustrates just how important, and difficult, it is for agencies to cultivate their constituencies. Organizations and citizens regularly wield enormous influence over policymaking in the bureaucracy. This power, however, does not necessarily direct agencies toward noncontroversial and widely supported actions. Nor does the public necessarily pressure agencies in ways that foster effective decision making.

This chapter focuses on the bureaucracy's **clients,** those interests in society that agencies are charged to regulate and protect. It is organized around three *core questions:*

- *WHAT TYPES OF CLIENTS ARE MOST ACTIVE IN BUREAUCRATIC POLICYMAKING?* Although both economic and environmental interests made their voices heard on Bitterroot's recovery, it is often the case that important clients remain silent on matters being weighed by agencies.

- **THROUGH WHAT VENUES DO CLIENTS PARTICIPATE IN AGENCY POLICYMAKING?** Organizations and citizens can access the bureaucracy in a multitude of ways. Denied an opportunity to offer comments on the Forest Service's logging plan, environmentalists exercised their input via the legal system.

- **HOW MUCH INFLUENCE DO CLIENTS EXERT OVER AGENCY DECISIONS?** In the end the Forest Service was swayed not only by the logging industry's plea for rapid action but also by environmentalist arguments about the need to protect and restore Bitterroot's most treasured resources. Agencies, however, are not always responsive to clients and are sometimes accused of being out of control.

It may sound as if the politics of the Bitterroot harvest are not indicative of agency-client relations in general. In fact, the theoretical perspective adopted in this chapter—interest group mobilization—is based on the notion that client activism and influence vary systematically across time and policy areas. Characteristics of the issues at hand have important implications, in ways described in the next section, for both the behavior of clients and agency accountability and performance.

## The Benefits, Costs, and Politics of Public Policy

Public policies affect citizens, organized interests, and society itself in a plethora of ways. For example, the Federal Highway Administration allocates funds for road construction that benefits virtually all Americans, the Social Security Administration oversees the transfer of income from workers to retirees, and the Environmental Protection Agency (EPA) regulates the operation of firms that discharge pollutants into the air, ground, and water. One common feature of these policies and all others is that they deliver benefits and impose costs. The way in which these benefits and costs are distributed across agency clients varies, however.[6]

**Benefits** and **costs** can be concentrated or diffuse in their effects. Concentrated effects occur when benefits or costs accrue to specific segments of

# Figure 4.1 The Benefits, Costs, and Politics of Public Policies

**Benefits of Public Policy**

| | Concentrated | Diffuse |
|---|---|---|
| **Concentrated** (Costs of Public Policy) | Interest group politics | Entrepreneurial politics |
| **Diffuse** (Costs of Public Policy) | Client politics | Majoritarian politics |

*Source:* From James Q. Wilson, *Bureaucracy: What Government Agencies Do and Why They Do It* (New York: Basic Books, 1989). Copyright © 1989 by Basic Books, Inc. Reprinted by permission of Basic Books, a member of Perseus Books, L.L.C.

society, such as individuals with certain characteristics (for example, retirees) or firms doing business in particular industries. Effects are diffuse when broad swaths of the population feel the benefits or costs (for example, highway drivers).

Importantly, the benefits and costs of policies affect the mobilization of societal interests and ultimately the politics of the bureaucracy. Figure 4.1 summarizes these effects. When benefits are concentrated and costs diffuse, **client politics** characterize policies. Specific constituencies mobilized by the prospect of reaping significant rewards dominate such issues. Society in general subsidizes the rewards. With costs so widely spread, little incentive exists for broad public involvement in the policymaking process.

Nuclear power policy in the middle of the twentieth century offers a classic example of client politics.[7] At that time public utility companies and other economic interests pressed the Atomic Energy Commission to promote the production of nuclear power by readily approving the construction and operation of plants throughout the country. These efforts proved successful in part because they faced little opposition. The economic costs of building up the nuclear power industry were distributed widely across society, and the environmental consequences were not yet publicly apparent (the Three Mile Island accident and the Chernobyl disaster lay well in the future).

When both the benefits and costs of policies are concentrated, however, the mobilization of societal interests is not so one-sided. **Interest group politics** characterize such policies. Once again the general public is not actively engaged in, nor perhaps even aware of, the contest over the direction of policy. Rather, this contest is fought among specific constituencies whose interests are at odds with one another. Early in the twentieth century, the trucking industry emerged as a serious competitor to railroads as a way of moving goods and services around the country. In the decades that followed, each set of interests continually lobbied the Interstate Commerce Commission for regulations that would profit its mode of transportation and cripple the other. Over time this battle became a mismatch as the agency went from being accommodating to the railroads to being controlled by motor carrier organizations such the American Trucking Association.[8]

Interest groups do not dominate the political process when the benefits of policies are diffuse. The combination of diffuse benefits and concentrated costs instead produces **entrepreneurial politics. Policy entrepreneurs** are individuals, from inside and outside government, who take on organized interests in the name of the general public. In 1965 public interest advocate Ralph Nader published *Unsafe at Any Speed,* a book about the dangers of cars as they were then designed. This book, and Nader's efforts in general, galvanized the consumer movement and ultimately provided the impetus for the adoption of many automotive safety features, such as air bags and antilock brakes, that Americans now take for granted.[9]

Finally, when both the benefits and the costs of policies are diffuse, **majoritarian politics** result. With little stake in the policymaking process, specific interests and organizations do not mobilize in support of, or opposition to, government actions. Rather, the political debate centers on broad, often ideological, considerations that cut across society, such as the proper role of government in economic and social matters. Some of the most significant policies in U.S. history fall into this category, including the Sherman Antitrust Act of 1890, a seminal moment in the trust-busting movement. At that stage of the industrial revolution, public sentiment was turning against large corporations and the power they increasingly wielded over the lives of each and every American. The Sherman Act, however, did not target specific firms and industries but monopolistic practices in general. As a result, opposition to the act was diffuse and grounded in the constitutional argument that the federal government has no authority to break up industrial trusts or, more broadly, to foster economic competition.[10]

To sum up, the theoretical perspective adopted in this chapter suggests that organized interests can dominate policymaking in the bureaucracy but only under certain conditions. A key question then becomes: How often do these conditions materialize? Interestingly, the answer to this question has changed quite a bit over the past four decades.

## The Rise and Fall of Iron Triangles

A favorite pastime of journalists and pundits is bemoaning the fact that organized interests, especially business and industry, have captured the U.S. government. In 2001 the collapse of Enron, a once high-flying energy company, brought such criticism to bear on both the Clinton and Bush administrations. People accused officials in agencies such as the Department of the Treasury of doing the company's bidding over the years by failing to regulate some of its more controversial practices, practices that eventually contributed to Enron's downfall.[11] Although episodes such as this one are no doubt telling, they are often used to exaggerate the influence of special interests in contemporary American politics.

| Inside Bureaucracy with | Donna Shalala<br>*Secretary of Health and Human Services*<br>*(1993–2001)* |
|---|---|

"There are iron triangles in government today. You see it in education, where you have powerful education interests. You see it less in HHS. Interest groups get access because they contributed to the campaign. We had to be careful all the time. If we saw an interest group that contributed to the presidential campaign, we scheduled a meeting with the opponent. And we never let anyone into a room with me without a civil service notetaker. We had no private meetings. It sure didn't endear us to the White House, but it kept us clean! We heard the most from hospitals, nursing homes, and home health agencies. They were all helpful. They behaved badly in the process, but it was always important to know what their positions were. It was particularly important to know where powerful interests stood."

## Figure 4.2 The "Iron Triangle" of Politics

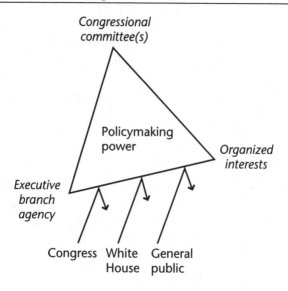

To be sure, interest groups have historically played a fundamental, and at times dominating, role in the political process. A half century ago many observers noted that public policy was at times the handiwork of **iron triangles.**[12] Figure 4.2 summarizes the essence of this observation. Iron triangles are issue-specific coalitions that consist of (1) the congressional committee of jurisdiction, (2) the relevant executive branch agency, and (3) those interests most directly affected by government actions in the area. These three parties jointly control policymaking by determining what issues make it onto the political agenda and how these issues will be resolved. Put differently, other interested parties, such as Congress as a whole, the White House, and the general public, are afforded very little influence over the scope and content of public policy. A prime example is agriculture policy. Legislators from farming areas secure seats on Congress's agriculture committees and work closely with the Department of Agriculture (USDA) and organized representatives of farming interests, such as the National Farmers Union, to produce profarmer policies. Largely shut out of this process are the tens of millions of Americans who consume agricultural products; so, too, are their elected representatives.

The grip of iron triangles over policymaking began to loosen in the 1960s for two principal reasons. One is that the number and nature of interest groups active in the political process underwent a dramatic transformation.

In 1960 there were 523 advocacy organizations with offices in Washington, D.C. By 1980 this number had grown more than tenfold, to 5,769.[13] A significant part of this growth came in the form of **public interest groups,** organizations promoting broad societal causes rather than the material gain of their members. Examples include environmental groups such as the World Wildlife Fund, founded in 1961, and consumer groups such as Public Citizen, which got its start a decade later.

The rise of public interest groups in and of itself was not enough to overcome the entrenched presence of iron triangles. One reason iron triangles were often successful in protecting their political turf was that they took great care to envelop themselves in positive **policy images.**[14] For decades the nuclear power industry promoted itself as a clean, cheap source of energy. As time went by, however, this positive policy image gave way to a far more negative one. Environmental groups and other opponents of nuclear power emphasized the dangers posed by mishaps at reactors and the difficulties associated with the storage of waste. Figure 4.3 illustrates that these tactics, no doubt strengthened by catastrophic and near-catastrophic events in the

## Figure 4.3  Positive and Negative Images in Media Coverage of Nuclear Power

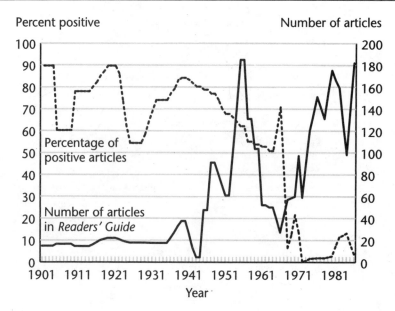

Percent positive                                    Number of articles

Percentage of positive articles

Number of articles in *Readers' Guide*

Year

*Source:* Policy Agendas Project, Center for American Politics and Public Policy, University of Washington, http://depts.washington.edu/ampol.aihome.shtml, February 28, 2003.

*Note:* The lines provide information about (1) the number of articles in the *Readers' Guide to Periodical Literature* on Nuclear Power and (2) the percentage of these articles that conveyed positive policy images.

nuclear industry, proved largely successful. Media coverage of nuclear power went from overwhelmingly positive through the 1950s to decidedly negative in later decades. Just as telling is the fact that the Nuclear Regulatory Commission, the successor to the Atomic Energy Commission, has not ordered a new nuclear power plant since the 1979 Three Mile Island accident.[15]

The shift in the locus of power in the area of nuclear energy is not unusual in that iron triangles of all sorts have lost their political monopolies. Today policymaking is often the domain of what are called **sloppy hexagons**[16] or, less colorfully, **issue networks.**[17] A constant flow of participants in and out of the decision-making arena, not limited access, characterizes issue networks. Some of these participants are traditional power brokers such as business and industry, while others include public interest advocates, economic and technical experts, and representatives of state and local governments. Because of this diversity, high levels of conflict among participants, rather than strict agreement, typify these networks. Such conflicts encompass not only the question of how best to resolve policy problems but also more fundamental questions such as: What is the nature of the problem? Is there a problem at all?

A great example of an issue network comes from the area of embryonic and fetal research, one of the most controversial areas of public policy in the early twenty-first century.[18] When it first came onto the national agenda in the 1970s, this issue was dominated by a small set of actors, most notably the scientific community. Researchers in universities and medical schools worked closely with the National Institutes of Health to establish a positive policy image grounded in the benefits of scientific autonomy and progress. Ultimately, the aim was to ensure a constant flow of government funding for research that some scientists believe holds the key to unlocking the mysteries of many of the world's most painful and deadliest diseases. Today this image, and the iron triangle it helped sustain, does not enjoy the monopoly it once did. Embryonic and fetal research raises fundamental moral concerns, such as the value of different forms of human life and the role of medical science in creating, enhancing, and destroying such life. These concerns are now being vigorously debated by ethicists, religious authorities, members of Congress, and activists on both sides of the abortion issue. Executive branch officials all the way up to the president have been involved in making decisions that generally serve to heighten, rather than diminish, the level of disagreement embodied in this issue network.[19]

The rise and fall of iron triangles illustrate three central points with respect to the benefit-cost approach to understanding societal mobilization and bureaucratic politics. The first is that the benefits and costs of policies vary not only across issues but over time as well. A closely related lesson is that perceived, as well as actual, benefits and costs play a critical role in determining the nature of the politics surrounding a policy area. Although the benefits and costs associated with nuclear power and embryonic and fetal research have undoubtedly evolved over the years, the demise of these long-standing iron triangles was in no small part a product of seismic shifts in the images through which potentially contentious issues were appraised and acted upon. Finally, such developments suggest there are now far fewer instances of client politics, and perhaps even interest group politics, than in years past. Although powerful interests and organizations still can, and do, exert extraordinary influence over the political process, the exercise of this power is not nearly as unchallenged as before.

## The Venues of Client Participation

Thus far this chapter has focused on the types of clients generally most active in bureaucratic policymaking as well as on how patterns of client activism have changed over the past several decades. Little has yet been said about the specific venues through which clients make their views known to agency officials. These venues run the gamut from commenting on proposed agency policies to prevailing upon politicians to intervene in bureaucratic proceedings. As will become apparent, venues are distinct in terms of the resources clients must bring to bear if they wish to participate regularly and effectively through these channels.

### *The Notice and Comment Process*

One of the central ways in which agencies make policy is through **rulemaking,** the bureaucratic equivalent of legislative lawmaking.[20] When engaged in rulemaking, agencies craft decisions that allocate governmental resources, redistribute these and other resources across segments of society, and regulate the behavior of particular societal actors. As an example, on January 31, 2007, Customs and Border Protection, an agency in the Department of Homeland Security, issued a rule regarding the responsibilities of importers of food, drugs, devices, and cosmetics. This action was one of twelve rules promulgated that day by federal agencies, an indication of just how common rulemaking is within the executive branch.

For more than a half century, rulemaking at the federal level has been governed by the Administrative Procedure Act (APA).[21] The APA generally requires agencies to provide public notice of their intention to take action by publishing a proposed rule in the *Federal Register.* Military and foreign affairs functions are not covered by this requirement, nor are actions where the agency, for good cause, finds prior notice to be "impracticable, unnecessary, or contrary to the public interest." In practice, about half of all agency regulations are not preceded by a **notice of proposed rulemaking.**[22] The APA also instructs agencies to offer interested parties the opportunity to comment on proposals. The **notice and comment process,** as this participation venue is known, is one of the most common ways in which clients come into contact with agency decision makers.[23]

"Implementation was everything. When we were in the midst of a rule-making process, we rarely saw anyone."

For any given rulemaking, the number of comments submitted is usually rather modest. Between November 2006 and January 2007, agencies issued thirteen rules considered "major."[24] **Major rules** are actions projected to have particularly pronounced consequences, such as annual effects on the economy of at least $100 million.[25] Despite their elevated significance, many of these thirteen actions generated small numbers of comments. For example, on December 21, 2006, the Securities and Exchange Commission (SEC) promulgated a rule pertaining to the financial reporting requirements of small public companies. The SEC received only 36 comments during the course of this rulemaking even though thousands of businesses stood to save as much as, or perhaps more than, a million dollars each in overall compliance costs.

On occasion, agencies are inundated with comments on their proposed rules. The Centers for Medicare and Medicaid Services received approximately 1,100 comments on a hospital payment action it took on November 24, 2006. In 1995 the Food and Drug Administration stirred up great public controversy by proposing to regulate the advertising, labeling, and sale of tobacco products to juveniles. This proposal precipitated the submission of about 700,000 comments, a volume that is only occasionally approached or exceeded by other rulemakings.[26] In recent years, numerous comments have been filed in rulemakings addressing the establishment of national organic standards, the setting of mercury emission levels, and rest and hours of service requirements for operators of commercial motor vehicles.[27]

Are there particular types of clients that participate most regularly in notice and comment rulemaking? It is well established that business and industry interests are often more likely to submit comments on proposed rules than are representatives of other segments of society.[28] For example, when the EPA proposed in 1994 to revise one of its hazardous waste regulations, 45 of the 60 comments it received came from corporations.[29] This kind of business domination, however, does not inevitably manifest itself in the commenting process. When the Department of Housing and Urban Development, also in

1994, crafted a rule pertaining to public housing for the elderly and disabled, only one comment (out of 268) was submitted by a corporation.[30] Similarly, the USDA's proposed organic standards generated hundreds of thousands of comments, mainly from consumers and small organic farmers.[31] In short, much depends on the nature of the rulemaking and the extent of business interest it evokes.

To what extent do client comments have an impact on the actions agencies ultimately take when promulgating policy through rulemaking? On the one hand, it is widely acknowledged that agencies carefully consider the viewpoints expressed in comments.[32] On the other hand, rules are often altered very little in response to the information provided by clients.[33] As one observer has put it: "Changes are made frequently enough during the comment phase of rulemaking, but they tend to be small and painful, and they are often subtractive rather than innovative or additive."[34]

Although the notice and comment process provides a solid foundation for client participation, it has its shortcomings. For example, rules sometimes take years to develop and are regularly subjected to lengthy litigation after being promulgated.[35] Unnecessary delays postpone the realization of the intended benefits of rules, which often include the prevention of illness and injury and the saving of lives.[36] Difficulties such as these are traceable in part to the inherently adversarial nature of notice and comment rulemaking. Under the APA, clients never come into direct contact with one another, but participate by submitting comments to agency officials. This lack of contact prevents clients from developing working relationships, shared understandings, and other connections that are useful in tamping down conflicts. Furthermore, client comments tend to stake out extreme positions and focus on pointing out flaws in agency proposals rather than identifying solutions to difficult rulemaking problems. With these limitations in mind, there has been a movement over the past three decades to augment the notice and comment process with a variety of collaborative approaches to client participation.

## Advisory Committees and Other Venues of Collaboration

In the early 1980s the Federal Aviation Administration (FAA) set about updating its rules on the maximum flight and duty time of pilots and other air carrier personnel.[37] As part of this process, the agency published several proposed rules in the *Federal Register*. These proposals elicited serious client objections, and the agency found itself unable to complete the rulemaking via the notice and comment process.

At this point the FAA turned to an advisory committee to help resolve the impasse. This advisory committee consisted of seventeen members, including representatives of the National Air Carrier Association, Aviation Consumer Action Project, Southwest Airlines, and International Brotherhood of Teamsters.[38] The agency charged these representatives with jointly developing a course of action that would garner the support of aviation stakeholders of all stripes.

**Advisory committees** are commissioned for such tasks all the time. About 1,000 advisory committees operate within the federal executive branch.[39] Advisory committees bring together clients who share a stake in specific policy areas. These clients receive the opportunity to offer their input in a variety of ways, such as by helping agencies set their policymaking agendas, drafting reports on specific issues that arise during rulemakings, and commenting jointly on agency proposals. Examples of advisory committees include the National Environmental Justice Advisory Council, Advisory Committee on Nuclear Waste, and Advisory Council on Children's Educational Television.

The **Federal Advisory Committee Act** (FACA) governs the operation of advisory committees. Under this statute, client representation on advisory committees must be balanced.[40] In other words, advisory committee members must consist of a representative cross section of the clients with a stake in the policy area under a committee's jurisdiction. The idea behind the balance requirement is to prevent a single constituency, such as business interests, from dominating advisory committee proceedings. Thus the National Drinking Water Advisory Council consists of five members from utilities and other water producers, five from state and local governments, and five from environmental, consumer, and other public interest groups. Such arrangements are commonplace among advisory committees.

Not all advisory committees, however, operate in a manner consistent with FACA at all times. In 1990, for example, the National Advisory Committee on Meat and Poultry Inspection did not have a single member affiliated with a consumer organization. Membership was dominated by industry interests such as the U.S. Meat Exporters Federation, American Association of Meat Processors, Veribest Cattle Feeders, and George A. Hormel and Company.[41] Other advisory committees have skirted client participation requirements by holding meetings in the State Department, Executive Office Building, and other restricted locations.[42] At times, there is vigorous debate regarding whether an advisory body is subject to the dictates of FACA at all. The Clinton administration's health care task force and President George W. Bush's National Energy Policy Development Group both operated outside the formal advisory committee system.

When advisory committees operate as envisioned in FACA, they embody the application of collaborative techniques to client participation. Clients interact directly with one another in an environment designed to foster the identification of mutually agreeable courses of action. This process paid dividends for the FAA in 1985, when the agency was finally able to revise its flight and duty time rules. This revision, which provided crew members with a nine-hour rest period prior to extended duty shifts, came about in no small part as a result of the input of the advisory committee charged with breaking the long-standing policy deadlock.

On occasion, advisory committees are used to facilitate a particular form of collaboration known as **negotiated rulemaking.** In negotiated rulemaking, advisory committees receive the authority to craft policy statements that are then published by agencies as proposed rules. The idea behind negotiated rulemaking is that comment periods and other subsequent venues of participation will proceed relatively quickly and harmoniously, as clients themselves have generated proposals with widespread, if not unanimous, concurrence.[43]

Most observers acknowledge, however, that the benefits of negotiated rulemaking are readily attainable only under certain circumstances.[44] For example, bargaining sessions are most likely to produce consensus when the number of stakeholders is limited. To put it differently, an auditorium full of people is likely to experience difficulty engaging in meaningful negotiations. For such reasons negotiated rulemaking has been used on a very limited basis. From 1983 to 1996 federal agencies undertook only sixty-seven negotiated rulemakings.[45] Similarly, of the 204 major regulations issued by agencies between March 1996 and June 1999, only four were developed with the help of negotiated rulemaking.[46]

Does negotiated rulemaking, on those occasions when it is used, have the effect of reducing delay and bringing about other desirable outcomes in bureaucratic policymaking? On the one hand, there have been instances where negotiated rulemaking has made a noticeable difference. Participants in several EPA negotiated rulemakings have reported greater levels of satisfaction with the substance of the regulations ultimately adopted than their counterparts in comparable rulemakings where negotiations were not an integral part of the process.[47] On the other hand, negotiated rulemaking has not generally proven faster and less contentious than notice and comment rulemaking, thus suggesting the limited applicability of advisory committees as consensus-building instruments.[48]

Advisory committees and negotiated rulemakings are not the only venues of collaborative participation. Agencies regularly hold **public meetings** and **public hearings,** where clients have the opportunity to testify and perhaps rebut one another's arguments in front of key executive branch officials. From March to May of 2000 the Federal Railroad Administration (FRA) held a series of ten hearings at locations around the country.[49] These hearings addressed the use of locomotive horns at highway-rail grade crossings. This issue is important from a public safety point of view in that trains collide with highway vehicles about 4,000 times during a typical year. In an effort to reduce property damage and personal injuries, the FRA proposed to require that locomotive horns be sounded as trains approach and enter highway-rail grade crossings.[50] During the hearings on this proposal, the FRA discovered that there is also a significant downside to the sounding of warning whistles, especially in the vicinity of communities normally characterized by peace and quiet. Tearful testimony was provided by residents linking sleep deprivation, and even the loss of livelihood, to horn blowing by trains passing nearby in the dark of night. Railroad conductors, too, recounted tales of personal trauma. One stated simply: "My ears have been harmed from too many train whistles." [51] The FRA responded to this vivid input and provided for exceptions to its whistle-blowing requirements, for example in areas designated as "quiet zones."[52] In general, public hearings and meetings, and collaborative instruments overall, can be useful venues for clients seeking to do more than submit written comments on agency proposals.

## Political Intervention

Another way in which clients seek to influence bureaucratic policymaking is by securing friendly interventions by prominent politicians. Such interventions have enabled Florida developers and business groups, for instance, to win concessions in environmental policy from federal, state, and local agencies. A key battleground in this area has been the Florida Everglades, an assortment of swamps and forests vital to southern Florida's water supply and home to many endangered species, including the greatly revered Florida panther.

In the early 1990s, when a prominent Florida developer, Ben Hill Griffin III, proposed the construction of a new institution of higher education—Florida Gulf Coast University—on 760 acres of donated land, biologists at the Fish and Wildlife Service expressed strong reservations. Griffin's plan, these scientists warned, would trigger "unprecedented" development for miles around the proposed campus, demolishing precious wetlands in the process.[53]

In the face of this warning, a Griffin lobbyist persuaded Sen. Bob Graham, D-Fla., to intervene on the developer's behalf. After a meeting between this lobbyist and Fish and Wildlife Service officials in Atlanta, the agency backed down from the confrontation. Next Griffin supporters won the allegiance of Florida's other senator, Republican Connie Mack. Mack contacted the Florida commander of the Army Corps of Engineers, urging the agency to approve a permit so the project could proceed expeditiously. Despite their reservations, corps officials issued the permit, and the university, an "ecological disaster" according to critics, admitted its first student—Mariana Coto—in 1997.[54]

The story of Florida Gulf Coast University is not unique. Clients of all types appear to make their views known to executive branch officials via legislators and other politicians. For example, firms located in districts represented on House committees with jurisdiction over the Federal Trade Commission are less likely to be sanctioned by the agency than firms lacking such representation.[55] The assumption is that this linkage is due to the fact that business groups apply pressure on particularly influential members of Congress, who in turn are inclined to communicate their constituents' preferences to the agency.

It would be a mistake to assume that business organizations are the only clients engaged in what might be called **political meddling.** Regulated firms face tougher enforcement by the Occupational Safety and Health Administration, as well as its state-level counterparts, in locations represented by congressional delegations sympathetic to labor interests.[56] The assumption here is that unions and other labor organizations urge like-minded legislators to insist the agency be vigilant when enforcing worker safety laws, at least within specific geographic jurisdictions. As long as reelection-oriented legislators consider these organizations to be important constituencies, such urgings are not likely to go unheeded.

### Client Participation and the Internet

In the spring of 2007, the Patent and Trademark Office (PTO) launched a new initiative hailed as "revolutionary."[57] Under this pilot project, patent examiners at the PTO use a Web-based system to access information about applications that would have been beyond their fingertips under traditional review methods.[58] The system is oriented around the idea of **community peer review,** not scientific writings and archival patent records. In a general way, the system resembles Wikipedia, the online encyclopedia that anyone can edit. It also incorporates features from eBay.com and Amazon.com, most notably a rating system that allows users to evaluate one another's contributions. The idea is to use digital technology to enhance both the expertise and openness of the patent review process. Although patent examiners continue to be the ultimate decision makers, their decisions are informed as never before by agency clients, especially those participants deemed by their peers to be particularly informative and useful.

An electronic, community-based review system is a far cry from the way patent examiners have historically gone about their jobs. At times, PTO officials have been prohibited from even using the Internet, lest they inadvertently reveal proprietary secrets during the course of their online searches.[59] Why, then, has the PTO become willing to move past such concerns and embrace the use of digital technology? In 2006, 4,000 examiners handled a record 332,000 patent applications, thus limiting the PTO's ability to conduct thorough reviews.[60] The aim is to use the new system to improve the PTO's performance in the face of such a massive workload as well as to make the patent process more accountable to the agency's expert client community.

The PTO is not alone in holding such aims. All across government, bureaucracies are turning to the Internet and other innovations in information technology for help in achieving their missions. Some of these innovations entail digitizing existing paper-based processes, as when agencies accept public comments on proposed rules via the Internet (in addition to, or in place of, comments sent by mail and fax). Other innovations, such as the community peer review patent project, transform the very structures and processes through which agencies engage their clients and make policy decisions.[61]

This wide-ranging enthusiasm for the promise of the Internet raises a variety of salient questions regarding clients and their participation in bureaucratic policymaking.

- Does the Internet attract new participants or simply provide established participants with additional ways of making their views known?
- Do online proceedings, and the virtually instantaneous communications they foster, reduce the time it takes agencies to make policy?
- What effects do digital technologies have on outcomes such as the quality and legitimacy of agency actions and the distribution of benefits and costs among stakeholders?

There are three basic schools of thought when it comes to addressing these kinds of questions. A first possibility is that the Internet will "change everything" for the better.[62] For example, if information technology facilitates broad-based client involvement in bureaucratic decisions, then it has the potential to enhance the democratic nature of policymaking in the executive branch. A second possibility is that digital technology will be associated with "politics as usual." For most individuals, life online—shopping, hobbies, working, entertainment—closely resembles life in the "real world."[63] That is to say, citizens who are not involved in public affairs offline are unlikely to be activists when it comes to the Internet. A third possibility is that the effects of information technology will be conditional.[64] Some innovations will transform agency processes and client behavior, while others will simply replicate already existing modes and practices.

Although the relative merits of these schools of thought are not yet fully apparent, it is not too early to make some preliminary assessments about agency experiences with information technology. For starters, most existing applications serve to digitize functions that have historically been paper based.

A prime example of digitization is agency Web sites. The vast majority of federal and state government Web sites provide departmental phone numbers and addresses.[65] Other common features allow clients to purchase hunting and fishing licenses, pay fines for overdue tickets, file consumer complaints, and print out and download reports and databases. Clearly, client interactions that have historically occurred over the telephone, through the mail, and in person are increasingly taking place on the Internet.

Some bureaucracies are faring better than others when it comes to digitizing their services. When rated on a variety of dimensions, the Web sites of agencies such as the FCC, Social Security Administration, and Internal Revenue Service emerge as pacesetters in the federal government.[66] On the other extreme, the Web sites of the Department of the Interior and the Department of Homeland Security are graded relatively poorly in terms of content, services, and usability. On the state level, the governments of Massachusetts, Texas, and Indiana are rated as the top e-performers, with Alaska, New Mexico, and Nebraska occupying places at the rear of the pack. Despite these differences in proficiency, agency Web sites for the most part share one important attribute, namely, their emphasis on digitizing existing functions rather than transforming agency-client interactions.

In 1998 the Department of Transportation (DOT) made history when it became the first agency to move its entire docket system to the Internet. **Dockets** are repositories that contain, on a rule-by-rule basis, detailed records of agency and client activities, including notices of proposed rulemaking, final rules, cost-benefit analyses, and comments and other forms of public participation. By moving its docket system online, DOT enhanced the ease with which information about its rulemakings could be submitted, stored, and retrieved, thus saving the agency more than a million dollars annually in administrative costs.[67]

This digitization also prompted expectations of a great outburst of client participation in DOT rulemakings. On rare occasions, this expectation has been borne out. For example, the DOT received more than 65,000 comments on its proposed corporate average fuel economy standards for light trucks.[68] For the most part, however, comparisons of online processes with prior levels of paper-based commenting show that overall patterns of commenting have been remarkably stable since the introduction on the online docket system. Figure 4.4 illustrates that clients submitted 100 or more comments in only

**Figure 4.4   Client Commenting before and after Online Docketing at the DOT**

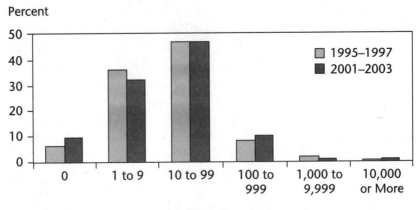

Percent

*Number of Comments*

*Source:* Steven J. Balla and Benjamin M. Daniels, "Information Technology and Public Commenting on Agency Regulations," *Regulation and Governance* 1 (March 2007): 46–67.

*Note:* Each bar represents the percentage of rulemakings in the period that fall into a particular category of comment activity.

about 10 percent of the rulemakings in both the 1995–1997 period (before online docketing) and 2001–2003 period (after digitization). In addition, about half of the rulemakings in both periods generated between 10 and 99 comments, the most common category of client activity.

At this point, it is too early to tell whether the DOT's experience is at all instructive for other bureaucracies. As part of the President's Management Agenda, the Bush administration launched an initiative, in 2002, to create the **Federal Docket Management System** (FDMS), a single portal through which all federal rulemaking materials will eventually be submitted, stored, and retrieved.[69] Thus far, sixteen agencies including the Department of Agriculture, Small Business Administration, and Office of Personnel Management have fully migrated their dockets to FDMS.[70] As this number grows, it will become increasingly possible to evaluate the impact of the digitization of public commenting on client involvement in rulemaking.

The PTO is not the only public bureaucracy that is using information technology to transform the way it interacts with clients and makes decisions.

In one of the first such transformations, the FAA, in 2000, held an online public forum addressing licensing requirements for small-scale rockets, the kind launched by amateurs for recreational or educational purposes.[71] For two weeks interested parties—educators, landowners, launch companies, and others—engaged in near-real-time discussions about various aspects of amateur rocketry and what actions the agency might take to regulate this increasingly sophisticated hobby.

Similarly, a year later, the EPA conducted an online dialogue when it was considering revisions to its public involvement policy. By a variety of metrics, the dialogue was deemed a "great success."[72] A total of 1,166 individuals representing a broad range of interests took part in the discussions. About three-fourths of these participants rated their experience positively, with over half indicating that their contributions were likely to have at least some influence over EPA decision making. On the downside, participants were concerned that there was "too much participation by 'experts' rather than average citizens."[73] One potential reason for this skewed pattern is the **digital divide,** the gap in computer use and skills between wealthy and poor Americans.

Despite these and other successful examples, there have been relatively few instances of agencies using the Internet to transform their client engagements. Most applications, such as electronic docket systems, have instead entailed the digitization of long-standing practices. Why have agencies been hesitant to embrace new modes of engagement? Generally speaking, emerging technologies do not act solely as agents of societal change and innovation. These technologies themselves are fundamentally shaped by existing institutions and power holders, including government agencies, thereby limiting the scope and speed of their transformations.[74] The impact of the Internet on the accountability and performance of public bureaucracies will be determined in no small part by decisions made inside the executive branch.

## Client Influence on Bureaucratic Policymaking

The popular image of clients, particularly organized interests, is that they are enormously resourceful and extraordinarily influential.[75] The overall accuracy of these perceptions, however, may be questioned for a number of reasons. First, interest groups differ dramatically in size, finances, membership, expertise, and credibility. All interest groups are certainly not created equal! According to *Fortune* magazine, the most powerful organized interests in America include the National Rifle Association (number six), Association of

Trial Lawyers of America (number five), and AARP (number one).[76] Many thousands of organizations fall well short of these lobbies in terms of personnel and budgetary resources as well as political clout.

Second, interest groups may be more effective in some settings than in others. Whereas Congress is designed to be highly porous and accessible, the bureaucracy, despite a multiplicity of participatory venues, is not fundamentally an institution of representative government. This means that resources such as campaign contributions and grassroots mobilization may not be directly useful to clients seeking influence over executive branch policymaking. As one bureaucrat has put it, "It's not a plebiscite. We're not doing rulemaking by vote."[77] Instead, economic, legal, scientific, and other forms of specialized information may be most relevant in affecting the course of agency decision making.

Third, interest groups, as we have already seen, are far more prominent in some policy debates than in others. To reiterate a central theme of this chapter, the significance of organized interests depends in part on whether the costs and benefits of policies are concentrated or distributed.[78] Fourth, interest group power ebbs and flows over time. Evidence suggests that organizational influence in the federal bureaucracy declined from the early 1970s to the mid-1980s, then rebounded somewhat.[79] Fifth, the influence of particular types of interest groups changes systematically over time. For example, Republican administrations tend to be more responsive to business organizations and conservative advocacy groups, while Democratic administrations tend to be more responsive to labor unions and advocacy groups with a liberal bent.

On this last score, the transition from the Clinton administration to the presidency of George W. Bush was typical and telling. In the days and months leading up to Inauguration Day, agencies issued tens of thousands of pages of rules.[80] These so-called **midnight regulations** represented a 51 percent increase in regulatory activity when compared with the same period during the three previous years.[81] Once in office, the Bush administration responded by releasing what became known as the **Card memorandum** (named after the White House chief of staff, Andrew Card). The Card memo called for agencies to "postpone the effective date of [recently issued but not yet effective] regulations for 60 days."[82] Specifically, the new president was targeting rules offensive to his key constituencies. Some rules, such as the ergonomics regulation discussed in Chapter 3, did not survive the partisan shift in administrations. Other rules, however, were eventually allowed to take effect. As a prime example, a sustained public outcry compelled President Bush to follow through on his predecessor's plan to tighten significantly the standards for acceptable levels of arsenic in drinking water.

Despite all of these qualifications, there is considerable evidence that interest groups exert highly regular influence over bureaucratic decision making. Although no cabinet secretary today would come right out and say "What's good for General Motors is good for the United States," business groups undoubtedly command the attention of executive branch officials. In at least two policy areas—the environment and consumer protection—public interest groups have become increasingly powerful in recent decades. In addition, state and local governments themselves have taken on the role of organized lobbyists, as when the National Governors Association seeks to shape the welfare reform decisions that emanate from federal offices.

## Business Organizations

The role of business in the policymaking process is uniquely important. As has long been acknowledged: "Businessmen generally and corporate executives

in particular take on a privileged role in government that is, it seems reasonable
to say, unmatched by any leadership group other than government officials
themselves."[83] Because maintaining low unemployment and strong economic
growth are high priorities for governments of all stripes, keen sensitivity to
business interests is apparent throughout the world. It is especially striking,
however, in the United States, where the private sector accounts for a relatively
large percentage of the nation's economic productivity.

Business organizations influence the bureaucracy because they possess
financial resources, policy expertise, and political clout. Financial resources
enable them to hire well-respected, experienced staff members, including former executive branch officials. These resources also enable them to conduct
research, finance receptions, and mobilize grassroots support. Policy expertise enhances their credibility when they present arguments to government
officials. Political clout helps to ensure their access to key decision makers.

The so-called **revolving door** between government agencies and the private sector offers an especially important source of business power. Officials
at the Federal Communications Commission (FCC) who used to work in the
broadcast industry are more likely to vote in support of the industry when
such issues come before the agency.[84] Even agency officials who have not previously worked in a particular industry may behave favorably toward it if they
hope to one day secure a job with a firm in that industry.

**Direct lobbying** is another useful strategy. In 1998 lobbyists from the
sugar industry helped to persuade the Army Corps of Engineers to reconsider
its water storage plans in the vicinity of Florida's Lake Okeechobee. Instead of
building a large reservoir on sugar lands, as originally intended, the agency
agreed to build underground storage systems, as proposed by sugar interests.[85]
In exercising this influence "the sugar companies not only survived the battle
over Everglades restoration; they guaranteed their future water supply."[86]

Similar conclusions have been reached for other agencies and policy arenas. Consider, for example, the EPA's authority, granted by the Federal Insecticide, Fungicide, and Rodenticide Act, to approve or cancel the registration of specific pesticides. One study found that over a fifteen-year period, the agency was less likely to cancel a pesticide's registration if a grower group intervened in the decision-making process.[87] A decision not to cancel a registration permits growers to use the pesticide despite any environmental concerns.

Business organizations influence not only federal agencies but state agencies as well. A study of public utility commissions in twelve states found that utility companies were moderately influential in one state and very influential in the other eleven.[88] Similarly, a study of environmental regulations in all fifty states found water pollution standards to be relatively weak in states in which the mining industry accounts for a particularly substantial share of economic activity.[89]

In general, business organizations fare better on issues where the glare of publicity is relatively dim. High issue salience generally works to the advantage of groups that can make strong appeals to the general public. Low issue salience, in contrast, generally favors economic interests with much narrower constituencies. The actions of the mass media, which both react to and promote high issue salience, help to explain this pattern. As it has been put, the role of the press is to "afflict the comfortable and comfort the afflicted."[90] In performing this role, journalists and other media officials draw attention to policy arrangements that benefit small numbers of producers at the expense of large numbers of consumers. In the end, however, although the influence of business organizations is mitigated by media coverage and other factors, this influence remains pervasive across agencies and levels of government.

## Public Interest Groups

At first glance the bureaucracy would not seem to be fertile territory for public interest groups, organizations such as Common Cause, the Consumers Union, and the Natural Resources Defense Council. Although bureaucratic decision making is surprisingly transparent, it is nonetheless more opaque than decision making in legislatures. This opacity enhances the difficulty for wide audiences seeking to participate in, and exercise influence over, agency proceedings. Moreover, issues addressed in bureaucratic settings tend to be more technical, more abstruse, and remoter than those resolved by legislatures. Such circumstances naturally favor experts, including agency personnel and the kinds of professionals public interest groups often cannot afford to maintain.

Despite these handicaps, public interest groups enjoy advantages today that they did not possess prior to the 1960s. The Freedom of Information Act and Government in the Sunshine Act make it easier for public interest groups, as well as other interested parties, to obtain important agency documents and to attend meetings where vital policy decisions are being considered. In addition, the National Environmental Policy Act and other statutes have created opportunities for public interest groups to challenge bureaucratic decisions in the courts.

The long saga of the spotted owl illustrates public interest groups' ability to shape bureaucratic decisions with a combination of direct lobbying and indirect intervention through the judiciary. In 1986 a small Massachusetts-based environmental group, GreenWorld, asked the Fish and Wildlife Service to list the spotted owl as an endangered species. When the agency failed to do so, the Sierra Club Legal Defense Fund initiated litigation against the government. In 1989 a federal district court judge issued the first of a series of rulings that would ultimately compel the agency to designate the spotted owl as endangered. Subsequent interventions by environmental groups resulted in decisions sharply curtailing the ability of the government to sell timber in the Northwest's old-growth forests, particularly in the vicinity of spotted owl habitats.[91]

Environmental groups have been particularly influential participants in bureaucratic policymaking. In addition to restrictions on timber sales, they

| Inside Bureaucracy with | Dan Glickman *Secretary of Agriculture (1995–2001)* |
|---|---|

"Some people believe that the Forest Service for years was so closely tied to timber interests that you had an iron triangle between Western-based senators, the timber industry, and the Forest Service bureaucracy. But during the Clinton administration that wasn't true. The Clinton Forest Service policy was very much more habitat protection oriented and species protection oriented. The environmental community was extremely active and was an equal match for the timber community. Frankly, it was one of the healthier areas of public policy because there was genuine debate, not only over legislative but also over regulatory issues. There was a kind of equality of engagement that you certainly did not see in farm policy, for example."

have used their power to promote reductions in livestock grazing and recreational use of national forests. It has been demonstrated that during the late 1980s and early 1990s, an "amenity coalition" of environmental groups and sympathetic government officials was more effective than a "commodity coalition" of ranchers and timber companies in shaping Forest Service planning decisions.[92]

Ultimately, the influence of public interest groups depends a good deal on the policy preferences of the bureaucracies whose behavior they are trying to shape. Some agencies are widely regarded as liberal in their preferences, while others are viewed as having conservative orientations. Agencies with liberal reputations include the EPA, Department of Housing and Urban Development, and Commission on Civil Rights. On the conservative side are organizations such as the Department of Defense, National Security Council, and Small Business Administration.[93]

Agency preferences, it is important to note, can change over time. Take, for example, the making of child care policy at the Department of Health and Human Services (HHS). The Children's Defense Fund and other child advocacy groups fared better in shaping the child care policies of the Clinton administration than in influencing comparable policies during the preceding Bush administration.[94] Olivia Golden, the head of the HHS's Administration for Children, Youth, and Families under President Clinton, was a former senior staffer at the fund, demonstrating that the revolving door can at times work to the advantage of public interest groups. In addition, Donna Shalala, the secretary of HHS, was very sympathetic to the fund and its aims. To top it off, first lady Hillary Clinton had once been a fund board member. Interestingly, though these institutional linkages did not exist before President Clinton took office, child advocacy groups had won some modest victories during the administration of George H. W. Bush.[95] These earlier victories testify to the power that public interest groups can now bring to bear on the policy-making process, regardless of the political climate.

## State and Local Governments

Governments themselves rank among the bureaucracy's most effective clients. Federal agencies hear all the time from state governments, local governments, and **professional associations** such as the National Conference of State Legislatures, Association of State Drinking Water Administrators, and National League of Cities. State and local governments enjoy special deference in the policymaking process because they authoritatively represent citizens in particular parts of the country. This deference is heightened when state and local officials work together, through organizations that allow them to speak with one voice.[96] The National Governors Association, to take one example, has been a particularly powerful force under recent presidents, several of whom had been governors themselves.

It is important to note that state and local governments often target Congress and the White House rather than executive branch agencies. Even working alone, many governors enjoy the stature and prestige necessary to arrange audiences with key members of Congress and the president's closest aides. From the perspective of such officials, why bother with the bureaucracy when you can confer with the bureaucracy's bosses?

State and local governments are in regular communication, however, with officials inside the bureaucracy. The rulemaking process is a common target for such interventions. For example, state and local governments file more than one thousand comments per year in EPA rulemakings deemed to be "major" or "significant."[97] Furthermore, in occupying well over 100 membership spots on EPA advisory committees, states and localities constitute one of the best represented clientele groups in the agency's advisory system.[98]

In recent years, state and local governments have repeatedly pressed federal agencies for waivers from rules and regulations. In the area of health care, states have pursued waivers allowing them to substitute managed care for fee-for-service medicine in their Medicaid programs. In education, state governments and local school districts have requested waivers enhancing their flexibility in administering education programs. In 1999 alone, the federal government received 174 waiver applications from states and local education agencies. In total, nearly a thousand such applications were submitted during the period between 1995 and 2004.[99]

In responding to waiver requests, the federal government has generally accommodated the states and localities while satisfying its own legal and political concerns. The Clinton administration was rather receptive to waiver requests.[100] When President Clinton took office, only one state—Arizona— had received the authority to create a statewide research and demonstration project under Medicaid. By the end of the Clinton administration, eighteen states were operating under such waivers.

The administration of George W. Bush has also looked favorably on waiver applications. In 2001 the Department of Education granted 85 of the 99 requests it received. In all, during President Bush's first term, the administration approved about 70 percent of the education waivers sought by state and local governments.[101]

As these data indicate, federal agencies occasionally deny state and local requests for waivers. In some instances the federal government denies such requests because it lacks the statutory authority to grant particular waivers. In other instances it denies requests because of expressed opposition. For example, the Clinton administration terminated New Mexico's managed care program for mental health after receiving extensive negative commentary from the Bazelon Center for Mental Health Law, a public interest group that enjoyed considerable credibility within the administration. This decision was reversed under President George W. Bush, whose administration was responsive to a different set of mental health interests.[102]

Direct intervention in a federal agency's deliberations is often accompanied by other approaches, such as expanding the **scope of conflict**.[103]

Democratic South Carolina governor Jim Hodges used a variety of strategies in opposing a Department of Energy (DOE) decision to ship plutonium from Colorado to his state. Hodges pleaded with energy secretary Spencer Abraham to stop the shipment and also asked Tom Ridge, director of Homeland Security, to intervene on South Carolina's behalf. When these efforts bore no fruit, Hodges ratcheted up the level of controversy by taking DOE to court and generating considerable mass media attention. He even threatened to lie down in front of any truck attempting to carry a plutonium shipment across South Carolina's border! Ultimately, Hodges was forced to acquiesce when a federal appeals court ordered him not to interfere with the plutonium shipment.[104] He won an important concession along the way, however. In a written letter, Abraham promised to seek legislation guaranteeing the removal of the plutonium if it could not be processed.[105]

## Clients and the Institutions of Government

The squabble between South Carolina and the federal government reinforces one of the central lessons of this, as well as the preceding, chapter. Client participation in bureaucratic policymaking does not occur in an institutional vacuum but via arrangements, such as the court system, established and maintained by political principals. As third-party intermediaries, individuals and organizations play a crucial role in determining the degree to which principals are well equipped to address issues of adverse selection and moral hazard and ultimately to mitigate the agency loss associated with the delegation of authority.

Principal-agent theory, however, does not directly speak to the desire and capacity of clients to take on the roles specified by executives, legislatures, and judiciaries. This is where the interest group mobilization framework comes in, pointing our attention to the benefits and costs associated with particular policy areas and choices. By offering a conditional perspective on client activism and influence, this framework recognizes citizens and interest groups as potentially powerful, and at times unwilling, participants in the hierarchical structures and processes of bureaucratic policymaking.

Importantly, agencies operate not only as agents on the receiving end of delegated authority but also as partners in networks that span agencies and governments as well as the public and private sectors. During his tenure as attorney general, Dick Thornburgh convened a body called the Financial Crimes Task Force. In the words of the attorney general, this organization "brought together on an interagency basis all the people who would be pursuing wrongdoing in that area," including agents from the Federal Bureau of Investigation. The task force, in other words, offered the possibility of coordination across a host of bureaucracies, all of which operated as agents to their own principals. The complexity of this arrangement, which is not at all uncommon, undoubtedly had implications for the mobilization of, and the influence exercised by, the intended beneficiaries and targets of executive branch activity in the area of financial crimes. These implications will become clearer after government networks are considered from a theoretical point of view in the following chapter.

## Client Participation: Three Lessons and Beyond

At first glance the bureaucracy often appears insular and impervious to outside intervention. Complaints about red tape and out-of-control agencies abound, and at times these complaints have merit. This chapter, however, has demonstrated that the bureaucracy is a surprisingly open and accessible set of institutions and organizations. Three lessons, in particular, seem appropriate to draw regarding the bureaucracy and its clients.

### Who Participates Varies

Both economic and environmental interests placed enormous pressure on the Forest Service during the debate over the revitalization of Bitterroot National Forest. This two-sided mobilization occurred even though the benefits of timber removal were to accrue narrowly to logging and other local interests, while the costs were to be borne by environmentalists all over the country. Although it might be tempting to conclude that agencies always hear from all relevant stakeholders, such a conclusion would ignore the variation in client participation that occurs over time and across policy areas. As noted above, in recent decades some iron triangles have been transformed into sloppy hexagons, making participation more fluid and uncertain than in previous eras. Within these hexagons the activism of particular clients varies across issues as benefits and costs take on unique distributions. Although business organizations will undoubtedly continue to participate extensively in bureaucratic proceedings, given their direct material stake in agency actions, the extent to which this participation will be met by other interests is best assessed on a case-by-case basis.

## Venues Vary

Just as the identities of client participants are remarkably diverse, so, too, are the venues through which these participants make their views known. When the Forest Service waived the public appeals process in its decision regarding logging in Bitterroot, environmentalists raised their grievances in the court system. In general, clients can communicate with agency officials through both direct and indirect channels. Direct channels, such as the advisory committee system, bring clients themselves before agencies. Indirect channels, in contrast, task legislatures and courts with addressing agencies on behalf of specific constituencies or parties. Importantly, venues are distinct in the resources clients must possess to take advantage of opportunities for participation. Clients seeking to comment on agency proposals are best off when exercising significant legal acumen, given the complexity of many contemporary rulemakings. When the goal is to entice legislators to intervene in bureaucratic decisions, clients are most capable when mobilizing large numbers of constituents or filling the campaign coffers of prospective benefactors.

## Influence Varies

Both sides got some of what they wanted when the Forest Service finally resolved the debate over Bitterroot's recovery. Many thousands of acres of burned trees were harvested, while the most pristine areas of the forest were left untouched. In other instances, however, influence accrues disproportionately to one interest or set of interests. When revising the way in which the Medicare program pays for physician services, the Health Care Financing Administration proved more responsive to comments submitted by specialists (for example, cardiologists) than to comments submitted by family practitioners and other general providers. These differences in influence were important because the agency had been charged by Congress with redistributing payments away from specialists.[106] The influence patterns, at least as witnessed in the notice and comment process, may have made it difficult for such an outcome to emerge from the rulemaking.

Issues of client influence raise a pair of broader, more normative questions: Does client participation make policymaking in the bureaucracy more democratic? Does this participation enhance the ability of agencies to make high-quality, defensible decisions? Although these questions do not have simple answers, this chapter has provided a framework for thinking about such concerns. Due in part to client participation, policymaking in the bureaucracy is a political process as well as an exercise in administration. Assessments of accountability and performance must be made with both aspects of bureaucracy in mind.

In the case of Bitterroot, the Forest Service's charge to foster multiple uses of the land under its domain would seem to make it difficult for the agency to act as an effective steward for any particular set of users, let alone all affected parties. The sustained activism of both environmentalists and local economic interests would seem to make the agency's task that much more difficult. Such client participation, however, can have exactly the opposite effect. In the words of former agriculture secretary Dan Glickman, "equality of engagement" among stakeholders can foster "genuine debate" and ultimately give rise to a policy community that is healthy and anchored by an agency that serves both its clients and the nation with distinction.

## Key Terms

Advisory committees, 107

Benefits, 96

Card memorandum, 117

Clients, 95

Client politics, 97

Community peer review, 111

Costs, 96

Digital divide, 115

Direct lobbying, 118

Dockets, 113

Entrepreneurial politics, 98

Federal Advisory
  Committee Act, 107

Federal Docket Management
  System, 114

Interest group politics, 98

Iron triangles, 100

Issue networks, 102

Major rules, 105

Majoritarian politics, 98

Midnight regulations, 117

Negotiated rulemaking, 108

Notice and comment process, 104

Notice of proposed
  rulemaking, 104

Policy entrepreneurs, 98

Policy images, 101

Political meddling, 110

Professional associations, 121

Public hearings, 109

Public interest groups, 101

Public meetings, 109

Revolving door, 118

Rulemaking, 104

Scope of conflict, 123

Sloppy hexagons, 102

*Unsafe At Any Speed*, 98

# 5 | Networks

As the population of the United States ages dramatically, the number of persons who could spend some portion of their lives in a nursing home increases. At its best, a nursing home provides high-quality medical care, plus tender loving care to make residents feel secure. At its worst, a nursing home is a smelly, noisy, scary place where frail and sick senior citizens suffer from indifference and neglect.

Government agencies run only about 5 percent of nursing homes. For-profit firms run the overwhelming majority of them; nonprofit organizations most of the rest.[1] Although government agencies seldom run nursing homes themselves, they are intimately involved in funding and monitoring them. The federal government funds nursing homes that care for Medicaid or Medicare clients. State human services agencies license all nursing homes, with additional oversight by the Centers for Medicare and Medicaid Services (CMS), the agency formerly known as the Health Care Financing Administration. State and federal laws require regular site visits by state officials, intermittent visits by federal officials.

All these organizations—federal and state agencies, for-profit firms, and nonprofit organizations—belong, in effect, to a network, albeit one that has no official name and is sometimes hard to detect. Other members of the network include state ombudsman offices representing nursing home clients, trade associations representing nursing homes, and citizens' groups representing clients and loved ones.

These arrangements typify what H. Brinton Milward has called the **hollow state.**[2] Instead of delivering social services, government bureaucracies frequently finance and scrutinize the delivery of such services by other organizations. This phenomenon, known as **contracting out,** originated in the "hard services" area (such as road repair and garbage pickup) but spread quickly to the social or human services (such as education and health). It is one element of a broader trend toward the **privatization** of public services.[3]

One way to view contracting out is through the lens of principal-agent theory. Just as CMS is the agent of Congress and the president, so, too, is the Manor Care nursing home in Bethesda, Maryland, an agent of the state of Maryland and the federal government. Contracts specify Manor Care's obligations to each of these government principals. The government entities have some leverage over their agent Manor Care (and other for-profit and non-profit nursing homes) because of their ability to withhold funds or to accelerate regulatory enforcement. As predicted by principal-agent theory, however, monitoring is a constant challenge.

Yet principal-agent theory may not be the best way to think about nursing home politics. Consider, for example, the relationship between the federal and state agencies that regulate the homes. Under our federal system, that relationship is not truly hierarchical, as principal-agent theory implies. While the federal government can tell the state of Maryland how to spend federal Medicaid funds, it does not enjoy the same degree of leverage when federal funding is not involved. Even when it comes to Medicaid, the federal government often treats states with kid gloves for fear of stifling innovation or provoking a negative political reaction.

Furthermore, Manor Care is more than just an agent of Maryland and the federal government. As a for-profit firm, it has obligations to its shareholders and its customers that may not coincide with the views of government agencies. Complicating matters even more is the fact that Manor Care in Bethesda is part of a chain of nursing homes. This implies yet another set of obligations. Of course, one might simply treat this as a case involving multiple principals. But even this adjustment does not adequately account for relationships not easily portrayed in hierarchical terms.

Ultimately, it may be more useful to apply network theory or, more broadly, a network approach to nursing homes and the agencies that occupy so prominent a place in the functioning of nursing homes. The network approach has several advantages. First, it can encompass both hierarchical and nonhierarchical relationships. Second, it seeks to measure information flows, which need to be modeled and documented if complex relationships between organizations are to be understood. Third, it recognizes the extent of interorganizational bargaining not just over programmatic details but also, more fundamentally, over programmatic goals. Organizations that belong to a network have their own goals, which they can pursue and promote to a greater degree than agents can. Fourth, the network approach highlights problems of accountability that seem to be growing as we shift from hierarchical organizational forms to other, more fluid and more complex kinds of relationships.

In this chapter we focus on networks that include bureaucracies—how they work, how they are changing, and how they might be changed to perform better. The following are the *core questions* we explore:

- *HOW DO FEDERAL AGENCIES RELATE TO STATE AND LOCAL GOVERNMENT AGENCIES AND WITH WHAT RESULTS?* Health policy and environmental policy are strikingly intergovernmental in character. Even education policy, once regarded as the province of local governments, has become increasingly intergovernmental.

- *WHAT ARE THE ESSENTIAL FEATURES AND KEY CHALLENGES OF PUBLIC-PRIVATE PARTNERSHIPS, SUCH AS CONTRACTING OUT?* For years public-private partnerships have marked such fields as trash collection and economic development. Recently, such arrangements have arisen in social policy as well, at times sparking considerable controversy.

- *HOW DO BUREAUCRACIES COORDINATE WITH OTHER BUREAUCRACIES?* Interagency task forces and cabinet meetings are among the traditional mechanisms employed. In recent years presidents have appointed "czars" to manage such complex domains as energy policy, drug policy, and homeland security—with mixed results.

More broadly, we consider the challenges of accountability and whether networks alleviate or aggravate these challenges. We also consider tools of government that may enhance the performance of networks comprising bureaucracies.

## Network Theory

A **network** is an institution linking organizations or persons. Students of bureaucratic politics find **interorganizational networks** of particular interest. Laurence O'Toole defines such networks as "structures of interdependence involving multiple organizations or parts thereof, where one unit is not merely the formal subordinate of the others in some larger hierarchical arrangement."[4] This definition, which we accept, is relatively broad. As long as two or more organizations are involved and their relationship is not strictly hierarchical, we posit that a network of organizations exists. The purpose of that relationship may be joint decision making or advocacy or information sharing or some combination of these goals.

Networks coexist with hierarchies, and they sometimes include hierarchical arrangements. For its part, network theory is a genuine alternative to principal-agent theory, even though a given relationship within a network may be between a principal and an agent. In some intergovernmental networks, a state government may be an agent of the federal government on one issue and a "free agent" on another. Within a given cabinet-level department, one unit may deliver services directly (a principal-agent relationship) while another unit delivers services through a variety of for-profit and nonprofit contractors (a network). One study of 14 public management networks found that managers spend the overwhelming majority of their time working within a hierarchy, only 15 to 20 percent of their time collaborating, and even less time collaborating within a network.[5] As Robert Agranoff has noted, networks have surely not displaced hierarchies, although the importance of networks appears to be growing.[6]

Whereas principal-agent theory originated in economics, network theory originated in sociology. For some sociologists it proved a useful concept for highlighting the surprising strength of weak ties between persons in social networks.[7] For others it proved a helpful tool in understanding how organizations share information.[8] More recently, students of public administration have seized upon the network as a vehicle for understanding how government agencies interact with other agencies and with private sector organizations.[9]

Unlike principal-agent theory, which treats the goals of principals as given and relatively fixed, network theory views goals as more fluid. Although each organization affiliated with a network undoubtedly has its own goals, the goals of the network itself evolve over time through a process of give-and-take.[10] This is probably a realistic perspective. Yet because a network's goals are more tentative and dynamic than those of an organization, and because a network's stakeholders are more numerous than those of a single organization, it is more difficult to evaluate a network's success.[11]

Students of networks, both social and organizational, have focused a good deal of attention on several key concepts, including centrality, density, size, complexity, multiplexity, and differentiation. **Centrality** refers to the degree to which information flows through a single individual or organization, strategically situated to serve as a clearinghouse or traffic cop. **Density** is defined as the number of actual connections among individuals or organizations divided by the number of potential connections among these individuals or organizations.[12] **Size** is the number of persons or organizations that participate in the work of the system. **Complexity** means the number of different service or product sectors represented by the members or member organizations.[13] **Multiplexity** refers to the number of separate relationships between two parties (for example, two mental health agencies might be linked through referrals, service contracts, and information sharing).[14] And **differentiation** refers to the degree to which there is functional and service specialization among the members or member organizations.[15] Together these concepts help us understand the "structure" of a network or patterns of social relations. It is sometimes useful, for example, to distinguish between a highly centralized and a highly decentralized network and between a high-density and a low-density network (see Figure 5.1).

At least one study has found that centrality and size are positively related, which means that larger networks find it necessary or desirable to route communications through one organization or subunit. It also appears that larger networks are more complex and more differentiated but less dense.[16] Interestingly, centrality and density are inversely related. In other words, the presence of a dominant individual or organization (high centrality) discourages connections with other individuals or organizations.

One way to think about networks is that they help to manage uncertainty caused by insufficient information about the content of a vexing social problem. Networks can be helpful in reducing this kind of uncertainty, which Joop Koppenjan and Erik-Hans Klijn call **substantive uncertainty.**[17] Networks can also help to manage **strategic uncertainty** (not knowing how other actors will respond to the problem) and **institutional uncertainty** (a lack of knowledge about the rules of the game in which actors must operate).[18] Network management requires skills that officials accustomed to a more hierarchical setting may or may not have. If they are to be effective, network managers must learn to manage accountability, legitimacy, conflict, design, and commitment within a network setting.[19] This requires a special brand of leadership.

Network theory can be particularly useful in certain fields, such as law enforcement. For example, the relative centrality of different individuals in a

## Figure 5.1 Networks with Different Characteristics

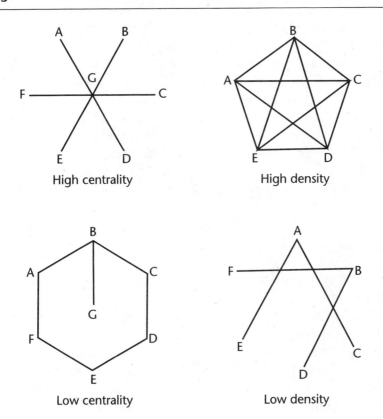

High centrality

High density

Low centrality

Low density

crime network can help investigators determine whom to target first. An-other useful concept is **equivalence.** As Malcolm Sparrow notes, "The dis-ruptive effectiveness of removing one individual or a set of individuals from a network depends not only on their centrality, but also upon some notion of their uniqueness. The more unique, or unusual, their role the harder they will be to replace. The most valuable targets will be both central and difficult to replace."[20] The concept of **weak ties** can also be instructive in that it alerts investigators to the utility of focusing attention on communication channels that are seldom used but indispensable to the network's success. As sociolo-gists have noted, weak ties are sometimes more important than strong ties (if you ever got a job through a friend of a friend, then you already under-stand the importance of "weak ties"). A criminal's chance encounter with an old acquaintance may lead to a burglary or some other type of crime. A law enforcement officer's conversation with a casual acquaintance may lead to an arrest.

In the wake of the September 11, 2001, terrorist attacks, some scholars have sought to understand that most infamous of modern networks, al-Qaida. In attempting to trace connections among hijackers, Valdis Krebs found that the organization's cells were characterized by extraordinarily low density, with few communications links among the conspirators. He concluded that "covert networks trade efficiency for secrecy."[21] Noting the absence of "moment-to-moment top-down management" in al-Qaida, Richard Rothenberg argued that leadership is essential at the planning stages "but may not be critical for the maintenance of the terrorist activity."[22] He also noted the organization's formidable barriers to entry and exit—another technique for ensuring secrecy.

## The Tools Approach

Although some political scientists have found network theory a fruitful source of insights into interorganizational behavior, a larger number of political scientists have found it more useful to import other ideas to understand networks and their consequences. One particularly promising line of inquiry is what is sometimes referred to as the **tools approach.** The essence of this approach is to understand that the choice of a particular policy tool typically implies the choice of a particular network or combination of organizations. Thus the effectiveness of a given network depends not only on the network's organizational characteristics but also on some of the distinctive characteristics of the underlying policy tool.

According to Lester Salamon, policy tools differ in several key respects, including coerciveness, directness, automaticity, and visibility. **Coerciveness** refers to the degree to which a tool compels a certain form of behavior, as opposed to merely encouraging it. **Directness** refers to the extent to which the organization authorizing, financing, or commencing an activity actually carries out that activity. **Automaticity** measures the extent to which a tool relies on existing structural arrangements as opposed to new ones. **Visibility** measures the degree to which resources devoted to a tool are featured prominently in normal budget and review processes.[23]

With these attributes in mind, it is possible to categorize a wide variety of policy tools, such as economic regulation, social regulation, grants, contracts, vouchers, direct loans, loan guarantees, labeling requirements, and information. For example, economic regulation tends to be high in coerciveness and directness, low in automaticity and visibility. In contrast, vouchers tend to be medium in coerciveness, low in directness, high in automaticity, and high in visibility.[24] When public officials choose vouchers rather than regulation, they inevitably advance one type of network rather than another. In the case of vouchers, the network will probably be decentralized and differentiated, with schools trying to establish a distinctive market niche. But the success or failure of vouchers will also depend on the distinctive characteristics of the vouchers themselves. Their high visibility, for example, helps to guarantee that they will be controversial. Their low directness fuels demands for systematic evaluations to demonstrate results.

The tools approach is closely linked to efforts to understand the phenomenon of **third-party government**.[25] Increasingly, public officials turn to third parties to deliver public services. These third parties include banks, day care centers, hospitals, nursing homes, schools, and other levels of government. To put it another way, the tools selected to deliver public services are more indirect than in traditional public sector arrangements. This makes it all the more important to look at relationships between organizations—or the inner workings of networks. It also raises questions as to whether the network form enables us to hold service delivery organizations accountable for their results.

To return to our nursing home example, whom shall we blame if we discover numerous patients with bedsores and dirty linens at a particular nursing home facility? Is it the owner of the nursing home? If the home is part of a chain, is it the owner of the nursing home chain? Is it the state agency that failed to oversee the nursing home? Is it the federal agency that failed to oversee the state agency? Is it the ombudsman whose intervention was too little, too late? In a hierarchical situation, it is relatively easy to affix blame. In the immortal words of Harry S Truman, "The buck stops here!" Accountability is more elusive in a network characterized by public and private partners, federal and state officials.

As Paul Posner has noted, third-party government involves at least five different kinds of accountability challenges.[26] First, federal goals are sometimes diverted or compromised because state and local officials do not support these goals. Second, state and local governments often receive fiscal windfalls, with the federal government supporting programs that recipient governments would otherwise have funded themselves. Third, federal support, through insurance and loan guarantee programs, creates moral hazard problems, encouraging third parties to take risks they would not otherwise take. Fourth, third parties frequently lack fiscal incentives to avoid waste, fraud, and abuse; it's not their money and they do not benefit from the correction of the problem. Fifth, third-party subsidies can encourage opportunistic behavior by organizations that seek to enhance their profits or, in the case of nonprofit organizations, their customer bases.

Despite these challenges, it is important to find ways of holding networks accountable because networks are becoming increasingly important in a variety of policy sectors. In health care, for example, networks of physicians, hospitals, and other health enterprises have grown dramatically since the rise of managed care.[27] In health care the network has become an attractive alternative to hierarchies (perceived as too rigid) and markets (perceived as unfair). More broadly, Laurence O'Toole believes that as policy problems grow more complex, the network becomes more attractive because of its flexibility and versatility.[28] You can, for example, create or dissolve a network much more easily than you can create or dissolve a government agency.

According to one careful study, 85 percent of significant new federal laws require the involvement of multiple actors at the implementation stage. Furthermore, the bureaucracy sometimes adopts rules requiring the involvement of additional actors, including state and local governments, private firms, and nonprofit organizations.[29] It is widely believed, though not firmly established, that network structures are growing in popularity and importance.[30]

At least three types of networks have been of interest to students of public administration: intergovernmental relationships, public-private partnerships, and interagency coordination. The first two involve third-party government and can be easily identified as networks. The third organizational form—interagency coordination—is often treated separately, as a useful coping mechanism employed by many hierarchical organizations, such as the federal government. Yet interagency coordination comprises "structures of interdependence involving multiple organizations or parts thereof, where one unit is not merely the formal subordinate of the others in some larger hierarchical arrangement."[31] From this vantage point interagency coordination clearly qualifies as a network, albeit one with a more limited scope than the scopes of the other two.

Although it is possible to use other theoretical frameworks to understand these phenomena (policy implementation theories for intergovernmental relations, principal-agent theory for public-private contracts, and public administration theories for interagency coordination), network theory and the tools approach are directly applicable to all three of types of arrangements. In the sections that follow, we examine each type of network, its accountability challenges, and ultimately its performance.

## Intergovernmental Relations

Because the United States is a federal system and because intergovernmental relations have become much more complex in recent years, the intergovernmental network is a particularly important type of arrangement. Many public policies involve some sort of shared decision making by federal, state, and local governments. There are at least three possibilities. First, Congress assigns responsibility for a program to a federal agency, which in turn delegates responsibility to run the program to a state or local government, subject to certain conditions. This phenomenon, known as **devolution,** increased during the 1980s and the 1990s. Second, Congress explicitly **mandates** states to implement a program or to perform certain tasks. Third, Congress appropriates **grants-in-aid** that may be used to entice states to participate in certain programs.[32]

### Environmental Protection

Following the passage of a slew of significant federal environmental laws in the 1970s, the Environmental Protection Agency (EPA) discovered it to be increasingly difficult to implement several important statutes on its own. Furthermore, many state governments pleaded for more flexibility, arguing that they could implement federal laws more successfully than the federal government because of their greater familiarity with the unique geographic, topological, economic, and political circumstances of their states. During the early 1980s, coinciding with President Reagan's first term, the EPA devolved considerable authority to run federal environmental programs to the states. In network theory terms, intergovernmental networks became less centralized. By the dawn of the twenty-first century, an average of two-thirds of the states were in charge of those programs that could in principle be delegated to them (see Table 5.1).

Clearly, the flow of information from the federal government to the states and vice versa is particularly important when programs have been delegated to the states. The federal government must specify its expectations clearly, distinguishing between federal minimum standards that must be upheld and other domains in which states are more or less free to do as they please. As for the states, they must furnish information on their policy outputs and policy

## Table 5.1 Number of States Authorized to Run Environmental Programs

|  | Yes | In Process | Partial | No | NA |
|---|---|---|---|---|---|
| ***Clean Air Act*** | | | | | |
| New Source Performance Standards | 39 | 1 | 9 | 1 | 0 |
| NESHAPS | 38 | 2 | 10 | 0 | 0 |
| Prevention of Significant Deterioration | 45 | 0 | 4 | 1 | 0 |
| Title V Operating Permit | 21 | 29 | 0 | 0 | 0 |
| New Source Review | 46 | 1 | 1 | 0 | 2 |
| ***Clean Water Act*** | | | | | |
| NPDES | 37 | 0 | 4 | 8 | 1 |
| Pretreatment/POTWs | 29 | 1 | 0 | 19 | 1 |
| State Revolving Fund | 48 | 0 | 0 | 2 | 0 |
| Sludge Management | 9 | 3 | 0 | 37 | 1 |
| Construction Grants | 46 | 0 | 0 | 3 | 1 |
| Wetlands | 2 | 0 | 0 | 42 | 6 |
| ***Resource Conservation and Recovery Act*** | | | | | |
| Subpart C, Base Program | 47 | 1 | 0 | 2 | 0 |
| Subpart C, Corrective Action | 31 | 3 | 0 | 16 | 0 |
| Subpart C, Mixed Waste | 39 | 1 | 0 | 10 | 0 |
| Subpart C, BIF | 19 | 4 | 0 | 27 | 0 |
| Toxicity Characteristics Revisions | 34 | 3 | 0 | 13 | 0 |
| LDR California Wastes | 37 | 2 | 0 | 10 | 1 |
| LDR 1/3 Wastes | 36 | 3 | 0 | 11 | 0 |
| LDR 2/3 Wastes | 21 | 3 | 0 | 26 | 0 |
| LDR 3/3 Wastes | 27 | 6 | 0 | 17 | 0 |
| Subpart D, Solid Waste | 29 | 1 | 8 | 3 | 9 |
| Underground Storage Tanks | 28 | 2 | 0 | 20 | 0 |

*(continued)*

outcomes to the federal government. Otherwise, the federal agency cannot know whether delegation has been successful, and accountability breaks down.

To improve the quality of information transmitted through the environmental policy network, the EPA established a new institution in 1995 known as the **performance partnership agreement,** or PPA. Under this arrangement, any state can negotiate a PPA with the EPA regional office responsible for that state. The EPA grants the state greater flexibility in the administra-

**Table 5.1** *Continued*

|  | Yes | In Process | Partial | No | NA |
|---|---|---|---|---|---|
| ***Safe Drinking Water Act*** | | | | | |
| Public Water System | | | | | |
| Supervision | 48 | 0 | 0 | 2 | 0 |
| Wellhead Protection Program | 36 | 1 | 0 | 4 | 9 |
| Underground Injection | | | | | |
| Control 1422 | 34 | 0 | 0 | 16 | 0 |
| Underground Injection | | | | | |
| Control 1425 | 35 | 0 | 1 | 9 | 5 |
| ***Federal Insecticide, Fungicide, and Rodenticide Act*** | | | | | |
| 23(a) State Cooperation, | | | | | |
| Aid, and Training | 44 | 1 | 1 | 0 | 4 |
| 23(b) State Cooperation, | | | | | |
| Aid, and Training | 44 | 1 | 1 | 0 | 4 |
| Endangered Species | 24 | 5 | 0 | 9 | 12 |
| Worker Protection | 48 | 1 | 1 | 0 | 0 |
| Groundwater Protection | 29 | 11 | 0 | 4 | 6 |

*Source:* National Academy of Public Administration, *Environment.gov* (Washington, D.C.: NAPA, November 2000), 137–138.

*Note:*

NA = not ascertained

NESHAPS = National Emission Standards for Hazardous Air Pollutants

NPDES = National Pollutant Discharge Elimination System

POTWs = Publicly Owned Treatment Works

BIF = Regulation of Burning of Hazardous Wastes in Boilers and Industrial Furnaces

LDR = Land Disposal Restrictions

tion of federal environmental programs and relaxes certain reporting requirements; in return, the state agrees to improve its environmental performance and to document those improvements better. Though voluntary, PPAs have been negotiated by thirty-three states.[33]

Part of a broader Clinton administration initiative known as the National Environmental Performance Partnership System (NEPPS), the PPA has received somewhat mixed reviews from outside observers.[34] Clearly, environmental performance measures at the state level are more widely used and more sophisticated than they used to be. NEPPS deserves some credit for this. Still, most states continue to rely more on output measures (such as the number of inspections conducted) rather than outcome measures (such as changes in air or water quality), despite the latter's greater importance.

By definition the PPA is a dyadic relationship between the EPA and a state environmental agency. In contrast, some environmental networks are regional in nature. These include initiatives to improve the Chesapeake Bay and the Great Lakes Basin. According to Barry Rabe, both initiatives have been successful, thanks to a combination of grants, technical assistance, coordination, and collective efforts to achieve uniform standards throughout each region.[35] Note the absence of coercive tools in these regional networks. In intergovernmental relations, coercion, though tempting, can be counterproductive. That is particularly true when federal and state officials agree on certain basic goals or values.[36]

In recent years state and federal agencies have formed hundreds of watershed partnerships in an effort to manage natural resources through voluntary cooperation. Such partnerships, which may also include third parties, reflect dissatisfaction with command-and-control approaches to environmental protection. They have arisen more often in watersheds characterized by severe pollution from nonpoint sources (for example, agricultural and urban runoff) and relatively weak agricultural interests.[37] Partnerships are more likely to arise in higher-income watersheds and less likely to arise in watersheds with a larger percentage of black and Hispanic residents.[38] In this respect, watersheds have not been an antidote to concerns over environmental justice, although they may have contributed to environmental protection.

The Suwannee River Project, which originated in north central Florida in 1998, illustrates the potential—but also the limitations—of watershed partnerships.[39] The partnership, which includes government officials, agricultural producers, and conservation groups, was created to reduce nutrient discharges when it appeared that a command-and-control strategy might be forthcoming if a voluntary approach did not succeed. Farmers participating in the partnership receive cash in return for pledges to adopt "best management practices" to reduce nitrogen loadings in the water basin. As of May 2003, the partnership had signed up 39 of 40 dairies, 131 of 139 poultry farms, and 207 of 300 crop farms in the basin.[40] The partnership's most conspicuous weakness has been its inability to convince environmental groups to join. Their reluctance to join is due to the fear that participation might compromise pending lawsuits against the state's environmental agency.[41]

## Health Policy

In dealing with the health care needs of the poor, the federal government has long relied on networks. The Medicaid program, established in 1965, sets up shared responsibility for funding the health care needs of the poor, with the federal government providing at least half of the funding and state governments providing the rest, under a fixed formula that favors states with lower per capita incomes. Under this program, state Medicaid agencies determine eligibility standards and benefits, subject to federal rules and regulations. A typical network includes federal and state agencies as payers and hospitals, nursing homes, and physicians as payees.

Beginning with the Nixon administration, the federal government expressed interest in developing managed care as an alternative to the traditional fee-for-service health insurance system, where insurance companies automatically pick up the full cost of health care. Although managed care takes many different forms, a common denominator is that health care providers have financial incentives to reduce unnecessary medical expenditures and procedures. Managed care originated on the commercial, or private, side of health care but eventually extended to the governmental, or public, side.

During the administration of George H. W. Bush, the federal Health Care Financing Administration, then responsible for overseeing Medicaid, was authorized to grant waivers to state governments that wished to extend managed care to Medicaid clients. Available waivers included **1915b waivers,** which allowed states to enroll some Medicaid clients in managed care plans, and **1115 waivers,** which allowed states even broader discretion as part of a research-and-demonstration effort. Such waivers, relatively few at first, escalated sharply during the Clinton administration. When President Clinton took office in 1993, fifty 1915b waivers were in effect; when he left office, one hundred such waivers were in effect. When President Clinton took office, only one state (Arizona) had an 1115 waiver; when he left office, eighteen states had such waivers.[42]

The trend toward Medicaid managed care ensured that health care networks would become more important and more complex. Because health care payments are no longer automatic, the standard operating procedures of health care service delivery organizations and government overseers become more important. Because health maintenance organizations (HMOs) limit access to physicians included in an HMO's "network," new norms have developed, with contractual arrangements that impose constraints on patients, physicians, and HMOs themselves.

**Donna Shalala**
*Secretary of Health and Human Services*
*(1993–2001)*

"There are enormous partnerships in adoption. Many states, including New York, long ago made a decision to involve private charity agencies in adoption. Our major partnerships at HHS were with HMOs. More generally, we increased contracting out to social service organizations."

To make matters even more interesting, Congress decided in 1997 to establish a new program, known as the Children's Health Insurance Program (CHIP). Modeled somewhat after Medicaid, CHIP nevertheless differed from it, having a somewhat more affluent clientele, somewhat more generous federal contributions, and somewhat more flexible rules. In implementing CHIP some states established a brand new program, others expanded Medicaid, and still others adopted a hybrid approach.

As implementation proceeded it soon became evident that better coordination was needed between the Medicaid network and the CHIP network. Some states, anxious to cash in on CHIP's more favorable matching rates and greater flexibility, enrolled children in CHIP who were in fact eligible for Medicaid. Such behavior exemplified poor coordination; it was also illegal. Eventually, thanks to federal pressure, states got better at assigning clients to the right program.

But additional problems remain, such as "churning" between the Medicaid and CHIP programs. Owing to changes in parental employment, income, and related factors, children eligible for CHIP may suddenly become eligible for Medicaid or vice versa.[43] This phenomenon makes it all the more important that the Medicaid network and the CHIP network work closely together. If the networks do so, children may enjoy a smooth transition from one program to another; if they do not, health care services may be interrupted, with harmful consequences for children's health.

Other continuing problems involve perverse financial incentives and the attraction of opportunistic partners, discussed earlier. Under the Medicaid program, for example, some states have charged the federal government for expenses they never truly incurred. By inducing hospitals and nursing homes to demand payment under higher Medicare rates, as opposed to lower Medicaid rates, states have extracted higher matching payments from the federal government. After the transfers occurred, the hospitals and nursing homes returned most of the money to the state government, thus resulting in federal matching dollars for fictional expenditures.[44]

Although federal health care funding is much more likely to be channeled through the states than through local governments, the latter are also important, particularly with respect to public health. In response to terrorist attacks, the visibility of our nation's public health network has increased sharply. The anthrax mailings of October 2001 exposed some of the weaknesses of our public health system. When the anthrax attacks commenced, many local health agencies floundered. Because half of all local public health departments did not have access to the Internet and because communications with the Centers for Disease Control (CDC) were often weak, many of them relied on the mass media for guidance.[45] At least one CDC official acknowledged coordination problems. Dr. Julie Gerberding, then acting deputy director of the CDC's Center for Infectious Diseases, told the *New York Times:* "In retrospect, we were certainly not prepared for layers and levels of collaboration among a vast array of government agencies and professional organizations that would be required to be efficient and successful in the anthrax outbreak."[46]

Immediately following the terrorist attacks of 2001, federal funding for state and local public health preparedness increased dramatically, from $67 million to $1 billion annually.[47] Within three years, the number of epidemiologists working in state and territorial health departments increased by 27 percent.[48] Despite these encouraging developments, the capacity of our public health network to respond to a catastrophe remains uncertain. Although the number of epidemiologists in state health departments increased, nearly one-third of them lack any formal training or academic coursework in epidemiology.[49] Also, whatever the capacity of state health departments, many local public health agencies do not appear to be ready for a public health emergency such as an infectious disease outbreak. Researchers at the RAND Corporation tested the readiness of nineteen local health agencies in eighteen states by reporting "urgent" cases in telephone calls to local public health officials. In a subset of calls, they described symptoms of botulism, anthrax, smallpox, and bubonic plague. Although some local officials responded appropriately by asking relevant questions and probing for details, others did not. After listening to a description of the classic symptoms of bubonic plague, one local health official told the caller not to worry and to "go back to bed" because no similar cases had been reported. Upon hearing about a case with symptoms of botulism, another local official said, "You're right, it does sound like botulism. I wouldn't worry too much if I were you."[50] These findings suggest that some local public health agencies would not respond well to a bioterrorist attack.

## Public-Private Partnerships

As is evident from some of the above examples, many networks involving government bureaucracies spill over into the private sector. Such networks may or may not include interagency or intergovernmental relationships. In some instances, they involve a direct contract between a government agency and a for-profit firm or nonprofit organization; in other instances, they involve a looser relationship where cooperative behavior emerges without an explicit contractual obligation.

### Contracting Out

The most common public-private partnership in the United States is contracting out, in which a government agency establishes a contractual arrangement with a for-profit firm or a nonprofit organization to deliver some service. Principal-agent theory can be applied to such relationships.[51] A contract, though, is a voluntary relationship between two independent organizations.[52] To the extent that a relationship between organizations involves bargaining rather than commands, network theory may be more suitable.

Contracting out appeals to government officials because it offers the promise—and sometimes the reality—of saving money. The privatization of garbage pickups, for example, seems to have resulted in cost savings, with no apparent diminution in the quality of services provided.[53]

But contracting out presents government officials with real challenges. Monitoring and controlling service delivery is difficult enough when those delivering the services are fellow government officials. When service deliverers are employees of some other organization, oversight becomes even more difficult. Without corrective steps, accountability becomes an elusive goal.

Accountability suffers if government officials lack sufficient information to distinguish between good and bad contractors. Accountability suffers if little or no competition exists. Accountability suffers if the government has poorly defined the contractor's responsibilities. Accountability suffers if government officials adopt a laissez-faire position after the contract has been awarded.

Another concern is that contracting out might ultimately transform non-profit organizations that receive the contracts—and not for the better.[54] As nonprofit organizations become more dependent on government for funding, they may find it advantageous to adjust their priorities, habits, strategies, and norms to secure additional funding. While this is not necessarily perverse, it can result in nonprofit organizations that come to behave a lot like for-profit firms.

## Energy Policy

The Department of Energy (DOE) relies more than most federal agencies on contracts with private firms. For every DOE employee, there are thirty-five contractor employees.[55] This has led Donald Kettl to describe DOE as "little more than an administrative shell over a vast empire of contractors."[56] Because there are so many contracts and the tasks being performed are so technical, DOE employees find it very difficult to monitor performance.

In 1989 government investigators uncovered serious problems at a nuclear weapons production facility in Rocky Flats, Colorado, run by Rockwell International. Investigators discovered numerous health and safety problems inside the plant, illegal dumping of hazardous wastes outside the plant, and gross insensitivity to environmental concerns. The severity of the problems, which ultimately led to an FBI raid on the plant, a temporary shutdown, and a new contractor, contrasted sharply with DOE's prior ratings of the plant, which had been quite positive.[57] Later it became evident that DOE's top managers had not been receiving accurate information. Without such information, it is impossible to hold an errant contractor accountable.

Part of the problem, one suspects, was a clash of organizational goals. For DOE, the production of nuclear weapons was a primary goal; environmental considerations were secondary but somewhat important. For Rockwell International, making a profit was the primary goal; environmental concerns mattered even less than for DOE. Under such circumstances, DOE managers had difficulty conveying the need to dispose of nuclear waste safely, securely, and legally.

## Mental Health Policy

As noted earlier, networks have been especially conspicuous in health policy. In particular, managed care has ushered in a new series of arrangements in which nonprofit organizations or for-profit firms under contract to state

Medicaid agencies provide vital health care services. This is true of both health policy generally and mental health policy in particular.

By using key concepts from network theory, some scholars have assessed the impact of managed care on the degree of system integration, which is generally regarded in positive terms. Following the introduction of managed care for the mental health system in Pima County, Arizona, both density and centrality increased for funding contract networks and also for referral net-works.[58] This finding is especially noteworthy given prior research suggesting an inverse relationship between centrality and density.

## Welfare Policy

Traditionally, welfare policy has been the province of federal, state, and local governments. As public discontent with welfare policy heightened during the 1990s, however, a number of state governments opted for public-private part-nerships as part of broader welfare reform efforts. Wisconsin, widely consid-ered the leader in state welfare reform initiatives, also became prominent in carving out a stronger role for the private sector in delivering welfare services. Under the state's Wisconsin Works (or W-2) program, county governments lost the exclusive right to run their welfare programs. Approximately 70 per-cent of Wisconsin's welfare caseload is now managed by for-profit firms and nonprofit organizations.[59] In Milwaukee County the local government no longer administers W-2 at all; instead, such organizations as the YMCA, Good-will Industries, and Maximus Inc. administer the program. Some of these or-ganizations use creative mechanisms to help clients succeed. For example, Maximus developed a "doorbell" service, which entails calling clients on the phone to ensure they wake up early enough to get their children off to school and themselves off to work.[60]

The privatization of welfare service delivery is part of a broader phe-nomenon, which Mark Rom describes as a shift from "the welfare state" to "Opportunity, Inc." Other examples of this phenomenon include child sup-port enforcement, employment and training, and even child welfare. At least twenty states use private firms or nonprofit organizations to assist in some aspect of child support collection, such as identifying parents or maintaining the payment system. In at least three states—Kansas, Michigan, and Texas—the child welfare systems are substantially privatized.[61] In each of these in-stances, public and private organizations belong to a network responsible for delivering social services to clients.

## Corrections

An equally interesting development has occurred in law enforcement, where a number of state governments have turned over the administration of some of their prisons to for-profit firms. In 1997 approximately 8.5 percent of all U.S. prisoners were in private facilities. This phenomenon has been most striking in the South. Tennessee, home of the firm then known as the Corrections Corporation of America (CCA), was an early supporter of private prisons. Texas, another early supporter, had nineteen private prisons in 2000.[62]

There is considerable debate about whether private prisons are more efficient than public prisons. Although private prisons sometimes cost less to run than their public counterparts, their lower wages have resulted in higher turnover, with attendant quality problems. One study found more assaults by inmates on both staff and other inmates in private prisons than in public ones. Another study found less reliable methods of classifying prisoners for security purposes in private prisons.[63]

Whatever the merits of private prisons, they do present accountability challenges. For instance, after securing approval to run a prison in Youngstown, Ohio, CCA seems to have misinformed state and local officials about security risks there. When five convicted murderers escaped from the prison in July 1998, company officials tried to cover up the escape. Ohio tried to terminate its contract with CCA but failed. Eventually, CCA agreed to move out of the Youngstown facility inmates unsuitable for a medium-security prison.[64] Of course, cover-ups are not unique to the private sector. Still, certain features of the public sector, including a relatively secure civil service, strong prodisclosure laws, and opportunities for judicial review, tend to discourage cover-ups.

## Partnerships without Contracts

Despite their enormous importance, contracts do not offer the only mechanisms for achieving collaboration between public and private organizations. In many instances, informal conversations and memorandums of understanding are sufficient to create relatively durable relationships between public agencies and other organizations. Many watershed partnerships, for example, rely on memorandums of understanding rather than formal contracts.[65] Much depends on the level of trust that exists between the relevant actors and the nature of the incentives to sustain informal agreements. If the level of trust is high and the incentives are compelling, contracts may not be necessary.

## Environmental Protection

In southern California, public officials, developers, and environmental groups have been participating in a cooperative governance arrangement that seeks to avoid the gridlock sometimes associated with enforcement of the Endangered Species Act. State and county parks and wildlife officials meet regularly with developers and environmentalists in an effort to anticipate problems with sensitive species and prevent the triggering of lengthy legal disputes. Under this program, developers receive permits to build on part of their land; in return, they agree to set aside some land for wildlife habitat and to fund environmental restoration work. In addition to participating in these negotiations, environmental groups provide volunteers to assist in restoration activities.[66] More than 450 habitat conservation plans like this one are in operation or in development in the United States.[67]

In many respects this kind of creative collaboration represents a constructive alternative to debilitating conflict. It brings together organizations with divergent goals that might otherwise be clutching at each other's throats. A potential danger, however, is that environmental groups might become co-opted by developers. As Steven R. Smith and Helen Ingram put it: "Democratic accountability may be compromised as environmental groups receive funding for collaboration in restoration activities they are supposed to monitor."[68] Fortunately, the very diversity of the environmental community means that any hint of co-optation is likely to trigger an outcry by other, more adversarial groups.

## Education

Public schools collaborate with a wide variety of partners in an effort to promote shared goals. In Chicago, for example, at least 90 businesses and nonprofit organizations have established informal partnerships with public schools in an effort to improve school management, the school curriculum, or auxiliary services. The Executive Service Corps, a consulting group, has established a work observation program that enables high school students to learn how a financial institution really works. The Suzuki-Orff School of Music through an outreach program with public and private schools has enabled thousands of children to develop a repertoire of songs and rhymes using rhythm instruments and xylophones. The Second Federal Savings Bank has established a student loan program. Other businesses that have established partnerships with Chicago public schools include McDonald's, JCPenney, the Wrigley Company (have they figured out how to remove gum from the bottom of students' desks?), and McKinsey & Company.

## Interagency Networks

The most fundamental of all networks in which bureaucracies participate is the interagency network. Within any given level of government (federal, state, or local), the executive branch seeks to coordinate its programs, activities, and public testimony. At the very least, coordination implies some information sharing; frequently, it also implies some effort to reach a consensus and to speak with one voice.

### The Cabinet

A familiar network within the executive branch is the president's cabinet. Ever since George Washington's time, the heads of the major departments have met on a regular basis to offer advice to the president, to learn from one another, and to hear what the president wants them to do. Contemporary students of the American presidency have not been very impressed by the cabinet as a policymaking institution or as a coordinating body. We know from Lyndon Johnson's presidency that cabinet officials sometimes concealed their true views of the war in Vietnam to avoid antagonizing a president who demanded fierce loyalty from his top officials.[69] We know from Richard Nixon's presidency that at least one cabinet member (the attorney general, no less) sanctioned illegal acts, including the infamous Watergate burglary.[70]

In general, political scientists have concluded that the cabinet has failed to live up to its potential. Its lack of coherence and limited ability to coordinate policy and management make the cabinet a weak institution.[71] Another problem is the selection process.[72] The president often seeks to placate particular constituencies and to make symbolic appointments that satisfy objectives such as ideological congruence (Reagan) and ethnic diversity (Clinton). After appointing individuals for all sorts of reasons other than their qualifications for the job, presidents, not surprisingly, often ignore their cabinet members' advice.

Yet cabinet meetings do facilitate exchanges between cabinet secretaries and their respective departments. The very knowledge that they will see one another again on a regular basis encourages cooperation.[73] Meetings involving

James Baker III
*Secretary of the Treasury (1985–1988)*
*Secretary of State (1989–1992)*

"In all the bureaucracies in Washington, there are historical positions that the various departments have taken. It's as the old saying goes: where you stand depends on where you sit. Every Wednesday, we had a breakfast meeting in the office of the national security adviser, Brent Scowcroft. It was Scowcroft, Dick Cheney, and me. We showed up with respective talking points from our departments. Only rarely did we have to take a matter to the president. We would work things out.

"There is a natural tension between State and the Pentagon. It is very important that the president make it clear that the secretary of state will be the primary spokesman on foreign policy, so that there won't be any doubt about that. Often there is tension between State and NSC, too. I think our administration was the exception rather than the rule. The rule seems to be godawful fights between State and the NSC. That happened during the Reagan years—knock-down, drag-out fights. It happened during the Clinton years, the Ford years, and the Carter years, resulting in Cyrus Vance's resignation as secretary of state.

"We did it right. Those tensions existed. They will exist. But it has to come from the president. We had a wonderful national security adviser in Brent Scowcroft. He said to me, 'I will never do a TV interview that you don't approve of.' It made it easy for me to say, 'Do as many as you like!' "

two or three cabinet secretaries are likely to be even more productive, particularly when they focus on a relatively discrete issue area, such as national security.

## Office of Management and Budget

In recent years the Office of Management and Budget (OMB), explicitly charged with coordinating government agencies and programs, has come to rival the cabinet in importance. On the budget side, OMB trims funding requests from individual agencies and departments and integrates the streamlined requests into a coherent budget document. To ensure official unity, especially for congressional testimony, OMB insists that all testimony by agency heads be cleared in advance. This doctrine, known as **legislative clearance,** helps the executive branch speak with one voice.

"The best way to coordinate across federal agencies is to build relationships over time, to make sure that the general counsels and inspectors general know each other. We convened groups from the Department of Justice and HHS and the Census Bureau on data issues, to make sure we knew what we were doing. For disease outbreaks, Agriculture and the EPA and HHS had to be coordinated.

"Coordination depends a lot on goodwill at the top and at the middle levels of the bureaucracy. On the Patients' Bill of Rights, Alexis Herman from DOL and I convened everybody and said, 'Look, we've been friends for years. Don't try to play us against each other! Work together!'

"Federal agencies are very turf conscious. Our biggest problem was always the FBI and the Department of Justice. They protected information and didn't share. The FBI simply would not share. The CIA and the security agencies were much more cooperative. The FBI was awful! And they didn't know anything! It's no different today."

By all accounts OMB has been less attentive to the management side of the equation, the most notable exception being the role OMB plays in reviewing major rules proposed by departments and other agencies. Ever since the Reagan administration federal agencies have been required to prepare a regulatory impact analysis for all proposed major rules. An agency submits the proposed rule and the impact analysis to OMB for its approval. OMB can approve the rule, ask for modifications, or sit on the rule indefinitely. A recent study demonstrates that OMB influences the content and ideological direction of rules promulgated by the EPA.[74] Interestingly, OMB speaks for both the president and itself. Depending on who is president, OMB will be harder or softer in its dealings with the EPA. Regardless of who is president, OMB will try to reduce the costs to be borne by regulated firms.

## Interagency Coordination

Despite efforts to promote specialization and differentiation, many agencies have overlapping jurisdictions. This is especially true in foreign affairs, which tends to be characterized by "bureaucratic interconnectedness."[75] The State

| Inside Bureaucracy with | Dick Thornburgh<br>*Attorney General (1988–1990)* |
| --- | --- |

"Our task force on savings and loans, our whole international schemata with respect to drugs—those are all networks. They depended on the exchange of information. They depended on personal relationships between people on the front lines and on a constant review of intelligence capabilities in the broad sense. We were networking before it was called networking. Part of it involves what Tom Ridge is up against now. You need to break down barriers between people who have related responsibilities. That's always been something I've been interested in. You beat people up. You make it clear to them that there's a high price to pay if they don't cooperate. Sometimes you can't beat people up because they're in other agencies, but we spent an awful lot of time on this. We had monthly meetings of all the levels of law enforcement agencies outside the Department of Justice. On a couple of occasions, I had the president speak and lay down the law. It wasn't contentious, but it was to make clear that we were all on the same team. The notion that intelligence or information would be withheld from an agency because it was the province of another agency was just wrong. Other agencies included the IRS, the Customs Service, the Bureau of Alcohol, Tobacco, and Firearms, and the Secret Service. We had the military intelligence people at these meetings. There are law enforcement components in almost every executive branch agency. Our task was to make sure that nobody was off on a frolic on their own."

Department has strong incentives to worry about the design and operation of the Defense Department and vice versa; the CIA has good reason to fret about the norms and decisions of the National Security Council and vice versa. In contrast, domestic agencies tend to be somewhat less dependent on one another and less tightly connected.

For agencies with overlapping jurisdictions, the interagency task force is a frequently used coordinating technique. For example, in 1999 and 2000 a Task Force on Export Control Reform brought together representatives from the Defense Department, Commerce Department, and State Department in an effort to modernize and liberalize the U.S. export control regime. The task force focused on how long it took to process licenses, which technologies should be easier to export, and how the United States should treat different countries. In 2007 President George W. Bush established an interagency task force, headed by the secretary of veterans affairs, to address problems in meeting the needs of veterans of the wars in Iraq and Afghanistan.[76]

Interagency task forces have sometimes aroused skepticism, especially among academics. Harold Seidman, for example, wrote: "Interagency committees are the crab grass in the garden of government. Nobody wants them, but everyone has them. Committees seem to thrive on scorn and ridicule, and multiply so rapidly that attempts to weed them out appear futile."[77] Nevertheless, interagency task forces abound because they serve a useful function. Despite their difficulties, they help individual agencies share information and look beyond their own narrowly defined missions.

## Czars

Another approach has been to create a **czar** to coordinate agencies and programs when a crisis suddenly erupts. President Nixon tried this approach in 1973 with the first energy crisis. The job of energy czar proved so challenging and frustrating that five individuals held the job within a memorable twelve-month period. The experience of former Colorado governor John Love was perhaps typical: despite a fancy title, he felt that he lacked both the staff and the authority to cope effectively with his duties.[78]

Since 1988 we have had a drug czar, who has the official title of director of the Office of National Drug Control Policy. That office, located within the Executive Office of the President, has been criticized by many observers as weak and ineffectual. Though it eventually received statutory authority, it has suffered from a lack of resources and authority. A key part of the problem is that responsibility for drug policymaking and enforcement is scattered across the

| Inside Bureaucracy with | Donna Shalala<br>*Secretary of Health and Human Services*<br>*(1993–2001)* |
| --- | --- |

"Bureaucrats solve problems by talking to each other a lot, particularly as a way of minimizing risk. They ask whether the problem to be solved will result in reward or punishment. The reward could be either financial or someone saying that was a good thing you did."

Dick Thornburgh
*Attorney General*
*(1988–1990)*

"Both presidents I served opposed the creation of the drug czar's office. President Reagan created a drug policy board chaired by the attorney general. I held that position until Bill Bennett was appointed as the drug czar. On the other hand, we didn't have any real differences with that office. Our relationships were positive. They had a better capability to be a mouthpiece for drug policy than the attorney general's office because we were so skittish about compromising particular cases. I think a case could be made that it was somewhat unnecessary, but on the other hand there are political reasons to do it."

federal bureaucracy, in more than sixty agencies.[79] Many of these agencies have different missions and cultures, making coordination extremely difficult.

Prior to the creation of the Department of Homeland Security in November 2002, the White House had tapped Tom Ridge, former governor of Pennsylvania, to serve as director of the Office of Homeland Security. When President Bush first announced Ridge's appointment as homeland security czar on September 21, 2001, the announcement provoked two strong reactions: praise for Ridge's leadership ability and skepticism that Ridge or anyone else would be able to function effectively without adequate authority.[80] Although some observers asserted that Ridge was the right man for the job, many experts believed he was being asked to perform an impossible mission.

The mission of the Office of Homeland Security was to "lead, oversee and coordinate a comprehensive national strategy to secure the United States from terrorist threats or attacks." [81] The executive order that had created the agency granted Ridge, as director, cabinet status. Ridge enjoyed an office in the West Wing of the White House, in close proximity to the president. In October 2001 Ridge emerged as the administration's leading spokesman on terrorism, holding press conferences two to three times a week.[82]

Despite these symbolic steps, the Office of Homeland Security and its director were severely handicapped. Their ultimate goal was to coordinate the forty or fifty federal agencies that shared responsibility for the nation's homeland defense. Unfortunately, however, the office had no direct line authority over any agency with significant staff or program responsibility. As of late

2001 Ridge directed only a skeleton staff of thirty.[83] Nor did Ridge possess any authority over other agencies' budgets. The fact that his very limited mandate was rooted in an executive order, not a statute, further weakened his legitimacy. The fundamental problem, though, lay in the executive order's lack of teeth.[84]

In a scathing editorial the *New York Times* put it bluntly: "Washington seems to have swallowed up Tom Ridge since he arrived in time last fall to take charge of domestic security. Instead of forcefully coordinating the work of a host of federal agencies, Mr. Ridge has bumped from one humiliation to another as various cabinet departments have openly flouted his advice and failed to address security problems identified by their own inspector general."[85]

Frustrated by these problems, President Bush reversed course and proposed the creation of a cabinet-level Department of Homeland Security. The new department, approved by Congress in November 2002, began operating in March 2003, with Ridge as the first secretary. Among other agencies, the department comprises the Coast Guard, Customs and Border Protection, Citizenship and Immigration Services, Secret Service, Federal Emergency Management Agency, and Transportation Security Administration.[86] Because the new department includes former employees from twenty-two other federal agencies (see Table 5.2), it continues to face considerable integrative challenges.

## Networks' Effectiveness

When are networks more effective? Some empirical research has been devoted to this subject. In a study of fifteen social service networks in upstate New York, Catherine Alter and Jerald Hage identified several factors that helped to predict a "performance gap" between the status quo and an idealized standard, based on the perceptions of caseworkers and administrators. As they expected, Alter and Hage found that vertical dependency was negatively related to performance and that network autonomy was positively related to performance.[87] From this finding, they inferred support for **resource dependency theory,** which says that a lack of control over resources weakens an organization or a cluster of organizations (a network). They also found that network complexity undermined performance but that a larger number of communication channels enhanced performance.

In a study that compared mental health networks in four cities, Keith Provan and H. Brinton Milward reached rather different conclusions.[88]

**Table 5.2 Agencies Shifted to Create the Department of Homeland Security**

| Agency | Moved from | Employees |
|---|---|---|
| Transportation Security Administration | Transportation | 44,000 |
| Coast Guard | Transportation | 43,639 |
| Immigration and Naturalization Service | Justice | 39,459 |
| Customs Service | Treasury | 21,743 |
| Secret Service | Treasury | 6,111 |
| Federal Emergency Management Agency | Independent | 5,135 |
| Animal and Plant Health Inspection Service | Agriculture | 2,000 |
| Federal Protective Services | General Services Administration | 1,408 |
| National Infrastructure Protection Center | FBI | 795 |
| Lawrence Livermore National Laboratory | Energy | 324 |
| Civilian Biodefense Research Programs | Health and Human Services | 150 |
| Chemical, Biological, Radiological and Nuclear Response | Health and Human Services | 150 |
| Plum Island Animal Disease Center | Agriculture | 124 |
| National Communications System | Defense | 91 |
| Critical Infrastructure Assurance Office | Commerce | 65 |
| Federal Computer Incident Response Center | General Services Administration | 23 |
| National Domestic Preparedness Office | FBI | 15 |
| National Infrastructure Simulation and Analysis Center | Energy | 2 |

*Source:* John Mintz, "Homeland Agency Launched," *Washington Post,* November 26, 2002, Sec. A. ©2002 the Washington Post. Reprinted with permission.

*Note:* Excludes agencies for which there is no information on employee transfers.

Defining network effectiveness as case managers' perceptions of the overall well being of severely mentally ill clients, Provan and Milward concluded that direct external control had a positive effect on network effectiveness. They also found that network integration, system stability, and substantial resources enhanced network performance.

In contrast to Alter and Hage, who focused on networks in a particular state, and Provan and Milward, who focused on networks in a particular policy sector, Eugene Bardach studied nineteen interagency collaboratives encompassing diverse geographic sites and diverse policy sectors.[89] He also used a qualitative research methodology, while the other scholars used a quantitative approach. Bardach concluded that four factors were most likely to produce effective networks: a technically clear mission, external demands to perform better, vigorous leadership, and a culture of pragmatism. More broadly, he concluded that network managers need to work hard to create and sustain an atmosphere of mutual trust. Edward Jennings, who examined state and local government efforts to coordinate employment and training programs, too, found leadership to be particularly important as a predictor of success. He also found it important to recognize that different programs have their own goals and that the various agencies should be treated with respect.[90]

Together these studies highlight the importance of network leadership and mutual respect, while raising questions about the desirability of external control. Because they reach somewhat different conclusions, the studies also suggest that the kind of network appropriate for one setting may be less appropriate for another. As Robert Axelrod and Michael Cohen have noted, the Linux computer software system proved itself an enormously successful network despite its being neither tightly controlled nor well funded.[91] Other observers have noted that "loosely coupled systems" can be quite effective under certain circumstances. For example, public transit in the Bay Area relies heavily on informal structures to achieve "coordination without hierarchy."[92] More ominously, al-Qaida offers a classic example of a loosely coupled system that has successfully pursued some of its goals.[93]

The most familiar and most celebrated of all networks is, of course, the Internet. Originally developed by the Advanced Research Projects Agency of the Defense Department as a tool for standardizing and integrating federal data, it quickly spread beyond the federal bureaucracy to academia, business, and ultimately wider society.[94] In recent years, Internet traffic has increased dramatically, by 100 percent per year.[95] By any reckoning, the Internet has been an extraordinarily successful network and, increasingly, a useful way for citizens to connect with government officials. In 2001, 55 percent of Americans who used the Internet went online to interact with the government.[96]

## Tools' Effectiveness

Public officials have many tools at their disposal. As we have seen, these tools differ in their characteristics. Which tools are effective and when? In our discussion below, we focus on three of the most essential tools: grants-in-aid, regulation, and information. Each of these tools is widely used by bureaucrats, though grants-in-aid must first be authorized by politicians.

### Grants-in-Aid

In intergovernmental relations, the federal government uses grants-in-aid to encourage state and local governments to spend more money on certain policy problems. Such grants-in-aid take different forms. **Categorical grants** must be used for a relatively narrow, specific program category. The Head Start program, which disburses money to local communities for the purpose of improving the school readiness of disadvantaged preschoolers, is a good example of a categorical grant. In contrast, **block grants** may be used for a variety of purposes, within a broad program area. The Child Care and Development Block Grant is a good illustration. These funds may be used to pay for child care for low-income families, to improve the availability of child care facilities, or to improve the quality of child care for all families.

Although grants-in-aid have many specific purposes, a key thrust of federal grants-in-aid has been to promote redistributive spending by state and local governments.[97] In general, state and local governments are less willing to allocate resources to disadvantaged residents for fear that poor citizens might migrate across political boundaries and take advantage of a specific locale's more generous social benefits. In the context of welfare policy, this phenomenon has sometimes been called the **welfare magnet effect** because states with higher welfare payments are thought to exert a magnetic pull on disadvantaged citizens.[98] Although welfare payment levels affect interstate moves less than other factors such as family ties, their effects can be considerable. For example, Michael Bailey estimates that if California increased its welfare benefits by 10 percent the net number of California households headed by single mothers would probably increase by more than 2,500 after five years.[99]

Some grants-in-aid programs have produced relatively clear and relatively positive results. The interstate highway program, inaugurated during the Eisenhower administration, within two decades produced a remarkable latticework of highways that facilitates interstate commerce and tourism. The Medicaid program, initiated during the Johnson administration, has enabled millions of poor persons, especially children and senior citizens, to receive timely medical care. The Head Start program, another Johnson-era initiative, has also generated generally favorable reviews, though doubts remain as to the persistence of its effects on cognitive development.[100]

Yet some federal grants-in-aid programs essentially substitute federal dollars for expenditures that state and local governments would have undertaken in any event. Students of fiscal federalism posited this phenomenon, known as the **crowd-out hypothesis,** years ago, and it has recently found empirical support.[101] The extent of crowd-out, however, seems to depend on tool design: the generosity of the federal match, whether there is a ceiling, or "cap," on matching funds, and related factors.[102] Through better tool design, public officials may be able to mitigate the phenomenon of state and local governments' substituting federal dollars for their own dollars.

Other problems have proved even more vexing. Whatever economic theories or theories of justice might suggest, political factors play a major role in determining how grants-in-aid will be distributed. As a result, the federal government allocates grants not just to the neediest of states and communities but to less needy governments as well. Another concern is that grants undermine accountability by creating a disjunction between the level of government that raises the money and the level of government that spends the money. If an intergovernmental program becomes embroiled in controversy, as the Medicaid program sometimes does, then who should be blamed? The federal government that failed to prevent abuse, or the state government that perpetrated the abuse?

In recent years, many grants-in-aid have taken the form of block grants, which permit state and local governments a considerable degree of flexibility in how they spend federal dollars. The Social Services Block Grant and the Community Development Block Grant are two examples. When OMB rated different types of government programs, using the Program Assessment Rating Tool, it awarded the block grant its second lowest rating among seven program types.[103] Block grants pose special problems because they are spent for a wider variety of purposes and because funding is typically determined by formula and population counts instead of merit or need.

After weighing the evidence, two careful students of grants-in-aid, David Beam and Timothy Conlan, concluded that "grants merit an overall moderate rating in terms of effectiveness." [104] When properly administered, grants-in-aid enable federal officials to promote redistributive goals and to compensate for externalities that spill across state boundaries (for example, air and water pollution). More broadly, grants-in-aid represent a hortatory control that can be extremely useful as an alternative to more coercive mechanisms that often produce dysfunctional results. [105]

## Regulation

If grants are carrots, regulations are sticks. By definition, regulation is a coercive policy instrument, though the degree of coercion varies considerably. A regulation requiring a coal-burning utility to use low-sulfur coal is far more coercive than a regulation requiring that same utility to open its doors to periodic inspections. A regulation requiring a day care center to maintain child-staff ratios of seven to one for preschool children is far more restrictive than a regulation requiring that center to arrange for periodic in-service training experiences for its professional staff.

Regulations can make a difference in policy outcomes. A careful study of state air pollution standards found that states with stronger regulatory standards experienced sharper reductions in sulfur dioxide and nitrogen dioxide. [106] A study of day care centers in four states found the poorest quality in the state with the weakest standards. [107] Regulatory enforcement can also make a difference. The imposition of monetary penalties by Occupational Safety and Health Administration inspectors improved the safety records of penalized firms. [108] Reduced surveillance of day care centers with reasonably good track records led to a higher number of code violations at the neglected centers. [109]

Critics argue that regulation is less efficient than reliance on markets or marketlike incentives. Certainly, under favorable circumstances marketlike approaches can produce good results. For example, the Clean Air Act authorizes **emissions trading** in an effort to encourage plants to agree to sharper than average emissions reductions in return for cash payments if they can make such reductions more cheaply than other plants. The early returns suggest that emissions trading has been a success. [110]

The case for or against regulation depends in part on the type of regulation involved. Consider, for example, **economic regulation,** which seeks to improve the functioning of certain markets through entry and exit restrictions or price controls. Such regulation is necessary when an industry is characterized by natural monopolies, in which the presence of competitive firms would be inefficient and inadvisable. For years analysts considered telephone companies and electric companies to be natural monopolies. With technological advances, however, it has become possible to achieve even greater efficiency through the introduction of competition or limited competition. Under such circumstances, **deregulation** makes sense. It can, however, backfire if pursued too zealously, as when California deregulated its electric utilities without providing for adequate safeguards.[111] As a result of hasty deregulation, California's electric utilities experienced dramatic increases in wholesale electricity prices. When utility companies could not pay their bills, some suppliers balked at selling electricity to them, resulting in intermittent blackouts throughout the state.

In contrast, **social regulation** seeks to curb or restrict behavior by individuals or firms that interferes with public health or safety. The case for social regulation is particularly strong when liability and tort systems prove cumbersome as mechanisms for correcting market failures.[112] But much depends on the willingness of individuals and firms to comply with regulatory requirements. Sometimes compliance is slow at first but picks up over time. When the federal government first required the use of seatbelts, many citizens balked at what seemed like a silly requirement. In time seatbelt use has become common enough to save thousands of lives, which in turn has encouraged even higher levels of seatbelt use.[113]

## Information

A central aim of interagency coordination is the sharing of information. Such information sharing may help agencies to specialize in different tasks, to share wisdom concerning best practices, or to move in tandem toward mutual goals. Information sharing is also important in intergovernmental relations and in public-private partnerships. Feedback on performance is one vital form of information sharing; clarification of goals and procedural rules another.

In recent years bureaucracies have devoted more resources to sharing information with the general public. The Federal Trade Commission has required cigarette manufacturers to place warning labels on their products, and the Food and Drug Administration has required companies to prepare nutritional labels to clarify the contents of foods and vitamins. The empirical literature on labeling suggests that it can have an impact. For example, one study found a decline in drinking during pregnancy beginning in 1990, eight months after the implementation of alcohol warning labels.[114] Nutritional labels may have contributed to a decline in fat consumption during the early 1990s, but total calorie consumption does not appear to have declined, and fat consumption seems to be rising again.[115]

Bureaucracies have also launched information campaigns aimed at discouraging drug use and promiscuous sexual behavior and at recruiting young people for military careers. Such campaigns have succeeded in some instances, though not in others. Energy conservation messages from the New York Public Service Commission proved more effective than identical messages from a private utility company.[116] Energy conservation messages from the Department of Energy proved more effective when less technical and less complex.[117]

Increasingly, bureaucracies have promoted the use of **organizational report cards,** which compare the performance of two or more organizations. Studies show that such report cards can affect both public and organizational behavior. Following the introduction of a hospital report card in New York state, deaths resulting from botched heart surgery declined more rapidly in New York than in other states.[118] Following the introduction of a public school report card in North Carolina, schools whose students had performed poorly on standardized tests did better the next time around.[119]

Congress mandated a different kind of report card in 1986, when it passed legislation creating the Toxics Release Inventory (TRI) to be prepared by the EPA with data supplied by private firms that release toxic chemicals into the atmosphere. The first round of disclosures negatively affected the stock market prices of some of the heaviest polluters.[120] In response, Monsanto and other top polluters announced ambitious air toxics reduction goals.[121] The TRI also provided environmental groups and journalists with valuable information that they were able to use in press releases, briefing reports, and news stories. Although the TRI clearly affected the behavior of private firms and supplied valuable information to interested parties, the general public's response was weaker. Only 11 percent of all citizens indicated that they were familiar with the law, and approximately half of these same citizens claimed to be familiar with a program that didn't even exist![122] Evidence of the TRI's effect on housing prices is mixed. Some evidence suggests that housing prices declined as proximity to publicly identified polluting plants increased while other evidence does not uncover such a link.[123]

When is information a useful policy tool? Janet Weiss, a careful student of the subject, argues that information is most useful under the following circumstances:

- when the problem is caused by information asymmetry or information that is difficult to obtain;
- when the targets of public policy are very broadly dispersed but not organized;
- when the interests of policymakers and those of targeted individuals or groups are closely aligned so that voluntary compliance is likely to occur;
- when there is broad agreement about desired outcomes; and
- when no legal or politically acceptable alternative tools are available or when policy outcomes occur in partnerships or coalitions in which command-and-control approaches are impermissible.[124]

We would add to these excellent observations that information is an especially potent tool when combined with other tools, such as financial incentives or the threat of government regulation.

## Networks: Some Conclusions

Although bureaucracies might prefer to act independently, much of what they do is done in concert with other bureaucracies, other levels of government, nonprofit organizations, and for-profit firms. In short, bureaucracies work through interorganizational networks. A key characteristic of such networks is that each organization has its own distinctive goals. Furthermore, organizations that belong to a network often differ in their political and economic resources. Another key characteristic is that the relationship between organizations is not purely hierarchical: one network member cannot simply tell another network member what to do.

For some networks to be effective, much is required. In many intergovernmental networks and in many public-private partnerships, some modus vivendi must be achieved between organizations with different missions and goals. Without this, organizations will be pulling in different directions and performance will suffer. In addition, some consensus must be reached on which organization is responsible for the success or failure of a particular task. Without this, citizens and politicians will be unable to hold networks accountable.

For other networks to be effective, less is required. Interagency coordination, for example, is sometimes a matter of information sharing. When one organization is not being asked to implement another organization's policies, it may be sufficient for organizations to share timely information about activities and initiatives so that agencies with overlapping jurisdictions can avoid conflict or duplication. One can easily underestimate the difficulty of information sharing across agencies. Still, it is, in principle, more feasible than changing another agency's point of view.

In thinking about networks, we have borrowed from two theoretical traditions. The first, from sociology, is called network theory. It emphasizes such concepts as centrality and density and seeks to map network structures. Some progress has been made in identifying key network characteristics and in linking such characteristics to network performance. On balance, however, the empirical literature is relatively sparse, especially when it comes to outcomes. The second tradition, from political science and public administration, is called the tools approach. While this literature is more scattered and diffuse, it is also more extensive. Its theoretical propositions are less cohesive, and its empirical applications often confined to a single type of network, such as public-private partnerships or intergovernmental relations. But the tools literature, unlike the network theory literature, almost always seeks to explain variations in performance rather than study communication for its own sake.

From the network theory literature we may conclude that networks function better if they possess ample resources and strong leadership. The role of external control is less clear. Although some research celebrates the advantages of network autonomy, other research finds that external control enhances performance, perhaps because it strengthens accountability.

From the tools literature we may conclude that the effectiveness of particular tools is highly contextual. Grants-in-aid can be useful tools for federal policymaking if designed to promote goals that state and local governments would not otherwise pursue (for example, redistribution) and to inhibit state and local governments from substituting federal dollars for their own resources. Contracts can be useful tools for officials at all levels of government if contractors are selected not just to reduce costs but also with the quality of services in mind. Regulations can be useful tools for officials at all levels of government, provided that the economics of a given industry (air transportation, child care, occupational safety and health) is carefully understood by government regulators.

As for information, it is the one indispensable tool that makes the other tools work. Without good information, federal policymakers cannot know how state and local officials are using federal tax dollars. Without good information, bureaucracies cannot be sure that contractors are accomplishing designated goals. Without good information, government regulators cannot correct for unexpected consequences that have the potential to undermine government policies. In this respect the network theory literature is right on target—communication between organizations that share responsibility for service delivery is essential. However, as the tools literature reminds us, what matters is not just who communicates with whom and how often but also what they say to one another and how much leverage the various parties have over one another.

## Key Terms

1115 waivers, 141
1915b waivers, 141
Automaticity, 134
Block Grants, 158
Categorical grants, 158
Centrality, 132
Coerciveness, 134
Complexity, 132
Contracting out, 128
Co-optation, 148
Crowd-out hypothesis, 159
Czar, 153
Density, 132
Deregulation, 161
Devolution, 137
Differentiation, 132
Directness, 134
Economic regulation, 160
Emissions trading, 160
Equivalence, 133
Grants-in-aid, 137

Hollow state, 128
Institutional uncertainty, 132
Interorganizational networks, 130
Legislative clearance, 150
Mandates, 137
Multiplexity, 132
Network, 130
Organizational report cards, 162
Performance partnership
    agreement, 138
Privatization, 129
Resource dependency theory, 155
Size, 132
Social regulation, 161
Strategic uncertainty, 132
Substantive uncertainty, 132
Third-party government, 135
Tools approach, 134
Visibility, 134
Weak ties, 133
Welfare magnet effect, 158

# 6 | The Politics of Disaster Management

MANY BUREAUCRATIC DECISIONS involve the application of standard operating procedures to routine situations. For example, when inspectors at the Environmental Protection Agency (EPA) conduct reviews of pesticide labels, these reviews are guided by a three-page inspection checklist.[1] Among other things, the checklist reminds inspectors to scrutinize the label for the name of the manufacturer, the company's EPA registration number, and the statement of product ingredients. In general, pesticide inspections entail clear chains of command and established patterns of interaction among agency officials, manufacturers, and other relevant parties.

Contrast all of this regularity with EPA decision making in the area of **climate change.** No EPA office has sole jurisdiction over the agency's policy response to this emerging threat to the planet. In fact, the U.S. Climate Change Science Program, which is run out of the Executive Office of the President, brings together more than a dozen federal agencies and departments.[2] When it comes to climate change itself, although many key facts are established (for example, temperatures are rising, human activities are negatively affecting the atmosphere), other fundamental aspects of the issue are not yet well understood. There is uncertainty, for example, regarding just how much warming will occur, how fast the warming will take place, and how increasing temperatures are likely to affect storms and precipitation patterns.[3]

Clearly, climate change represents in many respects a greater challenge to EPA decision makers than the review of pesticide labels. Generally speaking, catastrophic events and potentially disastrous threats provide public bureaucracies with some of their stiffest tests. That said, not all crises are alike in the nature of the specific difficulties they present to government agencies. Some crises are preceded by similar occurrences, such as the hurricanes that are spawned each summer and fall in the Atlantic Ocean. Other crises lack such precedent, as when terrorists used hijacked airplanes as bombs in their attacks on the World Trade Center and the Pentagon. On top of this, agencies are charged not only with reacting to crises, but also with taking steps to ameliorate or even avert disasters altogether.

Disasters also pose a tough test for the theories we have described and applied in the preceding chapters. All four of these approaches are designed to be general ways of understanding bureaucracies and their governmental and nongovernmental environments. How well do these general theories hold up in the unique context of disaster management? Do these theories provide us with a solid analytical basis for evaluating the successes and failures that bureaucracies experience in times of crisis?

In this chapter, we examine in some detail the bureaucratic responses to three different crises: Hurricane Katrina, a disaster with ample precedent; the terrorist attacks of September 11, 2001, an unprecedented tragedy; and an **avian influenza** pandemic, a potential threat that has not yet materialized. Our analyses of these cases focus on two *core questions:*

- *WHAT ACCOUNTS FOR THE BUREAUCRATIC SUCCESSES AND FAIL-URES THAT WERE AND ARE BEING REALIZED IN THE MANAGEMENT OF THESE DISASTERS?* In judging the relevant bureaucracies, we focus our attention on both key structural and procedural elements in agency decision making and the outcomes that resulted from these decisions.

- *CAN THE THEORIES AND CONCEPTS THAT HAVE BEEN INTRODUCED IN THE PRECEDING CHAPTERS INFORM OUR UNDERSTANDING OF HOW BUREAUCRACIES HAVE COPED WITH RECENT DISASTERS AND ARE PREPARING FOR FUTURE CATASTROPHIC THREATS?* All three of these crises have been examined by journalists, pundits, and public officials. Our aim is to take an analytical approach to understanding the politics of disaster management.

Before beginning, we should emphasize the importance of being frank in our assessments without setting the bar unreasonably high for bureaucracies operating in the midst of crises. Agencies experience accountability and performance failures in all of their activities, even routine tasks like pesticide label inspections. Using a sports analogy, we are asking whether a team can win the Super Bowl or World Series, whether it can succeed under the most trying of circumstances. Disaster management is, to be sure, a very demanding assignment for government bureaucracies.

## Hurricane Katrina: A Crisis with Precedent

The United States has thousands of miles of coastline, and, according to the 2000 census, 54 percent of Americans live within fifty miles of the East, West, and Gulf Coasts.[4] Inland, many of our oldest and largest cities are situated on the banks of major rivers and other significant bodies of water. As the U.S. population has moved westward over the years, more and more residents make their homes in locations that are particularly at risk of experiencing earthquakes and wildfires. In general, recurring natural disasters are a fact of life for millions of Americans who live in highly desirable, and highly vulnerable, parts of the country.

This certainty aside, specific weather events often strike in ways that defy pinpoint prediction. Tornadoes offer little warning to people caught in their fast-moving tracks. We know that weather disasters will occur, but we do not have the capacity to forecast beyond a reasonable doubt just when, where, and with what severity nature will unleash its fury. Also, earthquakes, much like extreme weather, vary tremendously in their magnitudes on the Richter scale.

This combination of certainty and doubt aptly describes Hurricane Katrina, one of the worst disasters in American history. On the one hand, it was not a surprise that a hurricane struck the Gulf Coast in late August of 2005. On the other hand, the sheer size and strength of the storm, combined with the proximity of its landfall to New Orleans, made Hurricane Katrina anything but a routine tropical weather event.

In the end, Hurricane Katrina took the lives of nearly two thousand Americans and caused more than $80 billion in damages.[5] Many government officials and organizations at the federal, state, and local levels came under heavy criticism in the aftermath of the storm. No bureaucracy endured more scorn than the **Federal Emergency Management Agency** (FEMA), the nation's primary disaster mitigation and relief organization. The FEMA director at the time of Hurricane Katrina, Michael Brown, lost his job, and the entire agency suffered great damage to its reputation (see Table 6.1 for some of the jokes that were told at that time by late-night comedians). What went so wrong in FEMA's preparation and response? Did anything go right in the bu-

**Table 6.1 Jokes about the Government's Bungled Response to Hurricane Katrina**

"No word yet on Mr. Brown's future plans, though sources say he does want to spend more time doing nothing for his family." —Jon Stewart

"Did you know you don't even have to be a lawyer to be on the Supreme Court? You don't even have to be a lawyer. Just like you don't have to be an emergency expert to work for FEMA." —Jay Leno

"Many Americans are calling on President Bush to fire the head of FEMA Michael Brown because of the slow response to the crisis. Unfortunately, due to the red tape, firing Brown will take 6 to 8 months." —Conan O'Brien

"Finally today convoys of troops and aid started to arrive along the Gulf Coast. Five days after the hurricane hit. Kind of makes you miss the innocent days when Bush only sat on his ass for seven minutes. It only took him four days to make a plan, but finally today he said he had a plan. Unfortunately, it's a faith-based plan that involves getting two of every animal onto a big boat." —Bill Maher

*Source:* About.com, http://politicalhumor.about.com/od/hurricanekatrina/a/katrina jokes.htm, March 26, 2007.

reaucracy's handling of Hurricane Katrina? A good place to start in addressing these questions is to take a historical look at the development of FEMA, both its high points and low points.

## FEMA's Evolution

For many years after its creation in 1979, FEMA was roundly criticized for being long on promises and short on results. In the wake of the agency's poor handling of relief efforts following Hurricane Hugo in 1989, Senator Ernest "Fritz" Hollings, D-S.C., referred to FEMA as the "sorriest bunch of bureaucratic jackasses I've ever known."[6] When FEMA responded ineptly to Hurricane Andrew in 1992, a local official appeared on national television and began to cry. "Enough is enough," she said. "Quit playing like a bunch of kids. Where the hell is the cavalry on this one? For God's sake, where are they?"[7]

All of this changed in 1993, when President Clinton appointed James Lee Witt as FEMA administrator. Witt was a longtime friend of the president and, unlike previous administrators, had extensive experience in disaster management, having served for four years as the director of the Arkansas Department of Emergency Services. Upon arriving at FEMA, Witt announced an "open door" policy so that employees would have easy access to him. On Witt's recommendation, the president filled political posts in FEMA with individuals who had backgrounds in disaster relief and intergovernmental relations. With this change in staffing orientation, FEMA was positioned to transform itself from the "political dumping ground" it had been for so many years.[8] To the surprise of many and consternation of some, Witt insisted that senior managers rotate jobs. The idea was that senior managers should not get too complacent or parochial, that they would perform better if they developed a keen sense of the agency's multiple responsibilities. As Witt himself put it, his goal was to "disassemble the stovepipe structure and reassemble it as a mass of connecting pipes."[9]

Under Witt's leadership, FEMA turned out to be one of the most impressive bureaucratic success stories of recent times. An agency that had been vilified won many new friends, including disaster victims, state and local officials, members of Congress, and an admiring press corps. Whereas the old FEMA waited for a disaster to strike before sending food, water, and equipment, Witt's FEMA sent supplies to the scene as soon as a disaster loomed. Whereas the old FEMA procrastinated in providing relief to victims, Witt's FEMA got checks to victims in record time.[10] Whereas the old FEMA often seemed more interested in credit claiming and blame avoidance than problem solving, Witt did his best not to upstage state and local officials. As Senator Bob Graham, D-Fla., put it, FEMA effected a "180-degree turnaround" from its response to Hurricane Andrew.[11]

One of Witt's more important changes was to articulate a clear mission for FEMA: "reduce the loss of life and property and protect our institutions from all hazards by leading and supporting the Nation in a comprehensive, risk-based emergency management program of mitigation, preparedness, response, and recovery."[12] This **all hazards approach** represented a marked departure from FEMA's historical preoccupation with preparation for a possible nuclear war. With FEMA's new stature as an effective, anticipatory, and responsive agency came a huge surge in agency morale. As one employee noted, "We don't have to wear bags over our heads when we go to meetings with other departments."[13] Another employee put it this way: "Everyone likes to wear their FEMA jackets now."[14]

And then things got worse. Upon assuming the presidency, George W. Bush appointed Joe Allbaugh as FEMA's director. Allbaugh, who had served as Bush's chief of staff in Texas and as his national campaign director in 2000, had good access to the president (like Witt) but no disaster management experience (unlike Witt). When the Mississippi River flooded Davenport, Iowa, in April 2003 for the third time in eight years, Allbaugh publicly upbraided local officials for not having built levees. He asked, "How many times will the American taxpayer have to step in and take care of this flooding, which could be easily prevented by building levees and dikes?"[15] Whatever the merits of his outburst, Allbaugh came off as blaming the victim. He subsequently apologized, but his credibility—and FEMA's—was damaged.

If public relations were a problem, internal changes were even more troublesome. Agency officials close to Witt were viewed with suspicion, and morale deteriorated. By the end of 2002, twenty-two senior staff members had quit or were fired.[16] At the same time, FEMA was struggling to rethink its mission in the wake of the September 11, 2001, terrorist attacks. In March 2003, FEMA was absorbed into the newly created Department of Homeland Security, despite protests from Allbaugh and Michael Brown, then the agency's recently appointed deputy director. When Tom Ridge was named to head the department, Allbaugh announced his resignation. Brown, whose résumé famously included a stint as director of the International Arabian Horse Association, took over as acting director and then became director.

FEMA fared poorly under the Department of Homeland Security. Instead of turning to FEMA to draft the **National Response Plan** for domestic incidents, Secretary Ridge asked the RAND Corporation to handle this assignment.[17] As a result, FEMA's role in drafting this important document was marginal at best. Authorized to reshape FEMA's budget virtually at will, Secretary Ridge reallocated substantial amounts of money from flood mitigation to the war on terrorism. He also transferred responsibility over preparedness grants from FEMA to state and local officials.[18] When a new secretary, Michael Chertoff, took over the department in early 2005, he reduced FEMA's authority even further. Although Brown argued against these changes, he lacked friends in high places. As one FEMA staffer put it, "Mike was often his own worst enemy. . . . He never cultivated any friends in the department or anywhere in Washington for that matter that I could see who were willing to go to bat for him. And the sad truth is FEMA suffered for it. FEMA suffered because people were making stupid decisions and Brown could not stop them."[19]

Despite the friction between FEMA and almost everyone else, the agency managed to respond reasonably well to a rapid series of four hurricanes that hit Florida in 2004. Politically and administratively, conditions were favorable.

Florida, perhaps more than any other state, was battle tested and prepared for the hurricane season. Governor Jeb Bush, the president's brother, was well situated to ask for and receive federal assistance. The fact that Florida was a key electoral battleground and that 2004 was a presidential election year may also have been important. Whatever the reasons, the federal government opened up its coffers to Florida, which made FEMA's job much easier. As two *Wall Street Journal* reporters put it, "Washington pulled out all the stops to ensure that the state—and its voters—got everything they needed."[20]

## Katrina Strikes

Hurricane Katrina struck the Gulf Coast with pitiless ferocity on August 29, 2005. In addition to the many hundreds of people who died, more than 200,000 homes were destroyed and another 45,000 residences were assessed as unlivable.[21] The storm also destroyed nearly 19,000 businesses.[22] Combined with Hurricane Rita, which made landfall near the Texas-Louisiana border less than a month later, damage was inflicted on more than 90,000 square miles of territory.[23] The toll was particularly heavy in New Orleans. In addition to those who died, about half of its nearly 500,000 residents never returned after the storm.[24]

All of this occurred, unfortunately, at a time when FEMA was particularly weakened. Approximately 500 of the agency's 2,500 positions were vacant, and eight of ten regional directors were working in an acting capacity when Hurricane Katrina struck.[25] Furthermore, lines of authority in the Department of Homeland Security were uncertain and untested in the face of such a massive natural disaster. Perhaps it is not surprising, then, that Terry Ebbert, head of emergency operations in New Orleans had this to say: "This is a national disgrace. FEMA has been here three days, yet there is no command and control."[26]

FEMA's blunders before, during, and after Hurricane Katrina were committed by officials all the way up and down the organization's **chain of command,** including those working for the scores of private firms with whom the agency had service contracts. Basic supplies—power generators, medical equipment, **emergency communications** systems—were not effectively transported to the areas where they were needed the most. "Where's my goddam ice?" was the question one state official heatedly posed during a telephone argument with Michael Brown.[27] FEMA even had great difficulty getting Jim Strickland, its designated Hurricane Katrina team leader, into New

Orleans.[28] With road signs down, Strickland's convoy accidentally separated on the way to the city. Without a scout or global positioning system (GPS), Strickland received faulty information about conditions in and around the Morial Convention Center, causing him to bypass the center city altogether and establish a base camp in the parking lot of a suburban Sam's Club.

FEMA, of course, was not the only bureaucracy overwhelmed by Hurricane Katrina's destruction. The mayor of New Orleans, C. Ray Nagin, made a colossal mistake by not issuing a mandatory evacuation order well in advance of the storm.[29] With education, economic development, and other pressing issues on the agenda, Nagin's administration had not placed much of an emphasis on improving the city's hurricane preparedness.[30] In fact, Nagin was one of the few public officials in the so-called hurricane belt who had not established a working relationship with Max Mayfield, the director of the National Hurricane Center (NHC).[31] Lacking a direct channel into NHC, Nagin missed out on valuable information and insights that may have changed his decision making and reduced Hurricane Katrina's toll on New Orleans.

## Applying the Theories

Without denying the role that lackluster leadership played in the bureaucracy's handling of Hurricane Katrina, the four theoretical perspectives direct our attention to other important considerations as well. When it comes to bureaucratic reasoning, decision makers put into practice a variety of elements of bounded rationality, both before and after Hurricane Katrina made landfall. The results were decidedly mixed.

In 2004 FEMA funded a week-long test designed to simulate what it would be like if a major hurricane hit New Orleans. The scenario, dubbed **Hurricane Pam,** was eerily evocative of what happened just a year later, with levee failures, ten-foot-high floodwaters, and a city teeming with hazardous debris.[32] Although simulations sometimes enhance boundedly rational decision making, this particular test was flawed in several key respects. Because of funding shortfalls, many FEMA officials were unable to attend the Hurricane Pam event and other exercises like it.[33] Furthermore, follow-up workshops were not convened until July 2005, too late to be of much use when Hurricane Katrina struck the following month.[34]

As documented in Chapter 2, bounded rationality often entails the application of standard operating procedures to recurring circumstances. In the aftermath of Hurricane Katrina, FEMA arranged, with great difficulty, for commercial airlines to evacuate remaining residents out of New Orleans. Then, consistent with its usual practices, the Transportation Security Administration insisted that all passengers and luggage be screened before any planes left Louis Armstrong International Airport.[35] This normally laudable practice was hindered by the fact that the electricity required to operate screening machines was not readily available in a city still without power! To make matters worse, the Department of Homeland Security mandated that undercover air marshals, a standard and useful element of contemporary aviation security, be present on all departing flights.[36] In the end, the evacuation took two long days to arrange, demonstrating how the invocation of standard operating procedures can sometimes produce dysfunctional outcomes. These particular procedures certainly made it more difficult for FEMA to do its job.

One of the main lessons of Chapter 3 is that the delegation of policymaking authority to the bureaucracy varies systematically across types of issues. Disaster management is high in both salience and complexity, a combination that often results in significant levels of discretion for agencies. This discretion, however, is often accompanied by procedural constraints on the exercise of delegated authority. For example, FEMA had the authority to purchase 145,000 trailers and mobile homes as a way of housing some of those displaced by Hurricane Katrina. Yet when more than 8,000 of these units went unused, procedures imposed on FEMA by Congress greatly restricted the agency's ability to sell the units or use them to house victims of subsequent disasters.[37] To be sure, in the acquisition process FEMA made its share of mistakes, such as purchasing modular homes that could not be used in flood zones.[38] That said, many of the problems associated with the units were ultimately attributable to delegation decisions made by political principals.

Some of FEMA's leadership shortcomings can also be traced back to elected officials. As discussed earlier, President Bush appointed a pair of FEMA administrators who lacked prior experience in disaster management. One of these agents, Michael Brown, did not serve his principal well during Hurricane Katrina, despite the president's now-infamous assertion "Brownie, you're doing a heck of a job." In retrospect, the appointment of Brown was an instance where adverse selection came back to haunt the administration.

But Brown was only part of the problem. Lines of authority changed abruptly when FEMA became part of the Department of Homeland Security. At a time when the administration (and the nation) was directing its attention more toward terrorist threats than natural disasters, even a highly competent, highly experienced FEMA director would have struggled to get his agency's mission noticed and funded. Furthermore, it was the secretary of homeland security, not the FEMA administrator, who was ultimately in charge of the federal government's actions. The day after Hurricane Katrina made landfall, Secretary Chertoff declared the disaster an "incident of national significance" and activated the National Response Plan.[39] Chertoff also named Brown as his "principal federal official," a designation that in some respects curtailed the FEMA administrator's ability to act independently.[40] At one point, Chertoff gave this order to Brown: "I don't want you running around, flying around all over the place, I want you to go to Baton Rouge and not leave Baton Rouge."[41] Brown was thus in the difficult administrative position of being closely monitored by one of his principals while at the same time attempting to direct the behavior of his own agents.

In general, these types of vertical communications were a major problem during Hurricane Katrina. In severe natural disasters, commercial landline and cellular phone systems are often compromised or destroyed, which means that emergency systems must be in place.[42] Unfortunately, adequate emergency communications systems were not in place in New Orleans. During a radio interview, Secretary Chertoff demonstrated a lack of awareness of just how dire things were getting for evacuees at the Convention Center: "Actually I have not heard a report of thousands of people in the Convention Center who don't have food and water."[43] As this lack of accurate information suggests, the ability of leaders at the top of the bureaucracy to communicate with agents in the field was drastically compromised during key moments in the rescue and recovery operations.

The seeds of New Orleans's destruction had been sown many years and decades before Hurricane Katrina unleashed its disruptive fury. Local officials consistently made shortsighted decisions to favor economic development over the protection of wetlands. Members of Congress made careers out of sanctioning public works projects that were of questionable merit. Historically, Louisiana has received more funding from the Army Corps of Engineers than any other state, with the lion's share of resources going to oil, fishing, and navigation projects.[44] Levees constructed along the Mississippi River had the effect of reducing the amount of silt carried out to the Gulf of Mexico, which in turn stunted the creation and preservation of coastal marshes and swamps. These wetlands, which serve as "hurricane speed bumps," have been vanishing at a rate of 24 square miles per year.[45] In addition, the Mississippi River Gulf Outlet, a man-made navigation channel connecting downtown New Orleans with the Gulf of Mexico, cuts right through a series of pristine marshes and natural levees. Its path, some experts say, has created a **hurricane superhigh-way** that amplifies the height and ferocity of storm surges, perhaps by as much as two feet during Hurricane Katrina.[46]

This combination of long-term conditions is strikingly reminiscent of what Chapter 4 described as "client politics." Water projects along the Mississippi River and Gulf Coast are usually characterized by concentrated benefits and diffuse costs. Local interests reap gains that are paid for by the nation as a whole. There is little wonder, then, that the Louisiana congressional delegation and Army Corps of Engineers have been able to secure a steady stream of funding for their preferred projects without needing to justify these efforts in the context of national water priorities. Although these projects have no doubt fueled economic growth beneficial to those living in and around New Orleans, they also played no small role in the chain of events that exacerbated the death and destruction left behind by Hurricane Katrina.

Client politics persisted after the storm as well. Well-connected firms received **no-bid contracts,** which meant they did not have to compete with other companies to prove they could do it better, faster, and cheaper. The Shaw Group, represented by former FEMA administrator Joe Allbaugh, won a $100 million no-bid contract to provide housing to displaced residents and another $100 million contract to pump water out of flooded New Orleans. A different Allbaugh client, KBR (a subsidiary of Halliburton), secured $88 million in contracts in just over a month.[47] Some of these awards were so egregious that the Department of Homeland Security was forced to reopen negotiations and allow other firms to enter the competitions. The bipartisan outrage that was directed at these awards points to the constraints client-based iron triangles face when diffuse constituencies become interested in issues they had formerly ignored.

In an ideal world, a network of public, nonprofit, and for-profit organizations would have responded promptly and vigorously to Hurricane Katrina. In reality, organizations both inside and outside government did too little too late. According to one estimate, as many as 533 organizations engaged in response operations after the hurricane struck. Few of these organizations intervened in advance of the storm, however, and many waited days or even weeks before taking action.[48] What eventually emerged was a **loosely connected network,** with an extremely low level of centralization.[49] This lack of centralization may have hindered the network's overall effectiveness, as there was no core agency or set of agencies through which organizational participants were connected to one another.[50]

One of the more notable **network failures** was the poor coordination between FEMA and the Red Cross.[51] According to Louise Comfort, the Red Cross did not get involved significantly until September 15, more than two weeks after Hurricane Katrina made landfall.[52] In fact, the Red Cross never opened up a shelter in New Orleans owing to its long-standing policy of not operating facilities in locations near or below sea level.[53] Even in areas where the Red Cross maintained an active presence, such as Houston and Baton Rouge, organization officials complained about FEMA's inability to process and respond in a timely manner to their requests for help.[54] For their part, FEMA officials found it difficult to work with the Red Cross's constantly rotating workforce of staff and volunteers.[55] In light of these failures, the National Response Plan was modified after Hurricane Katrina to place FEMA in charge of shelters, food, and first aid, and it relegated the Red Cross to a subsidiary role.[56] The relationship between these longtime network partners, in other words, was transformed into more of a hierarchical arrangement.

## The Coast Guard and Other Success Stories

Although FEMA was widely scorned for its performance during Hurricane Katrina, another federal agency, the **Coast Guard,** won nearly universal acclaim. The Coast Guard's leaders took decisive action two days before the storm. In anticipation of a major disaster, the agency moved its regional headquarters from New Orleans to St. Louis and established another command center in Alexandria, Virginia.[57] When Hurricane Katrina struck, the agency deployed 3,000 personnel to the region, along with a fleet of cutters and helicopters. Coast Guard employees, many of whom had lost their own homes in the flooding, demonstrated considerable valor and resourcefulness throughout the ordeal. What's more, they were indefatigable. As one official recalled, "The pace we kept up was amazing. When I say we were working around the clock, I mean it. Both boat and air. We were all go, go, go. Every minute of delay meant a possible loss of life."[58] Thanks to the Coast Guard's interventions, more than 33,000 people were saved.[59]

What enabled the Coast Guard to respond so effectively while other agencies dropped the ball? First, the Coast Guard performs a wide variety of missions, such as intercepting drugs, patrolling war zones, offering humanitarian relief, rescuing refugees on dilapidated boats, cleaning up oil spills, and identifying terrorist threats.[60] While employees tend to specialize in specific types of operational tasks, all personnel are trained to meet across-the-board standards. As a result, teams can quickly form up in emergencies, with each member knowing what every job entails and how it fits into the overall mission.[61] Second, the Coast Guard possesses an excellent emergency communications system. When the power went out throughout the Gulf region, the Coast Guard's system continued to function, enabling agency officials in disparate locations to communicate and coordinate with one another. Third, the Coast Guard has strong, experienced leadership. Thad Allen, the Coast Guard's chief of staff during Hurricane Katrina, had headed up the agency's maritime response to the September 11, 2001, terrorist attacks. At that time, Allen earned praise for acting decisively, by blocking the Potomac River and securing ports in New York and Boston. Within days of Hurricane Katrina, Allen was tapped to replace Michael Brown as the official in charge of federal recovery efforts in New Orleans.[62]

Other federal agencies also performed well during Hurricane Katrina. The National Weather Service provided accurate forecasts of the storm's intensity and location, which gave public officials enough time to mobilize an evacuation effort. Although many citizens remained behind, this was certainly not the fault of the National Weather Service, which warned that the storm would be fierce and devastating. One of its bulletins presciently stated: "Hurricane Katrina . . . A most powerful hurricane with unprecedented strength. . . . Most of the area will be uninhabitable for weeks . . . perhaps longer."[63] Likewise, the Forest Service behaved admirably during the ordeal, supplying more than 600,000 people with 2.7 million meals, 4 million gallons of water, and 40 million pounds of ice.[64] And when the delivery of Social Security checks was disrupted, the Social Security Administration responded resourcefully by making emergency payments to destitute senior citizens.[65]

Success stories such as these do not erase, of course, the failures in accountability and performance that plagued much of the bureaucracy before, during, and after Hurricane Katrina. These successes do remind us, however, that failure was not preordained. How, then, have the theories helped us understand the difference between bureaucratic victory and defeat?

All of the agencies and nongovernmental organizations we have considered applied standard operating procedures to the decisions they confronted during Hurricane Katrina. In many instances, these procedures broke down in the face of the sheer size and strength of the storm and the exceptional vulnerability of its Gulf Coast targets. The primary exceptions were those procedures explicitly designed to meet the specific challenges that emerged. For example, the Coast Guard's prior experience with dangerous air missions allowed the agency's operatives to carry out exceedingly difficult, and lifesaving, rooftop rescues.

The theories point out that standard operating procedures are designed to fulfill tasks handed to agencies by their bosses and requested by their clients. In many respects, these outside actors redesigned the bureaucracy for the worse prior to Hurricane Katrina. Many agencies, including FEMA, had shifted their emphasis toward terrorism and away from natural disasters. Agencies throughout the government had long pursued questionable policies that fostered development beneficial to Gulf Coast legislators, economic interests, and residents themselves. Ultimately, failures inside the bureaucracy were in no small part a reflection of failures in the larger political system within which the agencies were embedded.

## September 11, 2001: A Crisis without Precedent

Throughout its history, the United States has largely been free from foreign attacks on its own soil. Part of this security is due to the vast oceans that separate the United States from potentially hostile European and Asian regimes, while part of it is due to the worldwide economic and military power the country has projected since the early twentieth century. There have been occasions, of course, when this security has been disrupted. The British burned much of official Washington, D.C., including the White House, during the War of 1812. The Japanese attacked Pearl Harbor on December 7, 1941, a date President Roosevelt declared "will live in infamy." For the better part of two centuries, though, the U.S. mainland was essentially free from direct foreign intervention.

It is this freedom that made the terrorist attacks of September 11, 2001, such an unprecedented crisis. The attacks were also unprecedented in their origin (an international terrorist network), their scope (the use of airplanes at multiple sites to take approximately 3,000 lives), and their targets (civilians and buildings of economic and political significance). For many Americans, the attacks were very likely the most shocking world event of their entire lives.

That said, the idea that terrorists might target domestic sites was not completely foreign. On February 26, 1993, a car bomb was detonated in a parking garage beneath the World Trade Center. Sheik Omar Abdel Rahman was convicted of masterminding the bombing, and several other conspirators were imprisoned for their roles in planning and carrying out the attack, which claimed six lives and caused more than a thousand injuries.

In addition, intelligence agents had warned **Central Intelligence Agency** officials who warned the White House that "spectacular" terrorist attacks were being planned.[66] On two separate occasions in June 2001, Richard Clarke, the chair of the administration's Counterterrorism Security Group, informed Secretary of State Condoleezza Rice that **al-Qaida** personnel had predicted a pending attack and that the terrorist network's activity had reached a "crescendo."[67] A July 2001 memo from an FBI agent in Phoenix to bureau headquarters noted that an "inordinate number of individuals of investigative interest" were attending flight schools.[68] A month later, a memo from an FBI agent in Minneapolis to the CIA warned that an Islamic extremist, Zacarias Moussaoui, was learning how to fly.[69] A daily briefing prepared for President Bush by CIA analysts on August 6, 2001, carried the title "Bin Laden Determined to Strike US."[70]

In fairness, the federal government had been receiving warnings about possible terrorist attacks on U.S. soil for at least a decade. Furthermore, none of these reports was specific enough to allow decision makers to pinpoint a specific date or particular targets. As historian Roberta Wohlstetter has noted, it is "much easier *after* the event to sort the relevant from the irrelevant signals. After the event, of course, a signal is always crystal clear; we can now see what disaster it was signaling since the disaster has occurred. But before the event it is obscure and pregnant with conflicting meanings."[71]

Not surprisingly, the events of September 11, 2001, have been the subject of great debate and scrutiny. Arguably the most comprehensive investigation was carried out by the **National Commission on Terrorist Attacks Upon the United States,** an independent, bipartisan group chartered by Congress and President Bush. On June 22, 2004, this so-called 9-11 Commission issued a 567-page report covering everything from advance preparations to the immediate response to the prevention of terrorist attacks in the future. Given all of this general attention, our aim in this section is rather specific. What insights can the four theoretical perspectives provide when it comes to the bureaucracy's behavior before, during, and after the unprecedented crisis that occurred on September 11, 2001?

### The First Response

In New York City, the immediate response to the attacks on the World Trade Center entailed both individual heroism and systemic breakdown. Police officers and firefighters placed themselves in mortal peril, knowing full well they stood a good chance of dying in their efforts to rescue workers inside the burning towers. Thanks to their efforts, countless lives were saved that morning.

Hundreds of firefighters, however, entered the buildings with their hands figuratively tied behind their backs. Communications between firefighters and their superiors were poor. For example, although firefighters possessed new radios, they had not been trained to use these radios properly. Furthermore, coordination between the fire department and other key units—the police department, the Port Authority, the Office of Emergency Management—was severely limited by ineffective communications.[72] Some of these problems arose from the fact that the Office of Emergency Management was located inside 7 World Trade Center, a forty-seven-story building that was damaged and ultimately collapsed as a result of the attacks.[73] All told, 343 firefighters as well as 60 police officers perished in New York City on September 11, 2001.[74]

By contrast, the bureaucratic response to the attack on the Pentagon was relatively timely, safe, and effective. In large part, these differences are attributable to the fact that the logistics were much less daunting at the site in Arlington, Virginia, where a single airplane had crashed into a low-lying building. In addition, local officials were especially well prepared and organized. **Incident command** was established quickly, thanks to a formalized management structure for emergency response that had been put into place throughout the Washington, D.C., area prior to the attack.[75] Different agencies played different, well-defined roles. For example, the Arlington County fire department was the incident commander, with the Department of Justice serving as the lead federal agency.

These arrangements were familiar to many of the officials who were first on the scene, as federal, state, and local agencies regularly took part in regional events and training exercises. In fact, many of these agencies had been working together that very day on plans related to the World Bank–International Monetary Fund meetings that were to be held later that month in the nation's capital.[76]

This history of communication and cooperation paid immediate dividends. Within five minutes of the attack, FBI officials had arrived and fire department commanders had established their headquarters at the scene.[77] Evacuation of the area impacted by the crash was ordered minutes before the building partly collapsed. As a result of this quick action, no **first responder** was injured by falling debris.[78]

A common thread that emerges from the Pentagon and World Trade Center experiences is that when disaster strikes dedicated public servants will immediately arrive upon the scene ready to do whatever they can to make things better. Can the theoretical perspectives offer any insight into how successful these responders are likely to be in their initial efforts?

At both locations, bureaucratic networks were crucial forms of organization. No one agency possessed all the tools necessary to cope with the multitude of problems that were occurring at the same time—fires, injuries, airplane crashes, building collapses. Nor was there a single agency, or even a small set of agencies, with the authority to command the large numbers of organizations that were responding from all levels of government. These attributes would appear to be general descriptions of the immediate aftermath of any major disaster, suggesting that networked arrangements are likely to be inevitable in this area of policymaking and implementation.

Network failures too would seem to be unavoidable in times of great crisis, especially failures related to communications of one sort or another. It is hard enough for principals to keep in touch with their own agents, let alone for officials to coordinate with one another across agency lines. Even at the Pentagon, cell phones proved to be of little value and radio channels quickly became overwhelmed. Although pagers turned out to be the most reliable means of communication, many first responders were not equipped with these particular devices.[79] In the end, well-established, well-functioning networks are organizational tools for mitigating, though not eliminating, the communication problems that threaten the lives of both disaster victims and their would-be rescuers.

## Bureaucracy after 9/11

Once the dust had settled, the events of September 11, 2001, precipitated one of the most significant transformations of public bureaucracy in recent times. Six weeks after the attacks, Congress passed and President Bush signed into law the **USA PATRIOT Act.**[80] The Patriot Act strengthened the power of bureaucrats all across the government, especially at the federal level. Officials were given greater authority to track electronic communications, investigate and disrupt money laundering, detain and deport individuals suspected of having terrorist ties, and obtain so-called sneak-and-peek (that is, covert entry) search warrants.[81]

A year later, many of these disparate bureaucratic functions were consolidated into a single organization when Congress and President Bush agreed to create the Department of Homeland Security. As mentioned in Chapter 3, this new cabinet department brought together 22 agencies and 170,000 employees. Figure 6.1 illustrates why this action has been called the "most complicated restructuring of the federal government ever."[82] Agencies ranging from the Department of Transportation to the Federal Bureau of Investigation to the General Services Administration were altered, sometimes in fundamental ways, by the changes instituted in the Homeland Security Act.

These changes in bureaucratic power and organization were inspired by the fact that members of al-Qaida had been living and training in the United States for months, even years, prior to carrying out the attacks. Although the suspicions of individual bureaucrats had been raised in certain instances, the failure to **connect the dots** and uncover the hijacking plot pointed to the need for an expansion and reconfiguration of government authority in the area of homeland security.

From the beginning, these changes were met with skepticism from various quarters. Civil libertarians were concerned that individual rights would be seriously and unnecessarily eroded. Conservatives were opposed to the creation of a new federal department and the increase in the size of the government workforce that was bound to go with it.

What impacts have these changes had on the accountability and performance of the homeland security bureaucracy? In terms of accountability, the years following September 11, 2001, can be fairly characterized as domination by one political principal (the president) over another (Congress). As Chapter 3 suggests, this situation was unusual in that there is normally a strenuous, multifaceted competition between the executive and legislative branches for influence over bureaucratic agencies. The Bush administration's advantage during this period was attributable to two main factors. First, after the midterm elections of 2002, both chambers of Congress were controlled by Republican majorities. These majorities gave President Bush considerable discretion in designing the Department of Homeland Security, and they devoted little sustained attention to overseeing the implementation of the Patriot Act. Second, many of the initial applications of the bureaucracy's new powers and organization came in the context of military interventions in Afghanistan and Iraq. Historically, presidents are much more formidable in the conduct of foreign affairs than in the making of domestic policy.[83] For example, after Democrats regained control of the Senate and House of Representatives in 2007, they found it difficult to influence policy regarding the withdrawal of U.S. troops from Iraq, even though the conflict was widely unpopular among the American people.

# Figure 6.1 Organizational Highlights of the Creation of the Department of Homeland Security

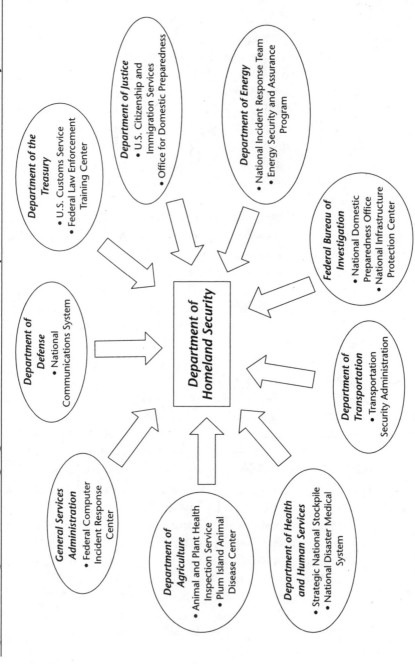

*Source:* "History: Who Became Part of the Department?" U.S. Department of Homeland Security, www.dhs.gov/xabout/history/editorial_0133 .shtm, April 25, 2007. Figure prepared by authors.

When it comes to performance, there have been both security success stories and **civil liberties** failures. Hundreds of millions of dollars in assets tied to international terrorist organizations and state sponsors of terrorism have been frozen by the U.S. government.[84] Most Americans have experienced nothing more than long lines at airport security checkpoints and other similar inconveniences as a result of tightened homeland security policies. A few citizens, however, have had their lives profoundly affected. In the fall of 2006, six Muslim imams were ordered off a flight from Minneapolis–St. Paul to Phoenix after passengers complained about their praying, conversation, and behavior.[85] At about the same time, the U.S. government agreed to pay $2 million to settle a lawsuit filed by Brandon Mayfield, an Oregon attorney who was mistakenly linked to train bombings in Madrid, Spain, that had killed 191 people two years earlier.[86] Mayfield and civil liberties advocates argued that his arrest and two-week detainment serve as reminders of just how easy it is for bureaucrats to abuse powers (for example, relaxed standards of probable cause) conferred by the Patriot Act.

### The Iraq War

It was in this uncertain post–September 11, 2001, environment that the Bush administration, with Congress's consent, embarked on a war in Iraq. The White House contended that Iraq was harboring terrorists and possessed **weapons of mass destruction** that could be used to inflict great damage upon American interests. In August 2002, for example, Vice President Dick Cheney asserted: "There is no doubt that Saddam Hussein now has weapons of mass destruction [and] there is no doubt that he is amassing them to use against our friends, against our allies, and against us."[87]

Assertions such as this ultimately proved false. The United States and its allies succeeded in toppling Saddam Hussein from power but never did locate the weapons of mass destruction that had served as such a crucial justification for the war effort. This startling failure has been the subject of much controversy and investigation. An independent, bipartisan commission came to this general conclusion: "the Intelligence Community was dead wrong in almost all of its pre-war judgments about Iraq's weapons of mass destruction."[88] From our perspective, this general finding begs more specific questions regarding bureaucratic accountability and performance. Why did intelligence agencies and other bureaucracies get it so wrong when it came to Saddam Hussein's weapons program? How might the theoretical perspectives provide insight into the mistakes that were made up and down the chain of command?

For starters, it is important to recognize that United Nations weapons inspectors had been absent from Iraq since 1998, making the intelligence community's job inherently difficult.[89] In this information vacuum, and based on the Hussein regime's past behavior, a prevailing assumption emerged that Iraq had resumed its weapons program.[90] This assumption affected the way in which the often sketchy information coming out of Iraq was interpreted and used. In bounded rationality terms, intelligence analysts had grounded much of their work in the idea that Iraq was making significant progress in developing biological, chemical, and nuclear weapons. These premises rendered unattractive other schools of thought and courses of action regarding the Hussein regime.

These limitations in decision making were magnified as information was passed through the bureaucracy from analysts up to policymakers. From the perspective of high-level officials, intelligence reports took on the appearance of making relatively certain claims when, in fact, there was much to be contested in their content.[91] For example, the **President's Daily Brief** often touched on Iraq's weapons program. These reports sometimes carried titles that were far more alarmist than the accompanying texts would seem to have called for. In addition, information about the credibility of the sources used to generate the intelligence was sometimes exaggerated or not discussed at all.[92] In this environment, the president and other principals faced a significant information deficit when it came to evaluating the orientation and work of their agents on the ground. These principals, in other words, confronted serious adverse selection and moral hazard problems, both of which appear to have contributed greatly to the poor policy choices that were eventually made.

These hierarchical problems were compounded by shortcomings in intelligence networks. There are many bureaucracies that collect intelligence information—the Central Intelligence Agency, the Defense Intelligence Agency, and the National Geospatial-Intelligence Agency, to name just three. Given this organizational diversity, it might have been useful if there had been a regularized way for intelligence agencies to coordinate their collection and analytical efforts. Unfortunately, no such central clearinghouse existed.[93] In fact, there was a bias in the intelligence community against sharing information across jurisdictional lines. The National Security Agency, for example, was hesitant to share its raw data with anyone from outside the organization.[94] In an effort to address this lack of centrality in the intelligence network, Congress and President Bush created, in late 2004, the position of director of national intelligence (DNI). At this point, it is too early to tell whether reforms such as this have enhanced the network's overall effectiveness, although some commentators have decried the DNI position as a "toothless figurehead."[95]

The conduct of the war itself and the reconstruction of Iraq were plagued by a host of problems as well. Although free elections were held in January 2005, the nascent government proved weak, and sectarian violence between Shiite and Sunni Muslims became all too common and deadly. Economic development stagnated, and Iraq's oil reserves were continually threatened by sabotage and corruption. By the spring of 2007, four years after the war had begun, more than 3,000 Americans had lost their lives, and a debate raged in Washington, D.C., regarding the imposition of a timetable for the withdrawal of combat troops.[96] By then, some intelligence reports were suggesting that the war on terror that had been launched after the September 11, 2001, attacks was being hindered by events in Iraq. Violent Islamic extremists were using the war as a tool for recruiting a new generation of terrorists who could be deployed around the world against American and allied interests.[97]

## Bureaucratic Theories and Future Terrorist Attacks

In the wake of September 11, 2001, bureaucracies from across the government have worked nonstop on preventing future attacks on American soil and responding to such attacks should they occur. The fact that no terrorist attack has occurred in the six years since that fateful day lends itself to two very different, yet not necessarily contradictory, interpretations. On the one hand, it may be that the efforts of bureaucrats and others have been successful in deterring al-Qaida operations in the United States. On the other hand, it may be that the terrorist network is biding its time, waiting for a good opportunity to strike again when it is least expected. What, then, are some of the specific steps that are being taken inside the executive branch in the ongoing war on terror? Do the theoretical perspectives provide any insight into the origins and likely impacts of these bureaucratic actions in the years ahead?

One crucial task of federal agencies is to provide information to state and local officials regarding potential terrorist threats inside their jurisdictions. The Department of Homeland Security, for example, has established a color-coded threat level system for the nation as a whole, as well as for specific industries and geographic regions. The department also issues Homeland Security Threat Advisories, which provide advance notice about potential incidents involving important assets and infrastructures. How do state and local agents rate these kinds of information tools? According to a survey conducted in 2005, most local officials agree, either somewhat or strongly, that homeland security information provided by federal principals is easy to understand.[98] However, the same officials report that information from state-level principals is even more easily understood. When it comes to timeliness, most local officials agree that homeland security information from the federal government reaches them in a timely manner. Once again, though, these officials report that information emanating from the state government is even timelier. Given the particular importance of federal information in anticipating and preventing terrorist attacks, it is clear that this information could be, and should be, disseminated more effectively. Without good information from principals, agents cannot perform designated tasks as intended.

This conclusion especially applies to local jurisdictions that are small in size. In cities with populations of more than 500,000, 78.1 percent of public health officials report that they have collaborated with the Department of Health and Human Services, the lead federal agency on matters such as bioterrorism. Unfortunately, the level of collaboration is much lower in smaller jurisdictions, with only 29 percent of local officials reporting these kinds of interactions with their federal counterparts.[99]

A survey of county and city officials in Florida suggests that intergovernmental networks have become stronger as a result of homeland security initiatives and expenditures. Increased levels of cooperation on homeland security since September 11, 2001, have been reported by 64 percent of county officials and 60 percent of city officials. Very few of these officials report a surge in conflict across jurisdictions.[100] Furthermore, 96 percent of counties and 92 percent of cities in Florida report having established a homeland security network with officials in Tallahassee, the home of Florida's state government. Smaller yet still sizable percentages—76 percent of counties and 84 percent of cities— report having established a homeland security network with officials in the federal government.[101] It would thus appear that, if developments in Florida are any indication, substantial progress has been made in fostering network arrangements in the area of homeland security. Within these networks, the bonds between local officials and state government are at this point stronger than the bonds between local officials and government at the federal level.

Although governments at all levels are better prepared for a terrorist threat than they were in 2001, the general public's level of awareness and information leaves much to be desired. Only 20 percent of all Americans are familiar with their state or local government's plan for a terrorist attack, and only 37 percent have worked out arrangements with family members and friends for responding to an emergency.[102] When asked how they would respond to a terrorist attack, Americans offer a wide variety of answers. This suggests that the public's response to an actual terrorist attack would be both varied and unpredictable.

A key reason for this is that bureaucracies have done little to educate the general public about proper preparation for and proper responses to an emergency. Bureaucracies have improved their own standard operating procedures, but have not assisted ordinary citizens in developing their equally important standard operating procedures. An exception is the city of Philadelphia, which recently held its first "Emergency Preparedness Month" aimed at improving the general public's ability to prepare for and respond to an emergency.[103] Without stronger public education efforts, the next terrorist attack on U.S. soil may find well-prepared public officials but poorly prepared citizens.

The mobilization of interest groups has implications, often not for the better, for decisions that are made in some areas of homeland security. Consider the allocation of **homeland security grants.** These are federal funds awarded to states and localities to shore up port security, protect critical infrastructure, equip and train first responders, and so forth. Sometimes these funds are allocated with an eye more toward constituency considerations than to objective need. In fact, for most homeland security grants, Congress has decreed that no state shall receive less than 75 percent of the average per capita grant allotment.[104] As a result of this decree, smaller states have received far more funding per capita than larger states with a preponderance of terrorist targets. For example, New York and New Jersey, which together handle 12 percent of the nation's cargo, received only 1 percent of the federal funds available for port protection.[105] This pattern is consistent with Congress's usual preference for distributing funds across many states and localities as a way of maximizing political support for federal programs.[106]

Within these broad contours, competition for homeland security grants has become a rather fierce business. During the course of the Bush administration, government **outsourcing** on homeland security has increased by $130 billion.[107] A particularly controversial example of this type of network arrangement occurred in early 2006, when it was revealed that Dubai Ports World, a firm controlled by the government of the United Arab Emirates, had come into a position to run ports in New York, New Jersey, Philadelphia,

Baltimore, Miami, and New Orleans.[108] Opponents argued that it would not be appropriate for this kind of authority to be given to a country that has "historically been used as a base of terrorist operations and financing."[109] Proponents countered that the decision had been approved by the Federal Bureau of Investigation and the Departments of Commerce, Defense, Homeland Security, and the Treasury. In the end, the transfer of authority never took place as Dubai Ports World bowed to political pressure and transferred all of its U.S. operations to a U.S. company.[110]

This episode illustrates two important points about homeland security and the war on terror as they are likely to be carried out in the years ahead. The first point is that public bureaucracies will surely retain primary, day-to-day responsibility for making decisions on everything from advance planning to first response to tactical operations. The second point is that the bureaucracy's bosses and clients will continue to use their influence and authority to shape bureaucratic decision making, but only in those instances where the political stakes are visibly elevated. Together these insights mean that it will not always be easy to assign credit and blame for homeland security successes and failures. All such efforts should naturally start with bureaucracies of the executive branch, but they need to recognize that these agencies function as part of a larger political system that itself is subject to various, often contradictory, outside impulses.

## Avian Flu Pandemic: A Crisis in the Making?

On June 4–6, 2004, an international agricultural conference held in California drew speakers and participants from all over the world. Unknowingly, some presenters were ill from a strain of avian influenza (also called "bird flu") and, during the course of the proceedings, transmitted the virus to other attendees. Within days, the news media were issuing reports of a sudden flu outbreak that had infected large numbers of people and had even resulted in some deaths. Health departments across the state were ordered to open mass clinics as a means of delivering a newly developed avian flu vaccine to all residents.

We can all be thankful that this scary-sounding series of events did not actually take place. Rather, the Yolo County Health Department created this mock scenario for a flu vaccination drill that it carried out in collaboration with other government agencies, the local Red Cross chapter, community health

**Table 6.2  Confirmed Bird Flu Cases and Deaths**

| Country | Number of Cases | Number of Deaths |
|---|---|---|
| Vietnam | 93 | 42 |
| Indonesia | 81 | 63 |
| Egypt | 34 | 14 |
| Thailand | 25 | 17 |
| China | 24 | 15 |
| Turkey | 12 | 4 |
| Azerbaijan | 8 | 5 |
| Cambodia | 7 | 7 |
| Iraq | 3 | 2 |
| Laos | 2 | 2 |
| Djibouti | 1 | 0 |
| Nigeria | 1 | 1 |
| Total | 291 | 172 |

Source: "Cumulative Number of Confirmed Human Cases of Avian Influenza A/(H5N1) Reported to WHO, April 11, 2007," World Health Organization, www.who .int/csr/disease/avian_influenza/country/cases_table_2007_04_11/en/index.html.

care institutions, and individual volunteers on June 10, 2004.[111] Drills such as this are one element, along with monitoring, scientific research, and economic and policy forecasting, of an overall preparation strategy for a public health catastrophe that has yet to, but one day very well might, affect the lives and livelihoods of millions of Americans.

The possibility of an avian flu pandemic, an outbreak of global proportions, is salient today in large part because of the ongoing spread of the H5N1 virus. H5N1 is a particularly virulent strain of avian flu that, since 2003, has infected 291 people around the world, killing 172 of them.[112] As Table 6.2 indicates, none of the reported cases has occurred in the United States. Nor has the virus thus far been detected in domestic poultry stocks. These conditions, however, are potentially at risk of deteriorating rapidly, given the ease of international travel and the fact that H5N1 is continually being carried to far-off locations by migratory birds.[113]

For H5N1 to spawn a pandemic, the virus would have to evolve from its current form, in which it can readily spread from an infected bird to a person but not from one person directly to another. If the virus were to acquire this latter ability, the results could be catastrophic, as humans possess little natural immunity to such mutated strains of influenza. Extrapolating from past pandemics, the U.S. Department of Health and Human Services estimates that somewhere between 200,000 and 2 million Americans would lose their lives, with tens of millions more suffering nonfatal illnesses.[114] In addition to these staggering losses, H5N1 has the potential to cause severe economic dislocations, impacting activities and industries as diverse as "travel, tourism, food, consumption and eventually, investment and financial markets."[115]

Clearly, an avian flu pandemic would provide public bureaucracies with a host of disaster management challenges. What is less certain is just when such an outbreak might occur as well as whether H5N1 is in fact the strain most likely to mutate into a human virus. As one scientist has put it, "There's no sense of 'imminence' here. . . . The virus could move closer to human-to-human transmission, and it could move farther away."[116]

When it comes to this disaster that has not yet happened, agency officials thus find themselves in a difficult spot. On the one hand, if they overestimate the likelihood of an H5N1 pandemic, they run the risk of misallocating valuable emergency preparedness resources, resources that could be utilized more effectively in getting ready for other prospective crises. In addition, by drawing extensive public attention to a crisis that does not in short order manifest itself, agency officials could unwittingly cast themselves in the role of Chicken Little, desensitizing citizens to dangers in public health and other important areas of collective concern. On the other hand, if the threat of an H5N1 outbreak is too steeply discounted, the bureaucracy might find itself woefully unprepared when poultry and people suddenly begin to exhibit symptoms in large numbers.

## National Strategy for Pandemic Influenza

More than a decade in the making, a national strategy for anticipating and responding to an influenza pandemic was announced by the Bush administration on November 1, 2005, and was followed, six months later, by the release of an accompanying implementation plan.[117] The strategy lays out three guiding principles—preparedness and communication, surveillance and detection, and response and containment. When it comes to implementing these laudable principles, the plan tasks the Department of Homeland Security with coordinating the overall federal effort, while it places the Department of Health and Human Services in charge of medical readiness and management. The primary responsibilities of the federal government are limited to working with international authorities; procuring and distributing vaccines and antiviral medications; modifying laws and regulations as needed; and offering guidance to states, localities, and other organizations. For their part, state and local governments are charged with managing both the medical and nonmedical impacts of the avian flu within their jurisdictions over the many months an outbreak is projected to last. This arrangement means that the "center of gravity" before and during a pandemic will be located not in Washington, D.C., but in communities all around the country.[118]

A number of the plan's features have come under criticism. By **fragmenting authority** across agencies and failing to empower a single, national leader on matters of avian flu preparation and response, the plan runs the risk of producing, as Newt Gingrich has put it, little more than "confusion, finger-pointing and neglect."[119] In addition, most state and local health departments are poorly equipped to carry out their designated responsibilities, such as instituting quarantines, delivering vaccines, and providing medical care to those who become sick.[120] The private sector may also be an unreliable partner for the federal government. In the area of vaccines, domestic manufacturing capacities are rather limited, which would make it difficult for drug companies to bring a newly developed pandemic treatment to the market in short order.[121] On top of this, owing in part to a dispute between the Bush administration and congressional Democrats, the United States is well behind other nations in stockpiling Tamiflu, an antiviral drug that is known to be efficacious when taken shortly after the onset of flu-like symptoms.[122]

An avian flu pandemic, then, has all of the markings of a crisis that may one day reveal deficiencies in everything from the bureaucracy's inclination and capacity to plan for prospective disasters to its ability to respond quickly and effectively once tragic sequences of events begin to unfold. That said, is it possible to be somewhat more specific in pointing out where failure is likely to be most profound as well as where there are potential bureaucratic success stories in the making? It is this difficult task that we now assign to our four theoretical perspectives.

## Using the Theories to Forecast

For starters, an avian flu pandemic would appear to be a case ripe for an application of the logic and lessons of bounded rationality. On the one hand, bureaucratic decision makers might very well know their preferences—to minimize the likelihood of an H5N1 pandemic; to contain illness, death, and harmful economic consequences were such a pandemic to occur. On the other hand, these decision makers likely find it extremely difficult to consider all or even most applicable prevention and response strategies, and they likely have an even harder time anticipating the outcomes that will follow from various policy choices. Satisficing, in other words, is more likely to be an apt descriptor of bureaucratic reasoning than is optimization.

As we pointed out in Chapter 2, satisficing has a lot to offer as a mode of decision making, in that it allows for quick actions that are often either close to right or right on target in their intended effects. Nevertheless, satisficing does sometimes lead to off-the-mark decisions and therefore has the potential to produce disastrous results when the stakes are extraordinarily high, as they obviously are in the context of the H5N1 virus. So what are some of the ways in which boundedly rational processes are being used in preparing for an avian flu pandemic?

One key element of bounded rationality is problem disaggregation, the breaking down of complex challenges into their component parts. Such disaggregation is evident throughout the *National Strategy for Pandemic Influenza.* Not only does the plan, as highlighted earlier, call for three distinct conceptual focal points, it also disaggregates in terms of specific activities and functions. The plan lays out more than 300 actions that are to be taken or are already being implemented by the federal government. Examples of these actions include establishing surveillance capacity in at-risk countries, developing standards for the isolation and quarantine of travelers, assembling vaccine stockpiles adequate to immunize millions of Americans, and providing guidance to law enforcement officials at the state and local levels.[123]

One advantage of problem disaggregation is that it opens the door for bureaucracies to conduct simulations and tests in areas of specific responsibility. The Yolo County Health Department focused its avian flu exercise on a handful of discrete tasks, including the delivery of mock vaccinations to several hundred volunteers within a short period of time.[124] The department did not concern itself at all with larger issues surrounding the development, manufacturing, and distribution of these vaccinations, duties that clearly fall outside of its immediate domain. With such a narrow focus, the department was readily able to evaluate the lessons, both positive and negative, that were learned from the drill. On the positive side, participants gained confidence with respect to the roles they would be called upon to play in the event of an actual avian flu outbreak. Conversely, the department discovered that its incident command center did not operate very effectively and that its control measures were inadequate for containing the spread of the virus.[125]

No matter how laudable, the department's simulation may ultimately be irrelevant if avian flu vaccinations never make it to Yolo County. This failure is a distinct possibility because of the current state of the domestic vaccine industry. Pharmaceutical companies, which collectively constitute one of the most powerful organized interests in contemporary American politics, have shied away from increasing their vaccine manufacturing capacities, primarily because of their concerns about liability and profitability.[126] This hesitancy has led some public health experts to call for an abandonment of the existing private sector system in favor of a government-led initiative, modeled perhaps after the World War II–era Manhattan Project.[127] As was made clear in Chapter 4, it would take entrepreneurial behavior on the part of such experts, along with similarly inclined officeholders, to impose concentrated costs on the drug industry in order to deliver potential benefits to a diffuse set of millions of Americans.

Questions surrounding the division of responsibility between the federal government and other public and private entities can be considered through the lens of principal-agent theory. This approach is particularly relevant in the context of the delegation of policymaking and implementation authority to state and local governments. In spite of the facts that Yolo County conducted a successful avian flu simulation and that governments in cities such as Seattle and New York have made significant progress in their planning efforts, it is nevertheless the case that the vast majority of local health departments remain ill-prepared to exercise their delegated authority in a reasonable manner.[128] These collective shortcomings might well be viewed as manifestations of adverse selection, with a principal (the federal government) selecting agents (local health departments) not well suited for the tasks at hand.

As discussed in Chapter 3, a common solution to the problem of adverse selection is for principals to screen agents carefully before delegating responsibilities. Unfortunately, the federal government has little choice in the matter because local health departments face little, if any, competition in their areas of jurisdiction. What this lack of competition suggests is that agency loss, here visible through poor planning and response on the part of local health departments, will be inherently difficult to mitigate in a serious way.

When it comes to networks, many interagency, intergovernmental, and public-private arrangements are reasonable candidates for theoretical scrutiny. Arguably the most important network arises out of the allocation of pandemic flu authority across multiple agencies of the federal government. In addition to the aforementioned duties of the Department of Homeland Security and the Department of Health and Human Services, at least six other agencies have jurisdictional responsibilities enumerated in the *National Strategy for Pandemic Influenza: Implementation Plan*—the Departments of Agriculture, Defense, Labor, State, Transportation, and the Treasury.[129]

Although such a division of authority is natural in the face of a multi-dimensional threat like the H5N1 virus, it immediately raises difficulties regarding cross-agency coordination and the manner in which policy disagreements are aired and resolved. Cognizant of these difficulties, officials who drew up the plan placed the secretary of homeland security in charge of the federal government's overall response to an avian flu pandemic. These policymakers also established a process for dealing with issues that cannot be successfully addressed at the departmental level. This process involves two organizations located inside the Executive Office of the President—the Homeland Security Council and the National Security Council.[130]

On the surface, secretarial and White House attention to the most pressing and stubborn problems in the area of avian flu preparation and response would appear to be exactly what is needed. A closer look, however, reveals that the key officials and organizations involved have portfolios extending well beyond the H5N1 virus. The day-to-day war on terrorism consumes much of the time and energy of these policymakers, a fact that might very well have the impact of diluting coordination and decisiveness when it comes to pandemic flu. As noted in Chapter 5, without sustained and vigorous leadership, interagency networks are not likely to be especially effective in achieving their core tasks.

In sum, the possibility that the H5N1 virus might mutate into a strain of pandemic influenza presents public bureaucracies in the United States with a host of accountability and performance challenges. This public health crisis in the making would seem to call for an aggressive federal planning effort, much like previous bureaucratic initiatives that resulted in the detonation of the atomic bomb and other successful responses to prospective dangers. At the same time, an avian flu pandemic would be the ultimate localized disaster, with its effects being felt in neighborhoods, schools, and workplaces throughout the country.

As our theoretical consideration of the avian flu case has demonstrated, there have been bureaucratic success stories in terms of both coordinated action and independent preparations. Boundedly rational actors at the federal and local levels have utilized problem disaggregation and simulations as ways of beginning to understand the scope and complexity of the problem they may one day confront. Nevertheless, if a flu pandemic were to strike the United States sooner rather than later, it is almost certain that bureaucracies at all levels of government would be quickly overwhelmed. At first glance, this verdict may read like an indictment of the bureaucracy. It bears emphasizing, though, that institutions throughout government, civil society, and the economy would find themselves in much the same situation, responding to a crisis that naturally stretches organizational capacities like few other disasters the world has experienced.

## Evaluating Bureaucracy in Light of the Theories

At the outset, we noted that emergency situations pose greater challenges for public bureaucracies than ordinary decisions made under routine circumstances. We also observed that the theoretical perspectives provide us with four vantage points from which to think systematically about the management of major disasters. Along the way, we have encountered examples of strong bureaucratic performance, as well as instances where agencies have taken courses of action that leave much to be desired. We have also argued that some agency successes and failures emanate from pressures external to the bureaucracy, such as directives from political principals and claims raised by societal clients. Our final task, then, is to look for general patterns that come out of the experiences of Hurricane Katrina; the September 11, 2001, terrorist attacks; and the H5N1 avian influenza. What, in the broadest sense, have we learned about bureaucracy and the politics of disaster management?

Five particular lessons stand out. The first is that simulations and tests are likely to be crucial elements in planning for and responding to disasters of all varieties, given the unusual nature of especially large crises, both natural and man-made. Hurricane Pam and the Yolo County vaccination drill provided valuable information to first responders as well as to organizational supervisors. In the end, though, what matters are the concrete ways in which new information is used once the enthusiasm generated by a test fades away. In the case of New Orleans and the Gulf Coast, unfortunately, even a well-conceived simulation did not lead to needed changes in preparation and response protocols.

Second, communications, both horizontal and vertical, are crucial in preventing and reacting to disasters. Communication failures of both kinds are revealed when the September 11, 2001, terrorist attacks are considered. Well in advance of the attacks, intelligence officers in multiple agencies uncovered evidence that al-Qaida operatives were learning to fly various types of airplanes. These disparate pieces of information, however, were hard to assemble across a bureaucracy characterized by long-standing organizational boundaries and even rivalries. Once the hijacked airliners had struck their targets, police, fire, and rescue supervisors found it difficult, if not impossible, to keep in touch with their subordinates inside the World Trade Center although, for a variety of reasons, communications were better at the Pentagon.

Third, centralized networks appear to be a plus when it comes to managing disasters. As discussed earlier, no one agency or small group of agencies is likely to possess the personnel or the mandate to truly lead when it comes to making emergency preparations and responding to crises as they occur. Even if networks are not already in place prior to a disaster, such organizational arrangements are likely to emerge naturally in the immediate aftermath of the event. In this kind of environment, centralization is a commonly called for, if not always realized, component of disaster networks. It was conspicuously lacking in the days immediately preceding and immediately following the landfall of Hurricane Katrina. Similarly, the lack of centralization in planning for an H5N1 pandemic has led observers to worry about the sustainability of the bureaucracy's attention to what could turn out to be a disaster of historic proportions.

Fourth, political principals and societal clients sometimes help but often hinder the bureaucracy's ability to plan for and respond to emergency situations. The threat that Osama bin Laden and his terrorist network posed to the United States was well known among elected officials all the way up to the president many years before the September 11, 2001, attacks. These officials, however, failed to take a number of steps that experts agree would have been useful in reorienting the bureaucracy away from conventional, Cold War–era modes of operation to approaches more appropriate in the face of a new, very different type of threat. In the Gulf of Mexico region, economic interests pressured for continued expansion in shipping, tourism, and other industries, even when such growth came at the expense of valuable natural buffers that would have protected New Orleans and other low-lying areas from a storm everyone anticipated and feared.

Finally, as these last statements indicate, the level of death and destruction associated with major disasters is a function of not only the immediate event itself but also the forces that operate over the long run. If the H5N1 virus ever mutates into a global health crisis, its personal and economic toll will be determined in no small part by preparations that are under way now and have been for many years. These preparations include steps being taken by innumerable individuals and organizations here in the United States and around the world. With such a diverse cast of characters, it is naturally rather difficult to sort out cause-and-effect relationships, to associate particular outcomes with actions that were, or were not, taken by specific actors. This inherent interconnectedness signals just how hard it is to evaluate bureaucracies that are operating inside larger political systems.

The four theoretical perspectives have been extremely useful in unpacking these types of complex problems. The theories have pointed to processes and institutions that are especially crucial to consider when trying to understand certain decisions and outcomes. The theories have also provided useful criteria by which to judge decision makers, criteria that are linked to well-established social scientific benchmarks. In the end, the theories have painted what we think is a realistic portrait of bureaucratic accountability and performance under some of the most difficult circumstances in which public servants find themselves.

## Key Terms

All hazards approach, 170

Avian influenza, 167

Central Intelligence Agency, 180

Chain of command, 172

Civil liberties, 185

Climate change, 166

Connect the dots, 183

Coast Guard, 177

Emergency communications, 172

Federal Emergency Management Agency, 168

First responder, 181

Fragmenting authority, 193

Homeland security grants, 189

Hurricane Pam, 173

Hurricane superhighway, 176

Incident command, 181

Loosely connected network, 176

National Commission on Terrorist Attacks Upon the United States, 180

National Response Plan, 171

National Strategy for Pandemic Influenza, 194

Network failures, 177

No-bid contracts, 176

Outsourcing, 189

President's Daily Brief, 186

al-Qaida, 180

USA PATRIOT Act, 182

Weapons of mass destruction, 185

# 7 | Why Are Some Bureaucracies Better Than Others?

As the theoretical frameworks and case studies throughout the book have demonstrated, executive branch bureaucracies are policymaking organizations that operate as institutions of American democracy. As one observer has put it, agencies "shape decisions that influence the quality of the air you breathe, how safe your car is, which immigrants will enter and stay in this country, how airports will be protected from terrorism, what you can expect from your employer in terms of working conditions and pension, and how safe that hamburger is that you just put in your mouth."[1] In terms of affecting our lives on a day-to-day basis, the bureaucracy has no peer among government institutions.

Although this influence is exercised by organizations not directly connected to the elections that form the backbone of U.S. democracy, it is inaccurate to portray the bureaucracy as being aloof from citizens and their elected representatives. From oversight by powerful congressional committees to testimony by the most common of folk, agencies stay in constant contact with their political supervisors and those in society upon whom their actions bestow benefits and impose costs. In the context of these interactions, two standards have become paramount in judging agencies as public policymakers: accountability and performance. Accountability has been a concern since the bureaucracy emerged as a policymaking force early in the twentieth century. More recently, strength in performance has come to rival clear accountability as a desirable, even necessary, trait in public bureaucracies.

As we have seen, success in measuring up to accountability and performance standards varies from one agency to another. Such variation can also be seen within an agency, as the organization moves from issue to issue and from one policy area to another. Many of the reasons for these variations have been highlighted in the preceding chapters. We now bring these insights together and amplify them in important ways by taking on two *final questions*:

- *WHICH AGENCIES ARE THE HIGHEST, AND LOWEST, PERFORMING ORGANIZATIONS IN THE EXECUTIVE BRANCH?*

- *WHAT FACTORS, INCLUDING ACCOUNTABILITY, HELP TO EXPLAIN DIFFERENCES IN BUREAUCRATIC BEHAVIOR AND OUTCOMES?*

## Rating the Performance of Agencies

A few years ago, a team of researchers set out to document differences in the performance of federal agencies. To account for the fact that performance is a multifaceted concept, these researchers developed a rating scheme that evaluated agencies on thirty-four criteria in five crosscutting areas—financial management, capital management, human resources, information technology, and managing for results. After conducting hundreds of interviews with individuals from the legislative and executive branches, think tanks, the press, interest groups, academic institutions, and many other organizations, the researchers deliberated and reached conclusions about the performance of fifteen agencies.[2]

In 1999 the researchers published these performance ratings in *Government Executive* magazine,[3] with grades ranging from A (the Social Security Administration) to C– (the Immigration and Naturalization Service, since renamed Citizenship and Immigration Services). Over the next three years, twelve more agencies were evaluated, including the Postal Service (USPS) and the Army Corps of Engineers. The researchers also rated six agencies a second time in an effort to track changes in performance over time. In 2002, the last year of the **Federal Performance Project,** the Internal Revenue Service received a B–, a modest improvement over the C it had received in 1999.

These report cards confirm that some agencies perform better than others. On occasion, as in the case of the Social Security Administration (SSA) and Immigration and Naturalization Service (INS), these differences are dramatic. More often than not, however, the differences are much subtler. According to the researchers, the Federal Emergency Management Agency (FEMA) was a higher-performing agency in 1999 than the Environmental Protection Agency (EPA) but only by a small margin (FEMA received a B, while the EPA received

**Figure 7.1 Report Cards for Selected Federal Agencies**

| 1999 | Immigration and Naturali- zation Service | Customs Service | Health Care Financing Administration | Environmental Protection Agency | Social Security Administration |
|---|---|---|---|---|---|
|  | C– | C | C | B– | A |

| 2000 | National Park Service | Occupational Safety and Health Administration | Veteran Benefits Administration | Army Corps of Engineers | Coast Guard |
|---|---|---|---|---|---|
|  | C | C | B– | B | A |

| 2001 | Bureau of Indian Affairs | Bureau of Consular Affairs | National Aeronautics and Space Administration | Postal Service | National Weather Service |
|---|---|---|---|---|---|
|  | D | C | B | A– | A |

| 2002 | Immigration and Naturali- zation Service | Centers for Medicare and Medicaid Services | Internal Revenue Service | Federal Aviation Administration | Social Security Administration |
|---|---|---|---|---|---|
|  | D | C– | B– | B | B |

*Source: Government Executive,* February 1999, March 2000, April 2001, May 2002. Consolidated table prepared by the authors.

*Note:* In 2001 the Health Care Financing Administration was renamed the Centers for Medicare and Medicaid Services. In 2003 the Immigration and Naturalization Service was renamed Citizenship and Immigration Services.

a B–). Figure 7.1 presents grades for a selection of agencies that were evaluated in the Federal Performance Project.

## Explaining Variations in Performance

To what extent are these variations in performance systematic, as opposed to reflections of idiosyncrasies in agencies and their evaluators? To answer this question, we return to the insights generated by the theoretical frameworks and case studies. On the basis of these insights, we believe four factors are particularly relevant in distinguishing agencies in their performance: **tasks, relationships, political support,** and **leadership.** Some agencies confront relatively clear, easy, and manageable tasks; other agencies have more imposing responsibilities. Some agencies communicate and coordinate well with other organizations; other agencies experience great difficulties in building effective network ties. Some agencies benefit from sustained accountability to diverse sovereigns and clients; other agencies lack solid political support. Some agencies enjoy competent, sensitive, and creative leadership; other agencies suffer from leadership that fails in fundamental respects. From these key premises flow twelve specific propositions about the performance of public bureaucracies.

## Tasks

At times agencies engage in policymaking, while at others they implement decisions made elsewhere in the political system. Although implementation can pose significant problems, policymaking is, generally speaking, a more difficult responsibility. For this reason agencies that primarily engage in routine implementation tasks are likely to perform better than those whose central mission is resolving complex and contentious policy issues. This holds especially for implementation tasks viewed favorably by the agency's clients.

- *PROPOSITION 1: AGENCIES WHOSE PRIMARY TASK IS TO DISTRIBUTE MONEY TO INDIVIDUALS TEND TO PERFORM WELL.*

The SSA, which received an A in 1999 and a B in 2002, exemplifies this proposition. Much of what the agency does is write checks to retirees and disabled individuals. Once eligibility has been determined, the rest is really quite straightforward. The criteria for retirement payments are crystal clear, and agency officials have extensive documentation of individual work histories at their fingertips. Determining eligibility for disability payments is somewhat trickier, but even here statutory criteria exist and are supplemented by more specific administrative rules and judicial decisions.

By way of contrast, consider the Centers for Medicare and Medicaid Services (CMS), the lead agency in delivering health care services to the elderly, poor, and other segments of the population. In carrying out the Medicaid portion of this task, CMS relies on state governments to decide who is eligible for the program and who is authorized to provide the program's services. In turn state governments rely on hospitals, managed care plans, and other health care organizations to hire, deploy, and compensate personnel. Finally, health care organizations rely on physicians, nurses, and other medical professionals to deliver services in accordance with program rules. With such a long chain of responsible parties, performance difficulties are bound to arise.[4] Not surprisingly, then, CMS received a C– in 2002.[5]

Not all implementation tasks are created equal, however, or viewed with favor. At times agencies engage in routine behaviors that stakeholders do not find at all endearing, such as collecting money. Whereas agencies distributing money are likely to be blessed, agencies extracting money are likely to be cursed.

- **PROPOSITION 2: AGENCIES WHOSE PRIMARY TASK IS TO COLLECT MONEY TEND TO PERFORM POORLY.**

The Internal Revenue Service (IRS), which has never received a grade higher than a B–, epitomizes this proposition. It goes without saying that hardly anyone likes the IRS and many people fear it. Despite this fear, a number of taxpayers cheat, banking on the fact that the agency audits only a relatively small portion of tax returns. In fact, the IRS estimates that the **tax gap,** the difference between what taxpayers owe and what they voluntarily pay, is approximately $345 billion.[6] To combat this tax evasion, the IRS has over time increased the number of returns it audits and the resources it devotes to enforcing the tax code.[7] In the late 1990s, revelations that some IRS officials were overzealous in their tax collection efforts made it even more difficult for the agency to perform these auditing duties. In a series of highly publicized hearings and the subsequent **Internal Revenue Service Restructuring and Reform Act,** Congress made it clear that it wants the IRS to be relatively benign in its enforcement efforts. Congress also undoubtedly wants the IRS to offer better services, such as timely and accurate advice to taxpayers, but legislators have not provided the funding necessary to bring about such performance enhancements. Yet even if Congress increases funding levels for these improvements, the IRS, by the very nature of its task, would likely continue to suffer from a negative image.

The Office of Student Financial Assistance (OSFA) (today known as the Office of Federal Student Aid) is an interesting agency to consider because it both distributes money and collects it. Like the SSA, it writes checks, in its case mainly to students of relatively modest means who wish to attend college. These payments, however, are primarily loans that must eventually be repaid. Like the IRS, then, the OSFA is also a revenue collection operation. Its task is particularly difficult because recent college graduates, if saddled with substantial debt, may lack the resources necessary to make rent payments, car payments, and student loan payments at the same time. According to the **National Center for Education Statistics,** about half of all college students graduate with loan debt. This debt is, on average, $10,000 per student.[8] Although the default rate on student loans has declined significantly since 1990, it is still a not-so-trivial 5 percent.[9] Not surprisingly, the OSFA earned no better than a C in 2000.

Throughout the preceding chapters we have highlighted the **missions** bestowed upon agencies by political principals. These missions reflect the fact that public problems are often hard to solve, especially without running afoul of powerful constituencies. The Forest Service's delicate balancing act between the conservation of natural resources and the fostering of rural economic development offers just one example of such a mission. In general, ambiguity and conflict in missions make it difficult for agencies to satisfy the desires and needs of their stakeholders and political supervisors.

- *PROPOSITION 3: AGENCIES WITH AMBIGUOUS OR CONFLICTING MISSIONS TEND TO PERFORM POORLY.*

Citizenship and Immigration Services (CIS) is an example of a bureaucracy bedeviled by competing goals. The agency is expected to "keep out illegal immigrants but let in necessary agricultural workers" and to "carefully screen foreigners seeking to enter the country, but facilitate the entry of foreign tourists."[10] It is extremely difficult, and perhaps impossible, to reconcile these goals. A looser touch allows agricultural workers and foreign tourists in but unintentionally whisks in illegal immigrants and individuals seeking to harm the United States. The stakes of getting this trade-off right were never so apparent as on September 11, 2001. In 2002, several months after the terrorist attacks, the agency received a D, lower than the C– it received in 1999. Even today, years after the attacks, it remains difficult to strike a balance between the often competing economic and security rationales for the nation's immigration system.[11] Absent a consensus, CIS is likely to remain caught in the middle, unable to perform well on either dimension.

By contrast, the National Weather Service (NWS), which suffers no existential angst as it contemplates its raison d'étre, received an A in 2001. Everyone inside and outside the agency knows that the NWS is responsible for predicting the weather as accurately as possible. Nothing cloudy about that mission! Fully aware of its mission, and equipped with the personnel and technology to do it, the NWS tracks hurricanes and other disturbances in the atmosphere with considerable finesse and precision. An agency with such a clear mission is likely to perform well, especially when that mission enjoys wide support. No one doubts the need for good weather forecasts to anticipate emergencies and to enhance the quality of our lives. By acquitting itself admirably during the Hurricane Katrina disaster, the NWS demonstrated that it continues to provide these valuable services in an accurate and dependable manner.

The distinction between outputs (the activities of agencies) and outcomes (the results of these activities) is salient when thinking about performance. For example, the observability of these facets of bureaucratic behavior varies across policy areas and agencies.[12] As a result, the difficulty of the moral hazard problem facing political principals and their constituents is best not treated as constant.

In dealing with the SSA, one question the agency's supervisors and clients ask is, *How quick and accurate are Social Security payments?* Fortunately, for all concerned parties, the information necessary to gauge these outputs and outcomes is readily available. Similarly, it is relatively easy for those inside and outside the USPS to keep tabs on the agency's activities and results. No great mystery exists about how long it takes a letter carrier to deliver the mail or a first class letter to reach its destination.

Agencies such as the SSA and the USPS are known as **production organizations.** In such organizations, clarity in outputs and outcomes makes it relatively easy for agency leaders to see what is being done and what is being accomplished. This clarity also helps interested parties outside the organization; agency mistakes, for example, are relatively transparent to bosses and clients. For these reasons production organizations, in most cases, perform with considerable strength and precision.

- *PROPOSITION 4: AGENCIES WHOSE OUTPUTS AND OUTCOMES BOTH ARE OBSERVABLE TEND TO PERFORM WELL.*

The National Aeronautics and Space Administration (NASA), which received a B in 2001, would seem to qualify at least in some respects as a production agency. Granted, the long-term implications of space exploration are difficult to assess. For example, it is hard to say whether NASA's **Vision for Space Exploration,** which calls for manned flights to the moon by 2020, is being executed effectively.[13] However, there are immediate consequences of NASA's outputs that are easy to spot. In 2003 a piece of foam insulation broke off the main propellant tank of the space shuttle *Columbia* and struck the leading edge of the craft's left wing. This accident damaged the shuttle's thermal protection system, and the vehicle disintegrated when hot gases penetrated its structure upon reentry into the Earth's atmosphere, causing the deaths of all seven crew members.[14] Two and a half years later, safety modifications to the shuttle fleet's external fuel tank system were put to the test when *Discovery* lifted off from Florida's Kennedy Space Center. During the course of their two-week mission, *Discovery's* crew members engaged in a first-of-its-kind spacewalk to perform repairs on the International Space Station.[15] Both the repairs and the flight itself were resounding successes. In general, NASA has performed reasonably well in executing a very difficult, and decidedly observable, mission.

What about agencies whose outputs and outcomes are difficult to observe? Such agencies, known as **coping organizations,** often find it difficult to perform well.[16] Leading examples of coping organizations include public schools and police departments. Diplomacy—the State Department's stock in trade—is also emblematic of this state of affairs. Perhaps not surprisingly, then, the State Department's Bureau of Consular Affairs (BCA) received a C in 2001. The BCA takes care of American citizens overseas—reissuing lost passports, for example—and gives visas to foreigners who wish to visit the United States. Because the BCA's consulates are scattered throughout the world and because its information technology is antiquated, it is problematic for agency leaders to manage the organization's tasks and for members of Congress to keep tabs on what the organization is doing.[17] The BCA's weaknesses became painfully apparent to many would-be travelers in the spring of 2007, when the agency's backlog of passport applications escalated sharply as a result of new regulations governing international travel.[18] Many Americans did not know if their passport application had been approved until just prior to their scheduled departure.

The Interior Department's Bureau of Indian Affairs (BIA), which received a D in 2001, also possesses some coping organization characteristics. The agency's activities, such as supporting education on tribal reservations, are difficult to measure and monitor. Although test scores offer some indication of how much students have learned, it is exceedingly tough to disentangle the effects of teacher intervention from those of student initiative and home environment. In short, the BIA's management lapses arise in part from the complexity of the tasks it is charged with carrying out. Like the Bureau of Consular Affairs, the BIA also suffers from woefully outdated technology.[19]

The much-maligned CIS and related agencies such as Customs and Border Protection (whose predecessor, the Customs Service, received a C in 1999) suffer from multiple problems, including the difficulty of discerning their outputs and outcomes. To cite the clearest problem, illegal immigration is extremely hard to document because those who enter the country on the sly have compelling incentives to remain hidden from government authorities. It is, of course, possible to gather statistics on the number of individuals apprehended at U.S. borders. Between June 15 and August 15, 2006, 5,003 illegal border crossers were apprehended in Texas, New Mexico, Arizona, and California.[20] The ratio of successful to unsuccessful illegal border crossings is for all intents and purposes unknowable. However, a common estimate is that 12 million illegal immigrants currently reside in the United States.[21]

## Relationships

Despite the importance of agency tasks, many bureaucracies with identical missions perform very differently. For example, some state environmental agencies have effectively controlled air pollution, while others have not. Some local police departments have successfully reduced violent crime, while others have not. Many factors help to explain these differences, among them relationships between bureaucrats (for example, **communications**) and relationships between bureaucracies (for example, **coordination**). These relationships are so integral to the daily lives of bureaucrats that we often take them for granted. Yet just as winning in basketball depends on certain relationships (crisp passing, solid team defense), so too does good bureaucratic work.

The transmission of information, though lacking in glamour, is of critical importance if bureaucrats, their bosses, and their clients are to know what is happening and what is expected of them. This is true in both emergencies and more routine situations. Communications are an especially pressing concern for the National Park Service (NPS), which received a C in 2000. The NPS has tens of thousands of employees who serve more than 285 million visitors each year.[22] In recent years, the NPS has relied on focus groups to assess what the public knows about the agency, what visitors expect from parks, and how the agency can best communicate with its constituents. According to agency personnel, these communication efforts "help the agency better understand its future needs, as well as educate the public about the importance of natural resource stewardship."[23]

• **PROPOSITION 5: AGENCIES THAT ESTABLISH GOOD COMMUNICA-TION SYSTEMS TEND TO PERFORM WELL.**

Coordination has sometimes been described as an unnatural act between consenting adults. Unnatural though it may be, coordination between agencies is of vital importance. The challenges of coordination are especially acute in an intergovernmental setting, where bureaucrats work for different bosses and for organizations with different cultures and norms. These challenges help to explain why intergovernmental programs are rated so poorly. Consider the Chesapeake Bay Commission (CBC), a tri-state body charged with restoring one of the nation's most treasured natural resources. Membership is equally divided among the member states—Pennsylvania, Maryland, and Virginia.[24] As one EPA official put it in a critical assessment of the CBC: "If we go at the current rate that we're doing, we're talking about restoring the Chesapeake decades from now, a generation or two."[25]

• **PROPOSITION 6: AGENCIES THAT COORDINATE ACTIVITIES INTER-NALLY AS WELL AS WITH OTHER AGENCIES TEND TO PERFORM WELL.**

Sometimes embattled agencies learn to coordinate better. Over the years, the Bureau of Land Management (BLM) has been on the receiving end of numerous lawsuits filed by environmental groups. To decrease the frequency of these lawsuits, some BLM officials have opted to improve interagency planning and coordination. For example, BLM officials in the San Joaquin Valley led an effort to create an interagency council that developed a regional plan to protect biodiversity.[26] In the long run, such constructive efforts are likely to reduce levels of environmental litigation.

## Political Support

As has been emphasized throughout, accountability and performance are the two main standards by which public bureaucracies are judged. Though distinct in some respects, these standards are inextricably linked in others. For decades, one of the central ways in which chief executives, legislatures, and judiciaries have sought to foster bureaucratic accountability has been by influencing the processes through which agencies go about producing outputs. The Administrative Procedure Act, with its dictates regarding public notices and comments, is perhaps the classic example of this fundamental connection.

But what about the linkage in the reverse direction? In what ways does accountability facilitate performance? Are there forms of accountability, and political support more generally, that hinder the ability of agencies to perform their most crucial tasks?

In iron triangles, political support comes from narrow constituencies that stand to benefit greatly from bureaucratic decision making. Opposing, broader interests do not typically mobilize against these narrow constituencies. Such a pattern can lead to difficulties in both processes and results. For decades the Interstate Commerce Commission had the authority to regulate the rates charged by railroads and motor carriers. Working closely with these interests, the agency developed what has been called "congenital schizophrenia."[27] In other words, taking care of the rail and trucking industries' needs case by case took precedence over consistent application of particular standards or rationalizations, to the detriment of other interested parties, including consumers and members of Congress.

- **PROPOSITION 7: AGENCIES THAT ARE PRESSURED BY DIVERSE SETS OF CONSTITUENCIES TEND TO PERFORM WELL.**

In general, support from diffuse constituencies is a way to avoid the kinds of problems that eventually contributed to the demise, in 1995, of the Interstate Commerce Commission. The EPA is perhaps the leading example of an agency that, from its inception, has been exposed to diverse points of view, including business interests, environmental advocates, and state and local regulators charged with carrying out federal policies. At times this exposure has proved frustrating for agency officials, who must negotiate political minefields when making decisions. Such negotiations have to be undertaken with great care and deliberation, and as a result the agency seldom sets records for the speed of its policymaking. Nevertheless, the EPA's diverse constituency helps guarantee that it will pay at least some attention to both economic efficiency and ecological concerns whenever it makes a decision. As a case in point, reductions in air and water pollution over the past three decades owe a great deal to the persistent efforts of environmentalists, while technological advances and the enhanced importance of economic incentives reflect the input of regulated industries. Although the agency's grades have not been perfect (a B– in 1999 and a B in 2002), they almost certainly would have been worse had the agency been dominated by either business firms or environmental activists.

In contrast, the Customs Service suffered from lopsided external pressure prior to the terrorist attacks of September 11, 2001. Shipping interests, eager to speed the flow of goods and therefore to increase their profits, lobbied the agency to expedite checks at the nation's borders. Security interests were poorly represented in this lobbying process. In the aftermath of the attacks, investigations revealed that every year the agency had been allowing millions of containers to enter the country with minimal scrutiny for bombs or biological weapons. In retrospect, the C received by the agency in 1999 accurately captured an organization poorly prepared to prevent terrorists from gaining a toehold inside the United States.

- ### PROPOSITION 8: AGENCIES WHOSE PROGRAMS AND POLICIES ENJOY DIFFUSE SUPPORT TEND TO PERFORM WELL.

A closely related covariate of performance is the level of support enjoyed by the programs and policies under an agency's jurisdiction. Consider, at one end of the spectrum, the SSA, USPS, and NWS, three agencies that have received very good or excellent ratings. Social Security is probably the most popular income support program in the United States. Senior citizens anxiously wait to receive their monthly check in the mail, and most working Americans probably feel a little more secure knowing that when they retire they, too, will receive a minimum pension from the federal government. Mail delivery, which dates back to the nation's earliest days, also enjoys widespread public support, despite periodic increases in the price of stamps. Even with a growing number of alternatives to traditional mail delivery, such as faxes, e-mails, instant messaging, and Federal Express and similar private services, Americans continue to rely heavily upon the USPS for personal and professional communications. Though not as old as the USPS, the NWS is just as familiar and highly regarded. Weather reports are particularly useful for farmers and travelers. The work of the agency's forecasters is also of critical importance for those who find themselves in the path of blizzards, hurricanes, tornadoes, and other natural disasters. As each one of us can undoubtedly attest, this work helps to enhance the quality of our daily lives, as when we choose to picnic on Saturday rather than Sunday because the weather looks more promising.

At the other end of the spectrum, the BIA is an agency whose programs and policies enjoy specific support from some Native Americans but not diffuse support from the general American public. One reason is that in an effort to build consensus, the agency has deliberately disaggregated issues, thus conveying the impression that its actions will probably promote nothing more than local benefits.[28] Another reason is the succession of highly conflictive issues the agency has had to deal with in recent years, including various disputes over Native American treaty rights. Because such controversies tend to pit Native Americans against other Americans, these issues are unlikely to generate diffuse support for an agency badly in need of performance enhancements.[29]

Support, or a lack thereof, for agencies and their jurisdictions comes not only from societal clients but from political supervisors as well. These supervisors seek to foster accountability through several different techniques of control.

A **catalytic control** places on an agency's agenda an issue requiring some kind of response but allows the agency considerable discretion in crafting its approach. A **hortatory control** offers incentives, such as financial rewards, to encourage an agency to take specific actions. Finally, a **coercive control** compels an agency to behave in a certain way, regardless of the preferences of the agency's leaders, managers, and operations staff. As a general rule, coercive controls inhibit creative problem solving and produce unintended, negative side effects. Although coercion is sometimes necessary, as when civil rights or civil liberties are threatened, it is usually a suboptimal technique for controlling the bureaucracy.[30]

- *PROPOSITION 9: AGENCIES SUBJECT TO CATALYTIC CONTROLS OR HORTATORY CONTROLS TEND TO PERFORM BETTER THAN THOSE SUBJECT TO COERCIVE CONTROLS.*

Congress's intervention in the area of ergonomics policy offers a good example of a coercive control. Rather than relying on legislative appropriations and oversight hearings to encourage an ergonomics rule that reflected its priorities, Congress waited for the Occupational Safety and Health Administration (OSHA) to adopt a rule and then, with the help of the newly inaugurated George W. Bush administration, promptly overturned it. Repudiated by Congress, and consistent with the aims of its new leadership, the agency declined to revise and reissue the regulation. Rather, OSHA, in 2002, established a four-pronged approach designed to change the behavior of employers and workers through voluntary measures.[31] This approach includes guidelines, inspections, outreach, and the ongoing work of the National Advisory Committee on Ergonomics. On the one hand, the plan has been hailed by the U.S. Chamber of Commerce and other business interests as putting "science ahead of politics."[32] On the other hand, labor unions such as the AFL-CIO have argued that the plan provides "no real protections" against repetitive stress injuries.[33]

By way of contrast, Congress has historically given the USPS considerable discretion and autonomy. Under an arrangement dating back to 1970, an independent Postal Rate Commission makes recommendations on rate increases to an independent board of governors, which then makes the final decisions. The requirements that members be appointed to nine-year terms and can be removed only under the rarest of circumstances insulate the board from political pressure. Such noncoercive controls free the USPS to take actions that raise very little political ire, even when they entail rate hikes that are inevitably unpopular with consumers.

As these examples illustrate, political support is not an all or nothing proposition. Agencies that most clearly recognize the opportunities and constraints presented by different types of accountability put themselves in a position to generate the political capital necessary to perform their tasks effectively. This awareness often comes from the top, with skillful, visionary leaders.

## Leadership

Although it is commonly acknowledged that leadership matters in public bureaucracies, much less agreement exists regarding the specific ingredients that make for an effective leader. This lack of agreement should not be viewed as surprising, as the qualities that make for strong leadership at some agencies may not be the qualities that facilitate appropriate leadership at others. For example, a moribund agency with programs escalating in economic, social, and political importance may benefit from a bold leader willing to rock the boat, even if this rocking causes some inside and outside the agency to feel queasy. In contrast, an embattled agency with programs constantly being challenged may benefit from a coalition builder who can effectively reach out to influential constituencies prior to making crucial decisions. Still, despite these complexities and subtleties, several general propositions about bureaucratic leadership can be advanced.

Agency heads are appointed for a variety of reasons—their qualifications, their demographic characteristics, their long-standing friendship with the president, their support from influential backers or constituencies, and so forth. Of these factors, effective leadership derives primarily from professional expertise and prior work experience. Without these qualities, agency heads will probably flounder, no matter how much support key bosses and clients provide. With these qualities, success is much more likely, even for agency heads who are not the president's personal friends or closely aligned with powerful societal interests.

- **PROPOSITION 10: AGENCIES WITH LEADERS WHO POSSESS THE REQUISITE EXPERTISE AND EXPERIENCE TEND TO PERFORM WELL.**

Carol Browner, who led the EPA during the Clinton administration, had headed Florida's Department of Environmental Protection prior to serving in the federal government. Browner had also worked on Capitol Hill, assisting Sen. Al Gore, D-Tenn., on environmental issues. Importantly, Browner made good use of the substantive knowledge and political connections she had accumulated prior to her EPA stint. During her tenure the agency launched a number of major initiatives, including Project XL, which allows businesses and state and local governments to experiment with innovative, cost-effective approaches for achieving environmental goals.[34]

Consider as well the background of John D. Graham, who headed the Office of Information and Regulatory Affairs (OIRA) until October 2005 in the administration of George W. Bush. Prior to taking the reins at OIRA, Graham founded the Harvard Center for Risk Analysis and wrote several books and dozens of articles on topics such as automotive safety and environmental policy.[35] This body of work established Graham as one of the nation's leading experts on the application of analytical techniques to the setting of regulatory priorities, the weighing of risks, and the design of cost-effective public policies. It was this expertise that in part enabled Graham to survive the contentious Senate confirmation process that inevitably follows the president's nomination of a new **regulatory czar** (as the OIRA administrator is commonly known in policymaking circles). During his productive tenure, Graham not only blocked proposed regulations that did not pass analytical muster, but also prompted agencies to issue rules in a number of important areas that otherwise might have been neglected. The trans-fat labels that have become standard elements of food packaging are one example of how Graham's prior expertise in risk analysis served as the impetus for a policy change that is likely to benefit the health and well-being of millions of Americans.

Regardless of their experience, leaders can also enhance bureaucratic performance by taking actions that advance their agencies' long-term interests, even if such actions undermine their personal interests in the short run. By making such **credible commitments,** leaders foster a sense of cooperation and esprit de corps among agency managers and operators, which in turn boost the prospects that the organization will take major strides toward achieving its most fundamental goals.[36]

- **PROPOSITION 11: AGENCIES WITH LEADERS WHO MAKE CREDIBLE COMMITMENTS TEND TO PERFORM WELL.**

Credible commitments can be made and demonstrated in a variety of ways. For example, Greg Woods was brought in to lead the Office of Student Financial Assistance at a time when the agency had just received a C rating. Rather than take steps to immediately endear himself to the organization's bosses and clients, Woods set about giving the agency a complete makeover. Symbolically, he restated its mission in human terms: "We help put America through school." In terms of service, he reorganized the agency around its three central clientele groups—students, schools, and financial institutions. Facing perhaps his most daunting challenge, he took steps to streamline and integrate the organization's computer systems, which had been created haphazardly over a period of many years.[37]

The initial assessments of Woods's leadership were somewhat mixed. He received praise for his energy and enthusiasm as well as for assembling a strong management team. But he received criticism for, among other things, placing too much emphasis on Access America for Students, a new initiative that would allow students to manage their financial aid accounts over the Internet. At one level, the complaints were about the supposed diversion of Woods's attention from his most pressing task of revamping the agency's computer systems. At another level, the complaints were about politics, as the initiative was a pet project of presidential candidate Al Gore.[38]

Despite these controversies, Woods was eventually credited with pointing the Office of Student Financial Assistance in the right direction. Even former critics rushed to his defense when Secretary of Education Rod Paige tried to rein in Woods's authority. Emotions ran high in September 2002 when Woods stepped down from his post to devote his full energy to a life-threatening (and ultimately losing) battle with pancreatic cancer.[39] In the end many in the financial aid community agreed with this assessment of Woods's tenure: "The investments that have been made in modernization are beginning to return dividends to us. We cannot afford to start at square one again, because if we do, it'll be years before we get back to the point where we're making significant progress."[40]

Although some commitments of visionary leaders last well beyond their time in office, other accomplishments are undone by subsequent administrators. In 2007 the student loan industry became embroiled in a major controversy when it was revealed that loan companies often have close and inappropriate ties with the government and university financial aid offices.[41] In other words, the delicate and long-standing balance between these constituencies was upset by a variety of unsavory practices, such as loan companies providing trips and other incentives to schools and financial aid advisers. The losers in this arrangement were parents and students, who were then steered toward unnecessarily large and expensive loans offered by gift-giving companies. In one particularly egregious example, Columbia University agreed to pay a fine of $1.1 million and fired its financial aid director who held more than $100,000 of stock in a lender he frequently recommended to students.[42] In the end, the controversy cost Theresa Shaw, the leader of the Office of Federal Student Aid, her job as well.[43]

At times agencies need not leaders who shake up internal operations but ones adept at attracting external support. Leaders who are savvy in this respect find it relatively easy to capture the attention and enthusiasm of not only the democratic public but agency bosses and clients as well. Generating favorable coverage in the mass media has become an essential component of this leadership skill. Positive reputations can enhance performance by making it easier, for example, for the organization to attract valuable resources and political capital.

- **PROPOSITION 12: AGENCIES WITH LEADERS WHO HAVE A FLAIR FOR PUBLICITY TEND TO PERFORM WELL.**

Jane Garvey, who led the Federal Aviation Administration from 1997 to 2002, attracted nationwide attention by vowing to be airborne when midnight struck on January 1, 2000. Her promise, which she kept with great fanfare, was broadcast on nightly news programs and reported in morning papers all across the country. Garvey's publicity stunt was substantively important because it helped reassure the public that the safety of air travel would be not be compromised by the year 2000 (Y2K) computer bug.[44] Overall, the agency's performance improved markedly during Garvey's tenure, as indicated by its jump from a C in 1999 to a B in 2002.

William Bratton, the only person ever to be the chief of police in both New York City and Los Angeles, is also a master of publicity. In both cities, he has used the media to cultivate a brash and bold style that attracts both admirers and detractors. In New York, he famously spearheaded a crackdown, with the encouragement of Mayor Rudy Giuliani, on the city's infamous "squeegee men" and other forms of petty criminal behavior. Upon arriving in Los Angeles, he colorfully informed the department's commanders that he would not tolerate opposition to his strategies: "If you don't want to work in the department, get the hell out."[45] Bratton's signature achievement—crime rates in New York City that plunged to their lowest levels in decades—is in no small part a reflection of his ability to capture external attention and support.

Bratton's successful track record demonstrates that leaders hold in their hands one of the keys to effective performance in executive branch bureaucracies. They cannot, however, unlock the door to praiseworthy outputs and outcomes on their own. Leadership does not operate in a vacuum but in a context colored by the tasks assigned to agencies and the level of political support provided by agency bosses and clients.

What this implies is that agencies favorably situated on multiple dimensions are especially well equipped to perform at a high level. The SSA embodies such an organization. The agency's primary task is to distribute money, a popular mission easily observable in terms of both outputs and outcomes. The diffuse support the agency receives provides the resources and political capital necessary to perform well across presidential administrations and changes in the Social Security program. So long as the agency's leadership does not get in the way, the SSA is likely to continue its record of success in the years and decades ahead.

## Bureaucracy in the Twenty-First Century

As seen from the outset, public bureaucracies are institutions of democratic policymaking that are constantly evolving and being transformed. Consider the prominent, and by now familiar, example of education reform.

Many education reforms have been tried in recent years, ranging from smaller classrooms to stronger testing requirements to school voucher programs enabling disadvantaged children to use public dollars to attend private schools. One innovation that has attracted considerable interest is **Success for All,** a comprehensive reform model for elementary schools initiated in Baltimore in 1987 and now utilized in approximately 1,300 U.S. schools in forty-six states.[46]

Success for All, which focuses primarily on reading, seeks to ensure that virtually every student will reach the third grade on schedule with adequate basic skills and will build on those skills throughout elementary school. Its

## Figure 7.2 Mean Reading Scores: Success for All Schools vs. Control Schools

Reading scores

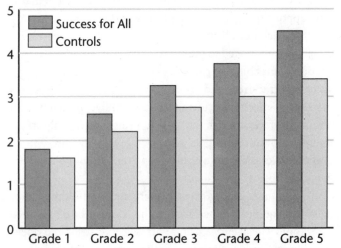

Source: Robert Slavin and Nancy Madden, "'Success for All' and African American and Latino Student Achievement," in *Bridging the Achievement Gap*, ed. John Chubb and Tom Loveless (Washington, D.C.: Brookings Institution Press, 2002), 80.

elements include a schoolwide curriculum, specially trained tutors, preschool and kindergarten programs, eight-week assessments of elementary school students, a family support team to work with parents, and a facilitator to help teachers implement the program.

A systematic comparison of Success for All schools with a group of control schools suggests that the program works. For each grade, from grade 1 through grade 5, Success for All students perform better on standardized reading tests than other students with similar socioeconomic backgrounds (see Figure 7.2). In general, numerous evaluations of Success for All have reached positive conclusions.[47] The program is especially noteworthy for its ability to improve the educational performance of African American and Latino students.[48]

The broader lesson is that bureaucratic innovations can make a difference. This is particularly encouraging in an area as challenging as elementary and secondary education. With ample opportunities for experimentation at the state and local levels, we should be able to determine which innovations work in an overall sense and which innovations are particularly advantageous for disadvantaged populations.

In bureaucratic policymaking, several broad trends encapsulate the changes that have been occurring recently and that will likely continue to occur in the years and decades ahead. First, the emergence of performance as a standard of evaluation has brought concepts from the private sector to bear on organizations at all levels of government. These concepts are articulated in actions such as the Government Performance and Results Act, which places great emphasis on strategic plans and the measurement and reporting of agency outputs and outcomes. There are, however, aspects of the movement toward performance that reflect the fact that bureaucracies are distinctly public institutions. For example, equity is an inescapable manifestation of performance for organizations charged with distributing and redistributing societal resources and with regulating the behavior of individuals, business firms, and other private actors.

Second, the authority vested in executive branch bureaucracies continues to increase, despite some appearances to the contrary. In his 1996 State of the Union address President Clinton declared, to much bipartisan applause, that "the era of big government is over." By only one measure is this claim sustainable. From 1968 to 2002 the number of full-time permanent civilian federal workers dropped from 2.3 million to 1.8 million.[49] Once the activities of institutions such as the **shadow government**—the nongovernmental positions created by public sector grants and contracts—are factored in, however, the size of the federal workforce exceeds 12 million. Add to this number the ever-burgeoning workforces at the state and local levels created to satisfy federal mandates, and the actual size of the federal workforce approaches 17 million.[50] Policymaking in the United States simply cannot be understood without paying close attention to executive branch organizations and their partners.

Third, as the bureaucracy continues to expand in scope and responsibility, the resulting organizational apparatus increasingly reflects a combination of hierarchical and network arrangements. Such a combination is certainly present in the newest federal agency, the Department of Homeland Security. The agency's leadership possesses stronger than normal authority to hire, fire, and reassign subordinate personnel. This authority provides principals inside and outside the department with an unusually robust way of dealing with adverse selection and moral hazard difficulties. At the same time, defending the nation's homeland inevitably entails public-private partnerships, such as those embodied in contracting-out relationships. Firms such as General Electric and L-3 Communications play a fundamental role in the area of transportation security by manufacturing the explosives detection devices that have been installed in airports in the aftermath of the September 11 terrorist attacks.

Fourth, public involvement in bureaucratic proceedings continues to evolve. During the past four decades, the portfolio of organized interests playing an active role in policymaking has diversified greatly. On the heels of this diversification has come a veritable revolution in the venues of public participation. The application of principles of bargaining and negotiation to the rulemaking process has been a significant addition in an area long governed by the notice and comment requirements of the Administrative Procedure Act. The Internet appears to be changing, at least in some ways, how agencies interact with the beneficiaries and targets of their activities.

In the face of all these changes, a set of analytical tools that transcends the particulars of agencies and policy areas is necessary to foster an ongoing understanding of the bureaucracy and its place in American democracy. The four social scientific frameworks presented here—bounded rationality, principal-agent theory, interest group mobilization, and network theory— offer just such an array of overarching perspectives. As the problems that agencies address, and the constellation of agencies themselves, evolve, these theoretical orientations toward the bureaucracy's people, bosses, clients, and networks will remain fruitful sources of guidance for students puzzling over policymaking inside the executive branch.

## Key Terms

Catalytic control, 212
Coercive control, 212
Communications, 208
Coordination, 208
Coping organization, 207
Credible commitment, 214
Federal Performance Project, 201
Hortatory control, 212
Internal Revenue Service
   Restructuring and Reform
   Act, 204
Leadership, 202

Missions, 205
National Center for Education
   Statistics, 205
Political support, 202
Production organization, 206
Regulatory czar, 214
Relationships, 202
Shadow government, 219
Success for All, 217
Tasks, 202
Tax gap, 204
Vision for Space Exploration, 206

# APPENDIX | Web Resources

## Agency Web Sites

These are particularly useful agency Web sites.

### Federal

CENTERS FOR DISEASE CONTROL AND PREVENTION (www.cdc.gov): This Web site provides information about diseases ranging from ADHD to tuberculosis, as well as links to vaccinations, safe food and water, and other travelers' health issues.

CENTERS FOR MEDICARE AND MEDICAID SERVICES (cms.hhs.gov): This Web site contains information about Medicare, Medicaid, and the State Children's Health Insurance Program.

DEPARTMENT OF AGRICULTURE (www.usda.gov): This Web site includes links to all of the offices, agencies, and mission areas of the department, including farm loans, child nutrition programs, and rural development.

DEPARTMENT OF HOMELAND SECURITY (www.dhs.gov): This Web site provides information about the color-coded national threat advisory, as well as how citizens, first responders, business, and all levels of government can enhance their emergency preparedness.

DEPARTMENT OF TRANSPORTATION'S DOCKET MANAGEMENT SYSTEM (dms.dot.gov): This Web site is where the Department of Transportation stores information about proposed and final regulations, copies of public comments on proposed rules, and many other useful documents.

ENVIRONMENTAL PROTECTION AGENCY (www.epa.gov): This Web site provides quick links to key topics such as asbestos, climate change, and enforcement.

FEDERAL COMMUNICATIONS COMMISSION (www.fcc.gov): This Web site provides information about the commissioners who are charged with regulating interstate and international communications by radio, television, wire, satellite, and cable, as well as upcoming meetings and auctions the commission holds to distribute licenses for the electromagnetic spectrum.

**FEDERAL EMERGENCY MANAGEMENT AGENCY** (www.fema.gov): This Web site contains a searchable map of counties that are currently designated for disaster and emergency assistance.

**FEDERAL RESERVE SYSTEM** (www.federalreserve.gov): This Web site provides access to the congressional testimony and public speeches of Federal Reserve officials, as well as information about monetary policy, banking regulation, and economic data and research.

**OFFICE OF MANAGEMENT AND BUDGET** (www.whitehouse.gov/omb): This Web site contains documents related to the president's budget and the management of agency regulatory activities, including letters that prompt agencies to initiate rulemakings and letters that return proposed rules to agencies for further consideration.

**U.S. EXECUTIVE BRANCH WEB SITES** (www.loc.gov/rr/news/fedgov .html): This Web site presents an official list of executive branch Web sites, including cabinet departments, independent agencies, and regulatory commissions.

## State

**CALIFORNIA STATE GOVERNMENT** (www.ca.gov/Government/State.html): This site features links to the governor's Web site, the online appointment system of the Department of Motor Vehicles, and state organizations and policies in areas ranging from business to health and safety.

**FLORIDA DEPARTMENT OF ENVIRONMENTAL PROTECTION** (www.dep .state.fl.us): This Web site provides information about breaking ecological news, the state's Clean Marina program, and opportunities for green lodging in Florida.

**MARYLAND DEPARTMENT OF HEALTH AND MENTAL HYGIENE** (www. dhmh.state.md.us): This Web site covers emerging issues such as bioterrorism, as well as traditional concerns such as nutrition, substance abuse, and the Medicaid program.

**NORTH CAROLINA STATE GOVERNMENT** (www.ncgov.com): This Web site provides a directory of all state agencies and departments, as well as access to a wide range of services for citizens and businesses.

## Research Web Sites

These are Web sites containing information that is useful across many policy domains.

*AEI-Brookings Joint Center for Regulatory Studies* (www.aei .brookings.org): This Web site, a joint effort on the part of the American Enterprise Institute and the Brookings Institution, provides analyses of existing regulatory programs and new regulatory proposals.

*Federal Advisory Committee Act Database* (fido.gov/facadatabase): This Web site contains information about the meetings, reports, and other activities of the nearly 1,000 advisory committees that operate in the executive branch.

*Federal Performance Project* (www.govexec.com/fpp/index.htm): This Web site contains the grades that the Federal Performance Project handed out to agencies, as well as articles that highlight particular success stories or examples of agencies that failed to measure up.

*Federal Register* (www.gpoaccess.gov/fr/index.html): This Web site provides access to every document published in the *Federal Register* since 1994.

*Government Accountability Office* (www.gao.gov): This Web site, which is updated daily, includes a list of Government Accountability Office reports on a plethora of topics as well as assessments of all major rules issued by federal agencies.

*Government Performance Project* (www.maxwell.syr.edu/gpp): This Web site contains a series of grade reports for the management capacity of the nation's 35 largest cities and 40 large counties.

*IBM Center for the Business of Government* (www.businessof government.org): This Web site publishes reports on public management, administrative leadership, performance measurement, and related issues. The goal of the center is to improve the business of government, in the United States and elsewhere.

*Library of Congress* (thomas.loc.gov): This Web site has information about legislative affairs, much of which pertains to the executive branch, including presidential nominations, appropriations bills, and delegations of authority from Congress to agencies.

**MERCATUS CENTER** (www.mercatus.org): This Web site provides links to research papers on a wide range of topics published by the Mercatus Center, which advances the idea of market-based solutions to public problems.

**RAND CORPORATION** (www.rand.org): This Web site presents the research of the RAND Corporation, a nonprofit organization that focuses on national security as well as business, education, health, law, and science.

**REGULATIONS.GOV** (www.regulations.gov): This Web site is a central clearinghouse for information about the regulatory activities of federal agencies.

# | NOTES

## Chapter 1

1. William Gormley Jr. and David Weimer, *Organizational Report Cards* (Cambridge: Harvard University Press, 1999).

2. Ling Gao, South Carolina Department of Education, personal communication with authors, April 27, 2007.

3. Eric Hanushek and Margaret Raymond, "Does School Accountability Lead to Improved Student Performance?" *Journal of Policy Analysis and Management* 24 (Spring 2005): 297–327.

4. Sam Dillon, "Most States Fail Demands Set Out in Education Law," *Washington Post*, July 25, 2006, Sec. A.

5. Maria Glod, "Educators Decry ESL Reading Ruling," *Washington Post*, October 29, 2006, Sec. C.

6. Maria Glod, "Fairfax Resists 'No Child' Provision," *Washington Post*, January 26, 2007, Sec. B.

7. Bill Turque, "Supervisors Step Up in 'No Child' Fight," *Washington Post* February 6, 2007, Sec. B.

8. Ibid.

9. Maria Glod, "Fairfax Schools Concede on Testing," *Washington Post*, April 19, 2007, Sec. B.

10. Richard Rothstein, cited in Beryl Radin, *Challenging the Performance Movement: Accountability, Complexity and Democratic Values* (Washington, D.C.: Georgetown University Press, 2006), 67.

11. Laura Hamilton, Mark Berends, and Brian Stecher, "Teachers' Responses to Standards- Based Accountability" (working paper WR-259 EDU, Santa Monica, Calif., RAND Corporation, April 2005).

12. Ibid., 30.

13. Ibid., 27–29.

14. Ibid., 30.

15. U.S. Food and Drug Administration, Office of Management, Budget Formulation and Presentation, www.fda.gov/oc/oms/ofm/budget/documentation.htm, May 2, 2007.

16. Robert Behn, *Rethinking Democratic Accountability* (Washington, D.C.: Brookings Institution Press, 2001).

17. Cornelius M. Kerwin, *Rulemaking: How Government Agencies Write Law and Make Policy*, 2d ed. (Washington, D.C.: CQ Press, 1999).

18. David Frederickson and H. George Frederickson, *Measuring the Performance of the Hollow State* (Washington, D.C.: Georgetown University Press, 2006), 132–137; see also James Q. Wilson, *Bureaucracy* (New York: Basic Books, 1989).

19. Barbara Romzek and Melvin Dubnick, "Accountability in the Public Sector: Lessons from the Challenger Tragedy," *Public Administration Review* 47 (May/June 1987): 229.

20. Ibid., 230.

21. William Gormley Jr., *Taming the Bureaucracy: Muscles, Prayers, and Other Strategies* (Princeton: Princeton University Press, 1989).

22. Steven J. Balla, "Administrative Procedures and Political Control of the Bureaucracy," *American Political Science Review* 92 (September 1998): 663–673.

23. John Brehm and Scott Gates, *Working, Shirking, and Sabotage* (Ann Arbor: University of Michigan Press, 1997).

24. Romzek and Dubnick, "Accountability in the Public Sector."

25. Joel D. Aberbach, *Keeping a Watchful Eye: The Politics of Congressional Oversight* (Washington, D.C.: Brookings Institution Press, 1990).

26. William Gormley Jr., "The Representation Revolution: Reforming State Government through Public Representation," *Administration and Society* 18 (August 1986): 179–196.

27. Paul C. Light, *The Tides of Reform: Making Government Work, 1945–1995* (New Haven: Yale University Press, 1997).

28. Gormley, "Representation Revolution"; Kathleen Bawn, "Political Control versus Expertise: Congressional Choices about Administrative Procedures," *American Political Science Review* 89 (March 1995): 62–73; David Epstein and Sharyn O'Halloran, "Administrative Procedures, Information, and Agency Discretion," *American Journal of Political Science* 38 (August 1994): 697–722.

29. Bob Woodward, *Maestro: Greenspan's Fed and the American Boom* (New York: Touchstone Books, 2001).

30. John M. Berry, "Nervous Eyes on Greenspan's Big Shoes," *Washington Post*, August 7, 2002.

31. Anne M. Khademian, *The SEC and Capital Market Regulation: The Politics of Expertise* (Pittsburgh: University of Pittsburgh Press, 1997).

32. Terry M. Moe, "The Politics of Structural Choice: Toward a Theory of Public Bureaucracy," in *Organization Theory: From Chester Barnard to the Present and Beyond*, ed. Oliver E. Williamson (New York: Oxford University Press, 1990).

33. Charles Goodsell, *The Case for Bureaucracy*, 3d ed. (Chatham, N.J.: Chatham House, 1994).

34. Justin Blum, "Anthrax Cited in 2 D.C. Postal Deaths," *Washington Post*, October 23, 2001, Sec. A.

35. Ben White, "Postmaster General Lauded Despite Mixed Performance," *Washington Post*, October 25, 2001, Sec. A.

36. U.S. Office of Management and Budget, *2006 Report to Congress on the Costs and Benefits of Federal Regulations and Unfunded Mandates on State, Local, and Tribal Entities*, www.whitehouse.gov/omb/inforeg/2006_cb/2006_cb_final_report.pdf.

37. Richard Nathan, introduction to *Quicker Better Cheaper? Managing Performance in American Government*, ed. Dall Forsythe (Albany, N.Y.: Rockefeller Institute Press, 2001).

38. U.S. General Accounting Office, *The Government Performance and Results Act: 1997 Governmentwide Implementation Will Be Uneven* (Washington, D.C.: GAO, 1997), 9.

39. U.S. General Accounting Office, *Managing for Results: Opportunities for Continued Improvements in Agencies' Performance Plans* (Washington, D.C.: GAO, 1999), 3.

40. Frederickson and Frederickson, *Measuring the Performance of the Hollow State*, 78.

41. See Radin, *Challenging the Performance Movement*, 159–163; see also U.S. General Accounting Office, *Results-Oriented Government: GPRA Has Established a Solid Foundation for Achieving Greater Results*, report no. 04-38 (Washington, D.C.: GAO, March 2004).

42. U.S. Office of Management and Budget and National Science Foundation, "Improving the Measurement of Program Effectiveness" (paper presented at OMB/NSF workshop Strengthening Program Effectiveness Measurement of Federal Programs, Arlington, Va., May 21, 2002).

43. John Gilmour, *Implementing OMB's Program Assessment Rating Tool (PART): Meeting the Challenges of Integrating Budget and Performance* (Washington, D.C.: IBM Center for the Business of Government, 2006), 12.

44. Ibid.

45. Ibid., 13.

46. John Gilmour and David Lewis, "Assessing Performance Budgeting at OMB: The Influence of Politics, Performance, and Program Size," *Journal of Public Administration Research and Theory* 16 (April 2006): 169–186.

47. John Gilmour and David Lewis, "Does Performance Budgeting Work?: An Examination of the Office of Management and Budget's PART Scores," *Public Administration Review* 66 (September/October 2006): 742–752.

48. *Performance and Purpose: Constituents Rate Government Agencies* (Washington, D.C.: Pew Research Center for the People and the Press, April 2000).

49. Senate Governmental Affairs Committee, *Reports on the Study of Federal Regulation* (Washington, D.C.: Government Printing Office, January/February 1997).

50. Bloomberg News, "Spitzer Criticizes SEC, Pitt," *Newsday*, July 26, 2002, 56.

51. Kathleen Day, "Harvey Pitt Raises a Promotion Commotion," *Washington Post*, July 25, 2002, Sec. E.

52. Guy Gugliotta, "New Staff, New Directions for NASA; Shake-Up is Part of Chief's Plan to Reach for the Moon (Again)," *Washington Post*, October 21, 2005, Sec. A.

53. Marc Kaufman, "NASA Looks to the Future With Eye on the Past," *Washington Post*, December 4, 2006, Sec. A.

54. Daniel P. Carpenter, *The Forging of Bureaucratic Autonomy: Reputations, Networks, and Policy Innovation in Executive Agencies, 1862–1928* (Princeton: Princeton University Press, 2001).

55. Ibid.

56. Eugene Lewis, *Public Entrepreneurship: Toward a Theory of Bureaucratic Practice* (Bloomington: Indiana University Press, 1980), 109.

57. Carpenter, *Forging of Bureaucratic Autonomy.*

## Chapter 2

1. William Gormley Jr., "Regulatory Enforcement: Accommodation and Conflict in Four States," *Public Administration Review* 57 (July/August 1997): 285–293.

2. Bryan Jones, Saadia Greenberg, Clifford Kaufman, and Joseph Drew, "Service Delivery Rules and the Distribution of Local Government Services: Three Detroit Bureaucracies," *Journal of Politics* 40 (May 1978): 332–368.

3. Gormley, "Regulatory Enforcement," 289.

4. Ibid.

5. Michael Powell, "N.Y. Rescuers Disorganized in 9/11 Attack," *Washington Post*, August 20, 2002, Sec. A.

6. Bryan Jones, *Politics and the Architecture of Choice: Bounded Rationality and Governance* (Chicago: University of Chicago Press, 2001).

7. Herbert Simon, *Administrative Behavior*, 4th ed. (New York: Free Press, 1997).

8. C. Edward Lindblom, "The Science of 'Muddling Through,'" *Public Administration Review* 29 (Spring 1959): 79–88.

9. John Kingdon, *Agendas, Alternatives, and Public Policies* (Boston: Little, Brown, 1995); Bryan Jones, Frank Baumgartner, and James True, "Policy Punctuation: U.S. Budget Authority, 1947–1995," *Journal of Politics* 60 (February 1998): 1–33.

10. George Akerlof, "The Market for Lemons," *Quarterly Journal of Economics* 84 (August 1970): 488–500; Burton Weisbrod, *The Nonprofit Economy* (Cambridge: Harvard University Press, 1988).

11. Simon, *Administrative Behavior*, 119.

12. Jonathan Bendor, *Parallel Systems: Redundancy in Government* (Berkeley: University of California Press, 1985), 85–118, 209–215.

13. Malcolm Sparrow, *The Regulatory Craft* (Washington, D.C.: Brookings Institution Press, 2000), 127.

14. J. Clarence Davies and Jan Mazurek, *Pollution Control in the United States* (Washington, D.C.: Resources for the Future, 1998), 59–63.

15. Simon, *Administrative Behavior*, 89.

16. Michael Lipsky, *Street-Level Bureaucracy* (New York: Russell Sage Foundation, 1980).

17. Robert Axelrod, *The Evolution of Cooperation* (New York: Basic Books, 1984), 73–87.

18. William Gormley Jr., *Everybody's Children: Child Care as a Public Problem* (Washington, D.C.: Brookings Institution Press, 1995), 113–117.

19. Jane Waldfogel, *The Future of Child Protection: How to Break the Cycle of Abuse and Neglect* (Cambridge: Harvard University Press, 1998), 148–151.

20. Jane Waldfogel, "The Future of Child Protection Revisited," in *Child Welfare Research*, ed. Duncan Lindsey and Aron Shlonsky (New York: Oxford University Press, forthcoming).

21. Ibid.

22. Sparrow, *Regulatory Craft*, 86–87.

23. Marsha Schachtel, "CitiStat and the Baltimore Neighborhood Indicators Alliance: Using Information to Improve Communication and Community," *National Civic Review* (Fall 2001): 253–265.

24. Robert Behn, "The Varieties of CitiStat," *Public Administration Review* 66 (May/June 2006): 332–40.

25. Ellen Perlman, "'Stat' Fever," *Governing* (January 2007): 48–50.

26. Simon, *Administrative Behavior*, 105.

27. Charles Perrow, *Normal Accidents: Living with High-Risk Technologies* (Princeton: Princeton University Press, 1999), 403.

28. Deborah Stone, *Policy Paradox: The Art of Political Decision Making* (New York: W. W. Norton, 2002), 256. It should be noted that Stone is describing, not endorsing, the rational choice model.

29. Simon, *Administrative Behavior*, 94.

30. Stone, *Policy Paradox*, 375.

31. Greenspan, quoted in Stone, *Policy Paradox*, 244.

32. Martha Feldman, *Order without Design: Information Production and Policy Making* (Stanford: Stanford University Press, 1989), 81, 106–114.

33. Jane Mansbridge, "The Rise and Fall of Self-Interest in the Explanation of Political Life," in *Beyond Self-Interest*, ed. Jane Mansbridge (Chicago: University of Chicago Press, 1990), 3–22.

34. Peter Clark and James Q. Wilson, "Incentive Systems: A Theory of Organizations," *Administrative Science Quarterly* 6 (September 1961): 129–166.

35. John Brehm and Scott Gates, *Working, Shirking, and Sabotage: Bureaucratic Response to a Democratic Public* (Ann Arbor: University of Michigan Press, 1997): 80–83.

36. Anthony Downs, *Inside Bureaucracy* (Boston: Little, Brown, 1967), 88.

37. Amartya Sen, "Rational Fools: A Critique of the Behavioral Foundations of Economic Theory," in Mansbridge, *Beyond Self-Interest*, 33.

38. Marissa Golden, *What Motivates Bureaucrats? Politics and Administration during the Reagan Years* (New York: Columbia University Press, 2000), 154–168.

39. Kenneth Meier, "Teachers, Students, and Discrimination: The Policy Impact of Black Representation," *Journal of Politics* 46 (February 1984): 252–263.

40. Thomas Dee, "A Teacher Like Me: Does Race, Ethnicity, or Gender Matter?" *American Economic Review* 95 (May 2005): 158–165.

41. Gormley, "Regulatory Enforcement."

42. Kenneth Meier and Jill Nicholson-Crotty, "Gender, Representative Bureaucracy, and Law Enforcement: The Case of Sexual Assault," *Public Administration Review* 66 (November/December 2006): 850–860.

43. Barry Rubin, *Secrets of State: The State Department and the Struggle over U.S. Foreign Policy* (New York: Oxford University Press, 1985), 124–129, 127.

44. Ibid., 127.

45. Joel Aberbach, Robert Putnam, and Bert Rockman, *Bureaucrats and Politicians in Western Democracies* (Cambridge: Harvard University Press, 1981), 84–112.

46. Amos Tversky and Daniel Kahneman, "Availability: A Heuristic for Judging Frequency and Probability," *Cognitive Psychology* 5 (1973): 207–232.

47. Perrow, *Normal Accidents,* 321.

48. Herbert Simon, "Why Public Administration?" *Journal of Public Administration Research and Theory* 8 (January 1998): 10.

49. Albert Hirschman, *Exit, Voice, and Loyalty* (Cambridge: Harvard University Press, 1970).

50. Herbert Kaufman, *The Forest Ranger* (Baltimore: Johns Hopkins University Press, 1960), 214–215.

51. Robert Katzmann, *Regulatory Bureaucracy: The Federal Trade Commission and Antitrust Policy* (Cambridge: MIT Press, 1980).

52. Simon, *Administrative Behavior,* 111.

53. Bendor, *Parallel Systems,* 117.

54. Anne Lamott, *Bird by Bird: Some Instructions on Writing and Life* (New York: Anchor Books, 1994), 18–19.

55. See Barry Rabe, "Power to the States: The Promise and Pitfalls of Decentralization," in *Environmental Policy in the 1990s,* 3d ed., ed. Norman J. Vig and Michael E. Kraft (Washington, D.C.: CQ Press, 1997), 35–36; see also Barry Rabe, "Permitting, Prevention, and Integration: Lessons from the States," in *Environmental Governance,* ed. Donald Kettl (Washington, D.C.: Brookings Institution Press, 2002), 14–57.

56. Sparrow, *Regulatory Craft,* 123–124.

57. A. Myrick Freeman III, "Economic Incentives and Environmental Regulation," in Vig and Kraft, *Environmental Policy,* 193.

58. Ibid., 191.

59. Nevada Barr, *Blind Descent* (New York: Putnam, 1998).

60. For more on the ethical implications of these choices, see William T. Gormley Jr., "Moralists, Pragmatists, and Rogues: Bureaucrats in Modern Mysteries," *Public Administration Review* 61 (March/April 2001): 184–193.

61. Eugene Bardach and Robert Kagan, *Going by the Book: The Problem of Regulatory Unreasonableness* (Philadelphia: Temple University Press, 1982).

62. Feldman, *Order without Design.*

63. Perrow, *Normal Accidents,* 170–231.

# Chapter 3

1. Cindy Skrzycki, "Aiming Rusty Legislative Artillery," *Washington Post,* March 6, 2001, Sec. E; Helen Dewar and Cindy Skrzycki, "Workplace Health Initiative Rejected," *Washington Post,* March 7, 2001, Sec. A; Helen Dewar and Cindy Skrzycki, "House Scraps Ergonomics Regulation," *Washington Post,* March 8, 2001, Sec. A.

2. Ellen Nakashima and Greg Schneider, "U.S. Likely to Miss Goal on Screening," *Washington Post,* November 28, 2001, Sec. A.

3. David Epstein and Sharyn O'Halloran, *Delegating Powers: A Transaction Cost Politics Approach to Policy Making under Separate Powers* (New York: Cambridge University Press, 1999).

4. Terry M. Moe, "The New Economics of Organization," *American Journal of Political Science* 28 (November 1984): 739–777; John D. Huber and Charles R. Shipan, "The Costs of Control: Legislators, Agencies, and Transaction Costs," *Legislative Studies Quarterly* 25 (February 2000): 25–52.

5. D. Roderick Kiewiet and Mathew D. McCubbins, *The Logic of Delegation: Congressional Parties and the Appropriations Process* (Chicago: University of Chicago Press, 1991).

6. Morris P. Fiorina, *Congress: Keystone of the Washington Establishment,* 2d ed. (New Haven: Yale University Press, 1989).

7. R. Douglas Arnold, *The Logic of Congressional Action* (New Haven: Yale University Press, 1990).

8. William Gormley Jr., "Regulatory Issue Networks in a Federal System," *Polity* 18 (Summer 1986): 595–620.

9. Ibid.

10. Lucy Drotning and Larry Rothenberg, "Predicting Bureaucratic Control: Evidence from the 1990 Clean Air Act Amendments," *Law and Policy Quarterly* 21 (January 1999): 1–20.

11. Ibid., 12.

12. The National Conference of State Legislatures provides information about session calendars, staff size, legislator compensation, and other salient characteristics on its Web site, www.ncsl.org/index.htm, January 18, 2007.

13. John D. Huber and Charles R. Shipan, *Deliberate Discretion? The Institutional Foundations of Bureaucratic Autonomy* (New York: Cambridge University Press, 2002).

14. Ibid., 7.

15. Ibid., 6.

16. State of Idaho Legislature, www.legislature.idaho.gov/about/citizenlegislature.htm, January 21, 2007.

17. Epstein and O'Halloran, *Delegating Powers.*

18. Ibid.

19. Morris P. Fiorina, "Congressional Control of the Bureaucracy: A Mismatch of Incentives and Capabilities," in *Congress Reconsidered,* 2d ed., ed. Lawrence C. Dodd and Bruce I. Oppenheimer (Washington, D.C.: CQ Press, 1981).

20. Richard E. Neustadt, *Presidential Power and the Modern Presidents: The Politics of Leadership from Roosevelt to Reagan* (New York: Free Press, 1990).

21. Fiorina, "Congressional Control of the Bureaucracy."

22. Terry M. Moe, "The Presidency and the Bureaucracy: The Presidential Advantage," in *The Presidency and the Political System,* 4th ed., ed. Michael Nelson (Washington, D.C.: CQ Press, 1995); Terry M. Moe and William G. Howell, "The Presidential Power of Unilateral Action," *Journal of Law, Economics, and Organization* 15 (March 1999): 132–179. For a much earlier yet similar argument, see Edward S. Corwin and Louis W. Koenig, *The Presidency Today* (New York: New York University Press, 1956).

23. Frank J. Murray, "Clinton's Executive Orders Still Are Packing a Punch; Other Presidents Issued More, but Many of His Are Sweeping," *Washington Times,* August 23, 1999, Sec. A.

24. Ibid.

25. William J. Olson and Alan Woll, "Executive Orders and National Emergencies: How Presidents Have Come to 'Run the Country' by Usurping Legislative Power," *Policy Analysis,* October 28, 1999.

26. James Risen and Eric Lichtblau, "Bush Lets U.S. Spy on Callers without Courts," *New York Times*, December 15, 2005, Sec. A.

27. Ibid.; Carol D. Leonnig, "Secret Court's Judges Were Warned about NSA Spy Data; Program May Have Led Improperly to Warrants," *Washington Post*, February 9, 2006, Sec. A.

28. Eric Lichtblau and David E. Sanger, "Administration Cites War Vote in Spying Case," *New York Times*, December 19, 2005, Sec. A.

29. David S. Broder, "Bucking Bush on Spying," *Washington Post*, February 9, 2006, Sec. A.; Charles Babington, "White House Working to Avoid Wiretap Probe; But Some Republicans Say Bush Must Be More Open about Eavesdropping Program," *Washington Post*, February 20, 2006, Sec. A.

30. Jonathan Weisman and Carol D. Leonnig, "No Compromise On Wiretap Bill; Focus Now on House Version," *Washington Post*, September 27, 2006, Sec. A.

31. Dan Eggen and Dafna Linzer, "Judge Rules against Wiretaps; NSA Program Called Unconstitutional," *Washington Post*, August 18, 2006, Sec. A.

32. Dan Eggen, "Court Will Oversee Wiretap Program; Change Does Not Settle Qualms about Privacy," *Washington Post*, January 18, 2007, Sec. A.

33. James Pfiffner, *The Modern Presidency* (New York: St. Martin's Press, 1994).

34. Ibid.

35. G. Calvin Mackenzie, *The Politics of Presidential Appointments* (New York: Free Press, 1981).

36. Ibid., 174.

37. G. Calvin Mackenzie, *Innocent until Nominated: The Breakdown of the Presidential Appointment Process* (Washington, D.C.: Brookings Institution Press, 2001).

38. Nolan McCarty and Rose Razaghian, "Advise and Consent: Senate Responses to Executive Branch Nominations, 1885–1996," *American Journal of Political Science* 43 (October 1999): 1122–1143.

39. B. Dan Wood and Richard W. Waterman, "The Dynamics of Political Control of the Bureaucracy," *American Political Science Review* 85 (September 1991): 801–828.

40. Linda L. Fisher, "Fifty Years of Presidential Appointments," in *The In-and-Outers: Presidential Appointees and Transient Government in Washington*, ed. G. Calvin Mackenzie (Baltimore: Johns Hopkins University Press, 1987).

41. Patricia W. Ingraham and Carolyn R. Ban, "Models of Public Management: Are They Useful to Federal Managers in the 1980s?" *Public Administration Review* 46 (March 1986): 152–160. See also Hugh Heclo, *A Government of Strangers: Executive Politics in Washington*, (Washington, D.C.: Brookings Institution Press, 1977).

42. Paul Blustein, "Treasury Bonds with Bono; Secretary and Rock Star Join in a Seriously Strange Tour of African Poverty," *Washington Post*, June 4, 2002, Sec. C.

43. Marilyn Weber Serafini, "Thompson Brings Pragmatic Approach to HHS," www.govexec.com/dailyfed/0201/020201nj.htm, May 2, 2007.

44. "Managing the Departments: Grades for Bush's Cabinet Secretaries," GovExec.com (National Journal Group), www.govexec.com/dailyfed/0103/012703nj2.htm, January 26, 2007.

45. J. Michael McGinnis, "Big Decision; How Your Weight Became a Federal Case," *Washington Post*, August 8, 2004, Sec. B.

46. Eliza Newlin Carney, "Rough Rider," GovExec.com (National Journal Group), www.govexec.com/features/1002/1002s5.htm, January 26, 2007.

47. Michael Abramowitz and Steve Vogel, "Army Chiefs Plead Ignorance, But Lawmakers Are Skeptical," *Washington Post*, March 6, 2007, Sec. A; Pauline Jelinek, "Army's Kiley Ousted in Walter Reed Furor," *Washington Post*, March 13, 2007, Sec. A.

48. See *Humphrey's Executor v. United States*, 295 U.S. 602 (1935).

49. Paul Kane and Dan Eggen, "Second Lawmaker Contacted Prosecutor," *Washington Post*, March 6, 2007, Sec. A.

50. Dan Eggen and Paul Kane, "Justice Dept. Would Have Kept 'Loyal' Prosecutors," *Washington Post,* March 16, 2007, Sec. A.

51. Ronald N. Johnson and Gary D. Libecap, *The Federal Civil Service System and the Problem of Bureaucracy: The Economics and Politics of Institutional Change* (Chicago: University of Chicago Press, 1994).

52. Paul C. Light, *The True Size of Government* (Washington, D.C.: Brookings Institution Press, 1999).

53. Patricia W. Ingraham, "Building Bridges or Burning Them? The President, the Appointees, and the Bureaucracy," *Public Administration Review* 47 (September–October 1987): 425–435.

54. Joel D. Aberbach and Bert A. Rockman, *In the Web of Politics: Three Decades of the U.S. Federal Executive* (Washington, D.C.: Brookings Institution Press, 2000).

55. "Division on Homeland Security Department: Labor Rights Issue Still a Stumbling Block," CNN.com: Inside Politics, www.cnn.com/2002/ALLPOLITICS/11/11/ homeland.security, November 11, 2002.

56. Robert Pear, "4 Unions Challenge Homeland Security Personnel Policies," *New York Times,* January 27, 2005, Sec. A.

57. Stephen Barr, "A Personnel Challenge at DHS," *Washington Post,* January 15, 2007, Sec. D.; Eric M. Weiss, "Appeals Court Vetoes Bush Plan to Alter U.S. Personnel Rules," *Washington Post,* June 28, 2006, Sec. A.

58. Richard H. Pildes and Cass R. Sunstein, "Reinventing the Regulatory State," *University of Chicago Law Review* 62 (Winter 1995): 1–129; William F. West, "The Institutionalization of Regulatory Review: Organizational Stability and Responsive Competence at OIRA," *Presidential Studies Quarterly* 35 (March 2005): 76–93.

59. William Gormley Jr., "Counterbureaucracies in Theory and Practice," *Administration and Society* 28 (November 1986): 275–298.

60. Steven Croley, "White House Review of Agency Rulemaking: An Empirical Investigation," *University of Chicago Law Review* 70 (Summer 2003): 821–885; Christopher C. DeMuth and Douglas H. Ginsburg, "White House Review of Agency Rulemaking," *Harvard Law Review* 99 (March 1986): 1075–1088; Pildes and Sunstein, "Reinventing the Regulatory State"; Mark Seidenfeld, "A Big Picture Approach to Presidential Influence on Agency Policy-Making," *Iowa Law Review* 80 (October 1994): 1–50.

61. E. Donald Elliott, "TQM-ing OMB: Or Why Regulatory Review under Executive Order 12,291 Works Poorly and What President Clinton Should Do about It," *Law and Contemporary Problems* 57 (Spring 1994): 167–184; Pildes and Sunstein, "Reinventing the Regulatory State."

62. Thomas O. McGarity, *Reinventing Rationality: The Role of Regulatory Analysis in the Federal Bureaucracy* (New York: Cambridge University Press, 1991); Stuart Shapiro, "Politics and Regulatory Policy Analysis," *Regulation* 29 (Summer 2006): 40–45.

63. Office of Management and Budget, "2006 Report to Congress on the Costs and Benefits of Federal Regulations and Unfunded Mandates on State, Local, and Tribal Entities," www.whitehouse.gov/omb/inforeg/2006_cb/2006_cb_final_report.pdf, January 29, 2007.

64. Judith A. Hermanson, "Regulatory Reform by Statute: The Implications of the Consumer Product Safety Commission's 'Offeror System,' " *Public Administration Review* 38 (March–April 1978): 151–155; Mathew D. McCubbins, Roger G. Noll, and Barry R. Weingast, "Administrative Procedures as Instruments of Political Control," *Journal of Law, Economics, and Organization* 3 (Fall 1987): 243–277.

65. William V. Roth Jr. and William H. Nixon, *The Power to Destroy* (New York: Atlantic Monthly Press, 1999).

66. Fiorina, "Congressional Control of the Bureaucracy."

67. Terry M. Moe, "The Politics of Bureaucratic Structure," in *Can the Government Govern?* ed. John E. Chubb and Paul E. Peterson (Washington, D.C.: Brookings Institution Press, 1989.)

68. Terry M. Moe, "The Politics of Structural Choice: Toward a Theory of Public Bureaucracy," in *Organization Theory: From Chester Barnard to the Present and Beyond*, ed. Oliver E. Williamson (New York: Oxford University Press, 1990).

69. Ibid., 125.

70. Ibid., 326.

71. David B. Spence, "Managing Delegation Ex Ante: Using Law to Steer Administrative Agencies," *Journal of Legal Studies* 28 (June 1999): 413–459.

72. Cornelius M. Kerwin, *Rulemaking: How Government Agencies Write Law and Make Policy*, 2d ed. (Washington, D.C.: CQ Press, 1999).

73. Mark H. Tessler, Federal Railroad Administration, interview by author, March 11, 2002.

74. Steven J. Balla, "Between Commenting and Negotiation: The Contours of Public Participation in Agency Rulemaking," *I/S: A Journal of Law and Policy* 1 (Winter 2005): 59–94.

75. Mathew D. McCubbins, Roger G. Noll, and Barry R. Weingast, "Structure and Process, Politics and Policy: Administrative Arrangements and the Political Control of Agencies," *Virginia Law Review* 75 (March 1989): 431–482.

76. Steven J. Balla and John R. Wright, "Interest Groups, Advisory Committees, and Congressional Control of the Bureaucracy," *American Journal of Political Science* 45 (October 2001): 799–812.

77. McCubbins, Noll, and Weingast, "Administrative Procedures."

78. David B. Spence, "Managing Delegation Ex Ante: Using Law to Steer Administrative Agencies," *Journal of Legal Studies* 28 (June 1999): 413–459.

79. McCubbins, Noll, and Weingast, "Administrative Procedures."

80. David B. Spence, "Agency Policy Making and Political Control: Modeling Away the Delegation Problem," *Journal of Public Administration Research and Theory* 7 (April 1997): 199–219.

81. Balla, "Between Commenting and Negotiation."

82. Morris S. Ogul and Bert A. Rockman, "Overseeing Oversight: New Departures and Old Problems," *Legislative Studies Quarterly* 15 (February 1990): 5–24.

83. John F. Bibby, "Oversight and the Need for Congressional Reform," in *Republican Papers*, ed. Melvin R. Laird (Garden City, N.Y.: Anchor Books, 1968).

84. Joel D. Aberbach, *Keeping a Watchful Eye: The Politics of Legislative Oversight* (Washington, D.C.: Brookings Institution Press, 1990).

85. Ibid.

86. Richard F. Fenno Jr., *Learning to Govern: An Institutional View of the 104th Congress* (Washington, D.C.: Brookings Institution Press, 1997).

87. Carol Leonnig and Amy Goldstein, "Libby Guilty on 4 of 5 Counts," *Washington Post*, March 7, 2007, Sec. A.

88. Mathew D. McCubbins and Thomas Schwartz, "Congressional Oversight Overlooked: Police Patrols versus Fire Alarms," *American Journal of Political Science* 28 (February 1984): 165–179.

89. Steven J. Balla and Christopher J. Deering, "Police Patrols and Fire Alarms: An Examination of the Legislative Preference for Oversight" (unpublished manuscript).

90. Terry M. Moe, "An Assessment of the Positive Theory of 'Congressional Dominance,'" *Legislative Studies Quarterly* 12 (November 1987): 475–520.

91. James F. Spriggs II, "The Supreme Court and Federal Administrative Agencies: A Resource-Based Theory and Analysis of Judicial Impact," *American Journal of Political Science* 40 (November 1996): 1122–1151.

92. Christopher Banks, *Judicial Politics in the D.C. Circuit Court* (Baltimore: Johns Hopkins University Press, 1999).

93. Ibid., 42.

94. Ibid., 45, 82.

95. *Greater Boston Television Corp. v. Federal Communications Commission*, 444 F. 2d 841 (D.C. Cir. 1970).

96. *International Harvester Co. v. Ruckelshaus*, 478 F. 2d 615 (D.C. Cir. 1973).

97. Banks, *Judicial Politics*, 44.

98. *Vermont Yankee Nuclear Power Corp. v. Natural Resources Defense Council, Inc.*, 435 U.S. 519 (1978).

99. See, for example, *Motor Vehicle Manufacturers Association of the U.S. v. State Farm Mutual Automobile Insurance Co. et al.*, 463 U.S. 29 (1983).

100. Charles Lane, "Clean-Air Authority of EPA Is Upheld," *Washington Post*, February 28, 2001, Sec. A; *EPA v. American Trucking Associations, Inc. et al.*, 531 U.S. 457 (2001).

101. *Chevron U.S.A., Inc. v. Natural Resources Defense Council, Inc.*, 467 U.S. 837 (1984).

102. Reginald Sheehan, "Administrative Agencies and the Court: A Reexamination of the Impact of Agency Type on Decisional Outcomes," *Western Political Quarterly* 43 (December 1990): 875–885.

103. John R. Wright, *Interest Groups and Congress: Lobbying, Contributions, and Influence* (Boston: Allyn and Bacon, 1996).

104. Mancur Olson, *The Logic of Collective Action: Public Goods and the Theory of Groups* (Cambridge: Harvard University Press, 1965).

105. Helen Dewar, "Senate Passes Homeland Security Bill: Bush Calls Step 'Historic and Bold,' " *Washington Post*, November 20, 2002, Sec. A.

106. James T. Hamilton and Christopher H. Schroeder, "Strategic Regulators and the Choice of Rulemaking Procedures: The Selection of Formal vs. Informal Rules in Regulating Hazardous Waste," *Law and Contemporary Problems* 57 (Spring 1994): 111–160.

107. John Brehm and Scott Gates, *Working, Shirking, and Sabotage: Bureaucratic Response to a Democratic Public* (Ann Arbor: University of Michigan Press, 1997).

## Chapter 4

1. Scott Baldauf, "Fires Force US to Stretch for Crews," *Christian Science Monitor*, August 21, 2000, 1; Andrew Gumbel, "Singed Bear Cub Survives Forest Wildfires," *Independent*, August 22, 2000, 10.

2. Jim Robbins, "Logging Plan for West's Burned Forests Incites a Debate," *New York Times*, July 22, 2001, Sec. A; Todd Wilkinson, "Move to Log Fire-Damaged Trees Ignites Controversy," *Christian Science Monitor*, December 17, 2001, 2.

3. "Mission, Motto, Vision, and Guiding Principles," U.S. Department of Agriculture, Forest Service, www.fs.fed.us/aboutus/mission.shtml, February 12, 2007.

4. Katharine Q. Seelye, "U.S. Approves Timber Sale, Prompting Court Challenge," *New York Times*, December 18, 2001, Sec. A; Bill McAllister, "Forest Service Sued over Logging," *Denver Post*, December 19, 2001, Sec. A; Elizabeth Shogren, "Timber Sale Stalled to Allow Appeal," *Los Angeles Times*, December 20, 2001, Sec. A.

5. Eric Pianin, "Settlement Is Reached in Sale of Charred Trees," *Washington Post*, February 8, 2002, Sec. A; Jim Robbins, "Forest Service and Environmentalists Settle Logging Dispute," *New York Times*, February 8, 2002, Sec. A.

6. James Q. Wilson, "The Politics of Regulation," in *The Politics of Regulation*, ed. James Q. Wilson (New York: Basic Books, 1980); James Q. Wilson, *Bureaucracy: What Government Agencies Do and Why They Do It* (New York: Basic Books, 1989).

7. Frank R. Baumgartner and Bryan D. Jones, *Agendas and Instability in American Politics* (Chicago: University of Chicago Press, 1993).

8. Lawrence S. Rothenberg, *Regulation, Organizations, and Politics: Motor Freight Policy at the Interstate Commerce Commission* (Ann Arbor: University of Michigan Press, 1994).

9. Wilson, "Politics of Regulation"; Wilson, *Bureaucracy*.

10. Ibid.

11. Kathleen Day and James V. Grimaldi, "Lay's Lobbying Reached the Top of Treasury; Enron Chief Leaned Hard as Company Sought to Avoid U.S. Oversight of Derivatives Deals," *Washington Post*, February 21, 2002, Sec. E.

12. Samuel P. Huntington, "The Marasmus of the ICC: The Commission, the Railroads, and the Public Interest," *Yale Law Journal* 62 (April 1952): 467–509; Grant McConnell, *Private Power and American Democracy* (New York: Knopf, 1966).

13. Kay Lehman Schlozman and John T. Tierney, *Organized Interests and American Democracy* (New York: Harper and Row, 1986).

14. Baumgartner and Jones, *Agendas and Instability in American Politics*.

15. This period of inactivity may soon come to an end. Paul Guinnessy, "Stronger Future for Nuclear Power," PhysicsToday.org, www.physicstoday.org/vol-59/iss-2/p19.html, February 12, 2007. Dan Morgan, "Restarting Reactor Could Boost Nuclear Power Industry: TVA Board to Vote on $1.7 Billion Proposal to Switch on Mothballed Unit in Alabama," *Washington Post*, May 16, 2002, Sec. A.

16. Charles O. Jones, "American Politics and the Organization of Energy Decision Making," in *Annual Review of Energy*, ed. Jack M. Hollander, Melvin K. Simmons, and David O. Wood (Palo Alto, Calif.: Annual Reviews, 1979).

17. Hugh Heclo, "Issue Networks in the Executive Establishment," in *The New American Political System*, ed. Anthony King (Washington, D.C.: American Enterprise Institute, 1978).

18. Elaine B. Sharp, "The Dynamics of Issue Expansion: Cases from Disability Rights and Fetal Research Controversy," *Journal of Politics* 56 (November 1994): 919–939.

19. Rick Weiss, "House Passes Bill Relaxing Limits on Stem Cell Research," *Washington Post*, January 12, 2007, Sec. A.

20. Cornelius M. Kerwin, *Rulemaking: How Government Agencies Write Law and Make Policy*, 3d ed. (Washington, D.C.: CQ Press, 2003).

21. Each of the fifty states and the District of Columbia have their own administrative procedure acts, which govern rulemaking within their jurisdictions.

22. Steven J. Balla, "Between Commenting and Negotiation: The Contours of Public Participation in Agency Rulemaking," *I/S: A Journal of Law and Policy* 1 (Winter 2005): 59–94; Kerwin, *Rulemaking*.

23. Schlozman and Tierney, *Organized Interests and American Democracy*.

24. Major rules are cataloged by the General Accounting Office at http://www.gao.gov, February 15, 2007.

25. U.S. General Accounting Office, *Congressional Review Act* (Washington, D.C.: GAO, 1997).

26. U.S. General Accounting Office, *Food and Drug Administration: Regulation of Tobacco Products* (Washington, D.C.: GAO, 1997).

27. Steven J. Balla and Benjamin M. Daniels, "Information Technology and Public Commenting on Agency Regulations," *Regulation and Governance* 1 (March 2007): 46–67.

28. Balla and Daniels, "Information Technology and Public Commenting on Agency Regulations"; Scott R. Furlong and Cornelius M. Kerwin, "Interest Group Participation in Rule Making: A Decade of Change," *Journal of Public Administration Research and Theory* 15 (July 2005): 353–370; Jason Webb Yackee and Susan Webb Yackee, "A Bias toward Business? Assessing Interest Group Influence on the U.S. Bureaucracy," *Journal of Politics* 68 (February 2006): 128–139.

29. Marissa Martino Golden, "Interest Groups in the Rule-Making Process: Who Participates? Whose Voices Get Heard?" *Journal of Public Administration Research and Theory* 8 (April 1998): 245–270.

30. Ibid.

31. Stuart W. Shulman, "An Experiment in Digital Government at the United States National Organic Program," *Agriculture and Human Values* 20 (Fall 2003): 253–265.

32. Jason Webb Yackee and Susan Webb Yackee, "A Bias Toward Business?"; Susan Webb Yackee, "Sweet-Talking the Fourth Branch: The Influence of Interest Group Comments on Federal Agency Rulemaking," *Journal of Public Administration Research and Theory* 16 (January 2006): 103–124.

33. Marissa Martino Golden, "Interest Groups in the Rule-Making Process"; Kerwin, *Rulemaking;* Wesley A. Magat, Alan J. Krupnick, and Winston Harrington, *Rules in the Making: A Statistical Analysis of Regulatory Agency Behavior* (Washington, D.C.: Resources for the Future, 1986); David C. Nixon, Robert M. Howard, and Jeff DeWitt, "With Friends Like These: Rule-Making Comment Submissions to the Securities and Exchange Commission," *Journal of Public Administration Research and Theory* 12 (January 2002): 59–76.

34. William F. West, "Formal Procedures, Informal Processes, Accountability, and Responsiveness in Bureaucratic Policy Making: An Institutional Policy Analysis," *Public Administration Review* 64 (January/February 2004): 67.

35. Philip J. Harter, "Negotiated Rulemaking: A Cure for Malaise," *Georgetown Law Journal* 71 (December 1982): 1–113.

36. Kerwin, *Rulemaking;* Cornelius M. Kerwin and Scott R. Furlong, "Time and Rulemaking: An Empirical Test of Theory," *Journal of Public Administration Research and Theory* 2 (April 1992): 113–138.

37. Neil Eisner, "Regulatory Negotiation: A Real World Experience," *Federal Bar News and Journal* 31 (November 1984): 371–376.

38. Department of Transportation, Federal Aviation Administration, "Notice of Establishment of Advisory Committee for Regulatory Negotiation and Notice of First Meeting," *Federal Register,* June 28, 1983, 29771.

39. The Committee Management Secretariat of the General Services Administration maintains an online database pertaining to advisory committees at http://fido.gov/facadatabase/, March 6, 2007.

40. Mark P. Petracca. "Federal Advisory Committees, Interest Groups, and the Administrative State," *Congress and the Presidency* 13 (Spring 1986): 83–114.

41. Steven J. Balla and John R. Wright, "Can Advisory Committees Facilitate Congressional Oversight of the Bureaucracy?" in *Congress on Display, Congress at Work,* ed. William T. Bianco (Ann Arbor: University of Michigan Press, 2000), 167–188.

42. Petracca, "Federal Advisory Committees, Interest Groups, and the Administrative State."

43. Lawrence Susskind and Gerard McMahon, "The Theory and Practice of Negotiated Rulemaking," *Yale Journal on Regulation* 3 (Fall 1985): 133–165.

44. Harter, "Negotiated Rulemaking."

45. Cary Coglianese, "Assessing Consensus: The Promise and Performance of Negotiated Rulemaking," *Duke Law Journal* 46 (April 1997): 1255–1349.

46. Steven J. Balla and John R. Wright, "Consensual Rule Making and the Time It Takes to Develop Rules," in *Politics, Policy, and Organizations: Frontiers in the Scientific Study of the Bureaucracy,* ed. George A. Krause and Kenneth J. Meier (Ann Arbor: University of Michigan Press, 2003), 187–206.

47. Laura I. Langbein and Cornelius M. Kerwin, "Regulatory Negotiation versus Conventional Rule Making: Claims, Counterclaims, and Empirical Evidence," *Journal of Public Administration Research and Theory* 10 (July 2000): 599–632.

48. Coglianese, "Assessing Consensus."

49. Department of Transportation, Federal Railroad Administration, "Use of Locomotive Horns at Highway-Rail Grade Crossings," *Federal Register,* March 22, 2000, 15298; Mark H. Tessler, Federal Railroad Administration, interview by Balla, March 11, 2002.

50. Department of Transportation, Federal Railroad Administration, "Use of Locomotive Horns at Highway-Rail Grade Crossings," *Federal Register,* January 13, 2000, 2229.

51. Railton Roy (letter to Department of Transportation, January 20, 2000), http://dmses.dot.gov/docimages/pdf42/70969_web.pdf, March 3, 2003.

52. Department of Transportation, Federal Railroad Administration, "Use of Locomotive Horns at Highway-Rail Grade Crossings," *Federal Register,* December 18, 2003, 70586–70687.

53. Michael Grunwald, "Growing Pains in Southwest Florida," *Washington Post,* June 25, 2002, Sec. A.

54. Ibid. See also "Explore FGCU: Historical Perspective," www.fgcu.edu/info/HistoricalPerspective.asp, October 23, 2002.

55. Roger Faith, Donald Leavens, and Robert Tollison, "Antitrust Pork Barrel," *Journal of Law and Economics* 25 (October 1982): 329–342.

56. John Scholz and Feng Heng Wei, "Regulatory Enforcement in a Federalist System," *American Political Science Review* 80 (December 1986): 1249–1270.

57. Alan Sipress, "Open Call from the Patent Office; Agency Web Site Will Solicit Advice," *Washington Post,* March 5, 2007, Sec. A.

58. Information about the project can be found at "Peer to Patent Project: Community Patent Review," http://dotank.nyls.edu/communitypatent/, March 8, 2007.

59. Sipress, "Open Call from the Patent Office."

60. Ibid.

61. Cary Coglianese, "E-Rulemaking: Information Technology and Regulatory Policy," www.ksg.harvard.edu/press/E-Rulemaking_Report.pdf, March 8, 2007.

62. Stephen M. Johnson, "The Internet Changes Everything: Revolutionizing Public Participation and Access to Government Information through the Internet," *Administrative Law Review* 50 (Spring 1998): 277–337.

63. Kevin A. Hill and John E. Hughes, *Cyberpolitics: Citizen Activism in the Age of the Internet* (Lanham, Md.: Rowman and Littlefield, 1998); Elaine Ciulla Kamarck and Joseph S. Nye, eds., *Democracy.com?: Governance in a Networked World* (Hollis, N.H.: Hollis, 1999); Michael Margolis and David Resnick, *Politics as Usual: The Cyberspace "Revolution"* (Thousand Oaks, Calif.: Sage, 2000).

64. Peter M. Shane, *Democracy Online: The Prospects for Political Renewal Through the Internet* (New York: Routledge, 2004).

65. Darrell M. West, *Digital Government: Technology and Public Sector Performance* (Princeton: Princeton University Press, 2005).

66. Ibid.

67. "Federal Rulemaking: Agencies' Use of Information Technology to Facilitate Public Participation," U.S. General Accounting Office, June 30, 2000, www.gao.gov, May 22, 2003.

68. Balla and Daniels, "Information Technology and Public Commenting on Agency Regulations."

69. Executive Office of the President, Office of Management and Budget, *The President's Management Agenda,* www.whitehouse.gov/omb/budget/fy2002/mgmt.pdf, March 9, 2007; see also www.regulations.gov/fdmspublic/component/main, March 9, 2007.

70. Jason Miller, "Regulations.gov to Nearly Triple Number of Rules Posted," *Government Computer News,* January 23, 2007, www.gcn.com/online/vol1_no1/42993-1.html, March 9, 2007.

71. Department of Transportation, Federal Aviation Administration, "Small-Scale Rockets, Notice of Public Meeting," *Federal Register,* December 30, 1999, 73597–73599.

72. Thomas C. Beierle, "Democracy On-Line: An Evaluation of the National Dialogue on Public Involvement in EPA Decisions," www.rff.org/Documents/RFF-RPT-demonline.pdf, March 12, 2007.

73. Ibid.

74. Jane E. Fountain, *Building the Virtual State: Information Technology and Institutional Change* (Washington, D.C.: Brookings Institution Press, 2001).

75. Jonathan Rauch, *Demosclerosis: The Silent Killer of American Government* (New York: Times Books, 1994).

76. Jeffrey H. Birnbaum, "Washington's Power 25: Which Pressure Groups Are Best at Manipulating the Laws We Live By? A Groundbreaking Fortune Survey Reveals Who Belongs to Lobbying's Elite and Why They Wield So Much Clout," CNNMoney.com, http://money.cnn.com/magazines/fortune/fortune_archive/1997/12/08/234927/index.htm, March 5, 2007.

77. Scott Hovanyetz, "FTC: No Campaign to Promote National DNC List," dmNews.com, www.dmnews.com/cms/dm-news/teleservices/20155.html, March 5, 2007.

78. Wilson, *Bureaucracy*.

79. Joel Aberbach and Bert Rockman, *In the Web of Politics: Three Decades of the U.S. Federal Executive* (Washington, D.C.: Brookings Institution Press, 2000).

80. Susan E. Dudley, "Reversing Midnight Regulations," *Regulation* 24 (Spring 2001): 9.

81. Ibid.

82. Ibid.

83. C. Edward Lindblom, *Politics and Markets* (New York: Basic Books, 1977), 5.

84. William T. Gormley Jr., "A Test of the Revolving Door Hypothesis at the FCC," *American Journal of Political Science* 23 (November 1979): 665–683.

85. Judith Layzer, *The Environmental Case: Translating Values into Policy* (Washington, D.C.: CQ Press, 2002).

86. Ibid., 308.

87. Maureen Cropper, "The Determinants of Pesticide Regulation," *Journal of Political Economy* 100 (February 1992): 175–197.

88. William T. Gormley Jr., *The Politics of Public Utility Regulation* (Pittsburgh: University of Pittsburgh Press, 1983).

89. Evan Ringquist, *Environmental Protection at the State Level* (Armonk, N.Y.: M. E. Sharpe, 1993).

90. Finley Peter Dunne, as quoted in Bill Kovach and Tom Rosenstiel, "Are Watchdogs an Endangered Species?" *Columbia Journalism Review* 40 (May/June 2001): 50.

91. Layzer, *Environmental Case*, 107.

92. Paul Sabatier, John Loomis, and Catherine McCarthy, "Hierarchical Controls, Professional Norms, Local Constituencies, and Budget Maximization: An Analysis of U.S. Forest Service Planning Decisions," *American Journal of Political Science* 39 (February 1995): 204–242.

93. Joshua D. Clinton and David E. Lewis, "Expert Opinion, Agency Characteristics and Agency Preferences," unpublished manuscript, Princeton University.

94. Sally Cohen, *Championing Child Care* (New York: Columbia University Press, 2001).

95. Ibid.

96. Anne Camissa, *Governments as Interest Groups: Intergovernmental Lobbying and the Federal System* (Westport, Conn.: Praeger, 1995).

97. Helen Boutrous, "Presidential Influence and Regulatory Review" (Ph.D. diss., Government Department, Georgetown University, 2002), 123.

98. Committee Management Secretariat of the General Services Administration online database, http://fido.gov/facadatabase/, May 2, 2007.

99. William T. Gormley Jr., "Money and Mandates: The Politics of Intergovernmental Conflict," *Publius: The Journal of Federalism* 36 (Fall 2006): 523–540.

100. William Gormley Jr., "An Evolutionary Approach to Federalism in the U.S." (paper presented at the annual meeting of the American Political Science Association, San Francisco, August 31, 2001).

101. Gormley, "Money and Mandates," 523–540.

102. Cathleen Willging, Rafael Semansky, and Howard Waitzkin, "New Mexico's Medicaid Managed Care Waiver: Organizing Input from Mental Health Consumers and Advocates," *Psychiatric Services* 54 (March 2003): 289–291.

103. E. E. Schattschneider, *The Semi-Sovereign People* (New York: Holt, Rinehart, and Winston, 1960).

104. Henry Eichel, "Appeals Court Bars Blockade of Plutonium," *Charlotte Observer*, August 7, 2002, Sec. A.

105. David Firestone, "South Carolina Battles U.S. on Plutonium," *New York Times*, April 12, 2002, Sec. A.

106. Steven J. Balla, "Administrative Procedures and Political Control of the Bureaucracy," *American Political Science Review* 92 (September 1998): 663–673.

# Chapter 5

1. Lester Salamon, *America's Nonprofit Sector* (New York: Foundation Center, 1992), 65.

2. H. Brinton Milward, "Symposium on the Hollow State," *Journal of Public Administration Research and Theory* 6 (April 1996): 193–195.

3. E. S. Savas, *Privatization: The Key to Better Government* (Chatham, N.J.: Chatham House, 1987); William Gormley Jr., "The Privatization Controversy," in *Privatization and Its Alternatives*, ed. William Gormley Jr. (Madison: University of Wisconsin Press, 1991), 3–16; and Harvey Feigenbaum, Jeffrey Henig, and Chris Hamnett, *Shrinking the State: The Political Underpinnings of Privatization* (Cambridge: Cambridge University Press, 1998).

4. Laurence O'Toole, "Treating Networks Seriously: Practical and Research-Based Agendas in Public Administration," *Public Administration Review* 57 (January/February 1997): 45–52.

5. Robert Agranoff, "Inside Collaborative Networks: Ten Lessons for Public Managers," *Public Administration Review* 66 (December 2006, special issue), 57.

6. Ibid.

7. Mark Granovetter, "The Strength of Weak Ties," *American Journal of Sociology* 78 (May 1973): 1360–1380.

8. Edward O. Laumann and David Knoke, *The Organizational State: Social Choice in National Policy Domains* (Madison: University of Wisconsin Press, 1987), 206–225.

9. Keith Provan and H. Brinton Milward, "A Preliminary Theory of Interorganizational Network Effectiveness: A Comparative Study of Four Community Mental Health Systems," *Administrative Science Quarterly* 40 (March 1995): 1–33; O'Toole, "Treating Networks Seriously."

10. Walter J. M. Kickert, Erik-Hans Klijn, and Joop F. M. Koppenjan, "Introduction: A Management Perspective on Policy Networks," in *Managing Complex Networks: Strategies for the Public Sector*, ed. Walter J. M. Kickert, Erik-Hans Klijn, and Joop F. M. Koppenjan (London: Sage Publications, 1997), 7–11; Paul Posner, "Accountability Challenges of Third-Party Government," in *The Tools of Government: A Guide to the New Governance*, ed. Lester Salamon (New York: Oxford University Press, 2002), 546.

11. Keith Provan and H. Brinton Milward, "Do Networks Really Work? A Framework for Evaluating Public-Sector Organizational Networks," *Public Administration Review* 61 (July/August 2001): 416.

12. John Scott, *Social Network Analysis: A Handbook*, 2d ed. (Beverly Hills, Calif.: Sage Publications, 2001), 82, 71.

13. Catherine Alter and Jerald Hage, *Organizations Working Together* (Newbury Park, Calif.: Sage Publications, 1993), 155, 157.

14. We are indebted to Brint Milward for bringing this concept to our attention.

15. Alter and Hage, *Organizations Working Together*, 158.

16. Ibid., 163.

17. Joop Koppenjan and Erik-Hans Klijn, *Managing Uncertainties in Networks: A Network Approach to Problem Solving and Decision Making* (New York: Routledge, 2004), 19–38.

18. Ibid., 7.

19. H. Brinton Milward and Keith Provan, *A Manager's Guide to Choosing and Using Collaborative Networks* (Washington, D.C.: IBM Center for the Business of Government, 2006), 19.

20. Malcolm Sparrow, "The Application of Network Analysis to Criminal Intelligence: An Assessment of the Prospects," *Social Networks* 13 (September 1991): 266.

21. Valdis Krebs, "Mapping Networks of Terrorist Cells," *Connections* 24 (Winter 2001): 43–52, 46.

22. Richard Rothenberg, "From Whole Cloth: Making Up the Terrorist Network," *Connections* 24 (Winter 2001): 37.

23. Lester Salamon, "The New Governance and the Tools of Public Action: An Introduction," in Salamon, *Tools of Government*, 1–47.

24. Ibid., 24–37.

25. Ibid., 2.

26. Posner, "Accountability Challenges of Third-Party Government," 528–532.

27. Walter Zelman and Robert Berenson, *The Managed Care Blues and How to Cure Them* (Washington, D.C.: Georgetown University Press, 1998), 142–145.

28. O'Toole, "Treating Networks Seriously."

29. Thad Hall and Laurence O'Toole Jr., "Shaping Formal Networks through the Regulatory Process" (paper presented at the annual meeting of the American Political Science Association, Boston, August 30, 2002), 5, 27.

30. H. George Frederickson, "The Repositioning of American Public Administration," *PS: Political Science and Politics* 32 (December 1999): 705; Koppenjan and Klijn, *Managing Uncertainties in Networks*.

31. O'Toole, "Treating Networks Seriously," 45.

32. Denise Scheberle, *Federalism and Environmental Policy* (Washington, D.C.: Georgetown University Press, 1997), 13–14.

33. U.S. Environmental Protection Agency, *Reinventing Environmental Protection: 1998 Annual Report* (Washington, D.C.: EPA, March 1999), 26.

34. National Academy of Public Administration, *Environment.gov* (Washington, D.C.: NAPA, 2000), 135–153.

35. Barry Rabe, "Power to the States: The Promise and Pitfalls of Devolution," in *Environmental Policy: New Directions for the Twenty-First Century,* ed. Norman Vig and Michael Kraft (Washington, D.C.: CQ Press, 2000), 43.

36. William Gormley Jr., *Taming the Bureaucracy: Muscles, Prayers, and Other Strategies* (Princeton: Princeton University Press, 1989), 3–31, 173–193.

37. Mark Lubell et al., "Watershed Partnerships and the Emergence of Collective Action Institutions," *American Journal of Political Science* 46 (January 2002): 148–163.

38. Ibid., 158.

39. Ayşin Dedekorkut, "Suwannee River Partnership: Representation Instead of Regulation," in *Adaptive Governance and Water Conflict: New Institutions for Collaborative Planning,* ed. John T. Scholz and Bruce Stiftel (Washington, D.C.: Resources for the Future Press, 2005), 25–39.

40. Ibid., 36.

41. Ibid., 31.

42. William Gormley Jr., "An Evolutionary Approach to Federalism in the U.S." (paper presented at the annual meeting of the American Political Science Association, San Francisco, August 31, 2001).

43. Centers for Medicare and Medicaid Services, *The State Children's Health Insurance Program: Annual Enrollment Reports* (Baltimore: CMS, February 6, 2002).

44. Dan Morgan, "States Given Breaks on Medicaid Funding Loophole," *Washington Post*, November 4, 2000, Sec. A.

45. Tara O'Toole, "Institutional Issues in Biodefense," in *Governance and Public Security*, ed. Alasdair Roberts (Syracuse, N.Y.: Campbell Public Affairs Institute, 2002), 98–110.

46. Lawrence K. Altman and Gina Kolata, "A Nation Challenged: Anthrax Missteps Offer Guide to Fight Next Bioterror Battle," *New York Times*, January 6, 2002, Sec. A.

47. "Brief Report: Terrorism and Emergency Preparedness in State and Territorial Public Health Departments—United States, 2004," *Journal of the American Medical Association* 294 (August 3, 2005): 549–550.

48. "Assessment of Epidemiologic Capacity in State and Territorial Health Departments—United States, 2004," *Journal of the American Medical Association* 293 (June 22/29, 2005): 2993–2994.

49. Ibid., 2993.

50. Mike Mitka, "Readiness of Local Public Health Agencies to Respond to Bioterrorism Questioned," *Journal of the American Medical Association* 294 (October 19, 2005): 1885.

51. Steven Kelman, "Contracting," in Salamon, *Tools of Government*, 305.

52. Donald Kettl, "Managing Indirect Government," in Salamon, *Tools of Government*, 491.

53. Savas, *Privatization*, 124–131.

54. Steven R. Smith and Michael Lipsky, *Nonprofits for Hire* (Cambridge: Harvard University Press, 1993).

55. Paul Light, cited in Kettl, "Managing Indirect Government," 490.

56. Donald Kettl, *Sharing Power: Public Governance and Private Markets* (Washington, D.C.: Brookings Institution Press, 1993), 131.

57. Ibid., 134–138.

58. Keith Provan, H. Brinton Milward, and Kimberley R. Isett, "Collaboration and Integration of Community-Based Health and Human Services in a Nonprofit Managed Care System," *Health Care Management Review* 27 (Winter 2002): 26.

59. Mark Rom, "From Welfare State to Opportunity, Inc.: Public-Private Partnerships in Welfare Reform," in *Public-Private Policy Partnerships*, ed. Pauline Rosenau (Cambridge: MIT Press, 2000), 161–182.

60. Lawrence Mead, *Government Matters: Welfare Reform in Wisconsin* (Princeton: Princeton University Press, 2004), 172.

61. Ibid., 161, 170.

62. Anne Schneider, "Public-Private Partnerships in the U.S. Prison System," in Rosenau, *Public-Private Policy Partnerships*, 203.

63. Judith Greene, "Bailing Out Private Jails," *American Prospect*, September 10, 2001, 23–27.

64. Pauline V. Rosenau, "The Strengths and Weaknesses of Public-Private Policy Partnerships," in Rosenau, *Public-Private Policy Partnerships*, 227; Greg Jaffe and Rick Brooks, "Violence at Prison Run by Corrections Corp. Irks Youngstown, Ohio," *Wall Street Journal*, August 5, 1998, Sec. A.

65. John T. Scholz, personal communication, January 26, 2007.

66. Steven R. Smith and Helen Ingram, "Policy Tools and Democracy," in Salamon, *Tools of Government*, 565.

67. Charles Sabel, Archon Fung, and Bradley Karkkainen, *Beyond Backyard Environmentalism* (Boston: Beacon Press, 2000), 5.

68. Smith and Ingram, "Policy Tools and Democracy," 565.

69. David Halberstam, *The Best and the Brightest* (New York: Random House, 1972).

70. Carl Bernstein and Bob Woodward, *All the President's Men* (New York: Simon and Schuster, 1974).

71. Jeffrey Cohen, *The Politics of the U.S. Cabinet* (Pittsburgh: University of Pittsburgh Press, 1988), 33–42.

72. James Pfiffner, *The Modern Presidency* (New York: St. Martin's Press, 1994), 117–128.

73. For numerous examples of this general phenomenon, see Robert Axelrod, *The Evolution of Cooperation* (New York: Basic Books, 1984).

74. Helen Boutrous, "Presidential Influence and Regulatory Review" (Ph.D. diss., Government Department, Georgetown University, 2002).

75. Amy Zegart, *Flawed by Design: The Evolution of the CIA, JCS, and NSC* (Stanford: Stanford University Press, 1999), 52.

76. Josh White, "Dole, Shalala to Lead Troop-Care Panel," *Washington Post*, March 7, 2007, Sec. A.

77. Harold Seidman, *Politics, Position and Power* (New York: Oxford University Press, 1970), 171.

78. David Howard Davis, *Energy Politics,* 2d ed. (New York: St. Martin's Press, 1978), 93.

79. Luis Payan, "Cops, Soldiers, and Diplomats" (Ph.D. diss., Government Department, Georgetown University, 2001), chap. 3, 41.

80. Edward Walsh, "Challenges Familiar to Bush Pick," *Washington Post,* September 22, 2001, Sec. A.

81. Michael Wermuth, "Mission Impossible? The White House Office of Homeland Security," in Roberts, *Governance and Public Security,* 31.

82. Mike Allen, "White House to Increase Ridge's Exposure," *Washington Post*, October 28, 2001, Sec. A.

83. Eric Pianin and David Broder, "Ridge Defends His Role as 'Coordinator,'" *Washington Post*, November 18, 2001, Sec. A.

84. For example, the executive order used the words *coordinate* and *coordinating* thirty-seven times but never used the words *direct* or *directing*. See Wermuth, "Mission Impossible?" 32.

85. Editorial, "Faltering on the Home Front," *New York Times,* May 12, 2002, Sec. 4.

86. Helen Dewar, "Senate Passes Homeland Security Bill," *Washington Post*, November 20, 2002, Sec. A; "Department Subcomponents and Agencies," U.S. Department of Homeland Security, www.dhs.gov/xabout/structure/#1, March 27, 2007.

87. Alter and Hage, *Organizations Working Together,* 210.

88. Provan and Milward, "Preliminary Theory of Interorganizational Network Effectiveness."

89. Eugene Bardach, *Getting Agencies to Work Together* (Washington, D.C.: Brookings Institution Press, 1998).

90. Edward Jennings, "Building Bridges in the Intergovernmental Arena: Coordinating Employment and Training Programs in the American States," *Public Administration Review* 54 (January/February 1994): 52–60.

91. Robert Axelrod and Michael Cohen, *Harnessing Complexity* (New York: Free Press, 1999), 52–58.

92. Donald Chisholm, *Coordination without Hierarchy* (Berkeley: University of California Press, 1989).

93. Charles Wise, "Organizing for Homeland Security," *Public Administration Review* 62 (March/April 2002): 132.

94. Jane Fountain, "Toward a Theory of Federal Bureaucracy for the 21st Century," in *Governance.com,* ed. Elaine Kamarck and Joseph Nye Jr. (Washington, D.C.: Brookings Institution Press, 2002), 120.

95. Joseph Nye Jr. "Information Technology and Democratic Governance," in Kamarck and Nye, *Governance.com,* 7.

96. Charles Colby and A. Parasuraman, *2002 National Technology Readiness Survey* (College Park: University of Maryland, Center for e-Service; Great Falls, Va.: Rockbridge Associates, 2002).

97. Paul Peterson, Barry Rabe, and Kenneth Wong, *When Federalism Works* (Washington, D.C.: Brookings Institution Press, 1986).

98. For an early study that found evidence in support of the welfare magnet theory, see Paul Peterson and Mark Rom, *Welfare Magnets: A New Case for a National Standard* (Washington, D.C.: Brookings Institution Press, 1990). For contrary evidence, see Sanford Schram, Lawrence Nitz, and Gary Krueger, "Without Cause or Effect: Reconsidering Welfare Migration as a Policy Problem," *American Journal of Political Science* 42 (January 1998): 210–230. The latest evidence supports the welfare magnet hypothesis; see Michael Bailey, "Welfare and the Multifaceted Decision to Move," *American Political Science Review* 99 (February 2005): 124–135.

99. Bailey, "Welfare and the Multifaceted Decision to Move," 133.

100. For a summary of the evidence on Head Start's short-term and long-term effects, see William Gormley Jr., "Early Childhood Care and Education: Lessons and Puzzles," *Journal of Policy Analysis and Management* 26 (Summer 2007).

101. For the original version of this hypothesis, see David Bradford and Wallace Oates, "Towards a Predictive Theory of Intergovernmental Grants," *American Economic Review* 61 (May 1971): 440–448. For the recent empirical work, see Brian Knight, "Endogenous Federal Grants and Crowd-Out of State Government Spending: Theory and Evidence from the Federal Highway Aid Program," *American Economic Review* 92 (March 2002): 71–92.

102. Knight, "Endogenous Federal Grants and Crowd-Out of State Government Spending," 88.

103. U.S. Office of Management and Budget, *Analytical Perspectives: Budget of the United States Government, Fiscal Year 2007* (Washington, D.C.: U.S. Government Printing Office, 2006), 12.

104. David Beam and Timothy Conlan, "Grants," in Salamon, *Tools of Government,* 371.

105. Gormley, *Taming the Bureaucracy,* 173–193.

106. Evan Ringquist, *Environmental Protection at the State Level* (Armonk, N.Y.: M. E. Sharpe, 1993), 126–154.

107. Suzanne Helburn, ed., *Cost, Quality, and Child Outcomes in Child Care Centers, Technical Report* (Denver: Economics Department, University of Colorado–Denver, January 1995).

108. Wayne Gray and John Scholz, "Does Regulatory Enforcement Work? A Panel Analysis of OSHA Enforcement," *Law and Society Review* 27 (1993): 177–213.

109. William Gormley Jr., *Everybody's Children: Child Care as a Public Problem* (Washington, D.C.: Brookings Institution Press, 1995), 113–117.

110. J. Clarence Davies and Jan Mazurek, *Pollution Control in the United States* (Washington, D.C.: Resources for the Future, 1998), 140–142.

111. Peter Schrag, "Blackout," *American Prospect,* February 26, 2001, 29–33.

112. Peter May, "Social Regulation," in Salamon, *Tools of Government,* 171.

113. According to the National Highway Traffic Safety Administration, seatbelts have saved approximately 135,000 lives since 1975. See Rick Popely and Jim Mateja, "Life Savers," *Chicago Tribune,* April 21, 2002, Sec. A.

114. James Hankin et al., cited in Janet Weiss, "Public Information," in Salamon, *Tools of Government,* 242.

115. David Weil et al., "The Effectiveness of Regulatory Disclosure Policies," *Journal of Policy Analysis and Management* 25 (Winter 2006), 170–171.

116. C. S. Craig, cited in Weiss, "Public Information," 240.

117. B. Farquhar-Pilgrim, cited in Weiss, "Public Information," 240.

118. William Gormley Jr. and David Weimer, *Organizational Report Cards* (Cambridge: Harvard University Press, 1999), 141–142.

119. Charles Clotfelter and Helen Ladd, cited in Gormley and Weimer, *Organizational Report Cards*, 156.

120. James Hamilton. "Pollution as News: Media and Stock Market Reactions to the Toxics Release Inventory Data," *Journal of Environmental Economics and Management* 28 (1995): 98–113.

121. James T. Hamilton, *Regulation through Revelation: The Origin, Politics, and Impacts of the Toxics Release Inventory Program* (New York: Cambridge University Press, 2005), 224–226.

122. Mark Atlas, Michael Vasu, and Michael Dimock, cited in Hamilton, *Regulation through Revelation*, 218.

123. Hamilton, *Regulation through Revelation*, 218–219; Weil et al., "Effectiveness of Regulatory Disclosure Policies," 171–172.

124. Weiss, "Public Information," 233–234.

# Chapter 6

1. "Pesticide Label Inspection Checklist," U.S. Environmental Protection Agency, www.epa.gov/compliance/resources/publications/monitoring/fifra/checklists/label.pdf, March 21, 2007.

2. U.S. Climate Change Science Program, www.climatescience.gov, March 21, 2007.

3. "Climate Change: State of Knowledge," U.S. Environmental Protection Agency, www.epa.gov/climatechange/science/stateofknowledge.html, March 21, 2007.

4. "Coasts," U.S. Army Corps of Engineers, www.vtn.iwr.usace.army.mil/environment/envcoasts.htm, March 26, 2007.

5. "Hurricane Katrina," Wikipedia, http://en.wikipedia.org/wiki/Hurricane_Katrina, March 23, 2007.

6. Douglas Brinkley, *The Great Deluge: Hurricane Katrina, New Orleans, and the Mississippi Gulf Coast* (New York: Morrow, 2006), 247.

7. Christopher Cooper and Robert Block, *Disaster: Hurricane Katrina and the Failure of Homeland Security* (New York: Times Books, 2006), 57.

8. Stephen Barr, "Transforming FEMA," in *Triumphs and Tragedies of the Modern Presidency: Seventy-Six Case Studies in Presidential Leadership*, ed. David Abshire (Westport, Conn.: Praeger, 2001), 268–270.

9. James Lee Witt and James Morgan, *Stronger in the Broken Places: Nine Lessons for Turning Crisis into Triumph* (New York: Times Books, 2002), 172.

10. In fiscal year 1998, FEMA took an average of eight days to get relief checks to disaster victims, down from a high of twenty days in 1992; see Jerry Ellig, "Learning from the Leaders: Results-Based Management at the Federal Emergency Management Administration" (Arlington, Va.: George Mason University, Mercatus Center, March 29, 2000), 2.

11. Ibid., 7.

12. Ibid., 8.

13. Ibid., 22.

14. Ibid.

15. Cooper and Block, *Disaster*, 72.

16. Ibid., 73.

17. Ibid., 82.

18. Ibid., 85–86.

19. Bill Carwile, quoted in Ibid., 90.

20. Cooper and Block, *Disaster*, 86.

21. Brinkley, *The Great Deluge,* 620.

22. "Katrina, One Year Later," *Washington Post,* August 29, 2006, Sec. A (editorial).

23. *Catastrophic Disasters: Enhanced Leadership, Capabilities, and Accountability Controls Will Improve the Effectiveness of the Nation's Preparedness, Response, and Recovery System,* Report no. GAO-06-618 (Washington, D.C.: U.S. Government Accountability Office, September 2006), 10.

24. Kevin F. McCarthy, D. J. Peterson, Narayan Sastry, and Michael Pollard, *The Repopulation of New Orleans after Hurricane Katrina* (Santa Monica, Calif.: RAND Corporation, 2006), www.rand.org/pubs/technical_reports/2006/RAND_TR369.pdf, May 2, 2007.

25. Donald Menzel, "The Katrina Aftermath: A Failure of Federalism or Leadership?" *Public Administration Review* 66 (November/December 2006): 808–812.

26. Josh White and Peter Whoriskey, "Planning, Response Are Faulted," *Washington Post,* September 2, 2005, Sec. A.

27. Cooper and Block, *Disaster,* 102.

28. Brinkley, *The Great Deluge,* 230–234.

29. Ibid., 34.

30. Ibid., 21.

31. Ibid., 57–58.

32. Ibid., 18–19.

33. Eric Klinenberg and Thomas Frank, "Looting Homeland Security," *Rolling Stone,* no. 990/991, December 29, 2005, 44–54.

34. See Menzel, "The Katrina Aftermath," 809.

35. Cooper and Block, *Disaster,* 202–203.

36. Ibid.

37. Spencer S. Hsu, "FEMA Taking Hit on Sale of Surplus Trailers," *Washington Post,* March 8, 2007, Sec. A.

38. Ibid.

39. Brinkley, *The Great Deluge,* 173.

40. Ibid.

41. Ibid., 170.

42. *Catastrophic Disasters,* 40.

43. Brinkley, *The Great Deluge,* 205.

44. Michael Grunwald and Susan Glasser, "The Slow Drowning of New Orleans," *Washington Post,* October 9, 2005, Sec. A.

45. Michael Grunwald, "Par for the Corps; A Flood of Bad Projects," *Washington Post,* May 14, 2006, Sec. B.

46. Cooper and Block, *Disaster,* 26–27; Grunwald, "Par for the Corps."

47. Klinenberg and Frank, "Looting Homeland Security."

48. Louise Comfort, "The Dynamics of Policy Learning: Catastrophic Events in Real Time" (paper presented at the annual meeting of the American Political Science Association, Philadelphia, September 1, 2006).

49. Ibid., 9.

50. Keith Provan and H. Brinton Milward, "A Preliminary Theory of Interorganizational Network Effectiveness: A Comparative Study of Four Community Mental Health Systems," *Administrative Science Quarterly* 40 (March 1995): 1–33.

51. *Catastrophic Disasters,* 30.

52. Comfort, "The Dynamics of Policy Learning."

53. Brinkley, *The Great Deluge,* 17–18.

54. Ibid., 588–589; Spenser S. Hsu, "FEMA to Take Lead Role in Coordinating Disaster Aid," *Washington Post,* April 18, 2007, Sec. A.

55. Hsu, "FEMA to Take Lead Role in Coordinating Disaster Aid."

56. Ibid.

57. Paul Purpura, "Coast Guard Stands Up Well to Its Biggest Task," *New Orleans Times-Picayune*, October 2, 2005, Sec. 1.

58. Brinkley, *The Great Deluge*, 213.

59. Stephen Barr, "The Coast Guard and Its Chief, Models of Excellence," *Washington Post*, April 20, 2006, Sec. D.

60. Ibid.

61. Stephen Barr, "Coast Guard's Response to Katrina a Silver Lining in the Storm," *Washington Post*, September 6, 2005, Sec. B.

62. Josh White, "Coast Guard's Chief of Staff to Assist FEMA Head Brown," *Washington Post*, September 7, 2005, Sec. A.

63. Brinkley, *The Great Deluge*, 79.

64. *Catastrophic Disasters*, 48.

65. Ibid., 50.

66. National Commission on Terrorist Attacks Upon the United States, *The 9/11 Commission Report: Final Report of the National Commission on Terrorist Attacks upon the United States* (New York: Norton, 2004), 257, www.9-11commission.gov/.

67. Ibid., 257.

68. Ibid., 272.

69. Ibid., 273–275.

70. Ibid., 260.

71. Roberta Wohlstetter, quoted in Ibid., 339.

72. Ibid., 301.

73. See Jonathan Mahler, "Aftershock," *New York Times Book Review*, November 12, 2006, 57.

74. Donald Kettl, *System under Stress: Homeland Security and American Politics* (Washington, D.C.: CQ Press, 2004), 1.

75. National Commission, *The 9/11 Commission Report*, 314.

76. Ibid.

77. Kettl, *System under Stress*, 29.

78. National Commission, *The 9/11 Commission Report*, 315.

79. Ibid., 315.

80. The name of this act is an acronym for Uniting and Strengthening America by Providing Appropriate Tools Required to Intercept and Obstruct Terrorism Act of 2001.

81. Kettl, *System under Stress*, 96–97.

82. Ibid., 49.

83. Bryan W. Marshall and Richard L. Pacelle Jr., "Revisiting the Two Presidencies: The Strategic Use of Executive Orders," *American Politics Research* 33 (January 2005): 81–105.

84. "Terrorist Assets Report," U.S. Department of the Treasury, Office of Foreign Assets Control, www.treas.gov/offices/enforcement/ofac/reports/tar2005.pdf, April 25, 2007.

85. Bob von Sternberg and Pamela Miller, "Uproar Follows Imams' Detention; The Removal of Six Muslim Clerics from a Twin Cities Flight Ignited Outrage," *Star Tribune* (Minneapolis, Minn.), November 22, 2006, Sec. A.

86. Dan Eggen, "U.S. Settles Suit Filed by Ore. Lawyer; $2 Million Will Be Paid For Wrongful Arrest after Madrid Attack," *Washington Post*, November 30, 2006, Sec. A.

87. Bob Woodward, *Plan of Attack* (New York: Simon & Schuster, 2004), 164.

88. Commission on the Intelligence Capabilities of the United States Regarding Weapons of Mass Destruction, *Report to the President of the United States*, March 31, 2005, www.wmd.gov/report/wmd_report.pdf.

89. Ibid., 157.

90. Ibid., 162.

91. Ibid., 172.

92. Ibid., 181.

93. Ibid., 166.

94. Ibid., 177.

95. Fred Kaplan, "You Call That a Reform Bill?" *Slate,* December 7, 2004, www.slate.com/id/2110767/.

96. Michael Abramowitz and Peter Baker, "Bush Keeps Vow to Veto War Spending Bill," *Washington Post,* May 2, 2007, Sec. A.

97. Karen DeYoung, "Spy Agencies Say Iraq War Hurting U.S. Terror Fight," *Washington Post,* September 24, 2006, Sec. A.

98. Carmine Scavo, Richard Kearney, and Richard Kilroy Jr., "Challenges to Federalism: Homeland Security, Disaster Response, and the Local Impact of Federal Funding Formulas and Mandates" (paper presented at the annual meeting of the American Political Science Association, Philadelphia, September 1, 2006), 23.

99. Ibid., 19.

100. Kiki Caruson and Susan A. MacManus, "Mandates and Management Challenges in the Trenches: An Intergovernmental Perspective on Homeland Security," *Public Administration Review* 66 (July/August 2006): 527.

101. Ibid., 529.

102. Paul Light, "What Citizens Don't Know," *Governing,* October 2005, A1.

103. Anya Sostek, "Master of Disaster," *Governing,* October 2006, A1–A4.

104. Peter Eisinger, "Imperfect Federalism: The Intergovernmental Partnership for Homeland Security," *Public Administration Review* 66 (July/August 2006): 537–545.

105. Klinenberg and Frank, "Looting Homeland Security," 44–54.

106. Donald F. Kettl, *Managing Community Development in the New Federalism* (New York: Praeger, 1980).

107. Klinenberg and Frank, "Looting Homeland Security."

108. "Bush, Congress Clash over Ports Sale," CNN.com, February 22, 2006, www.cnn.com/2006/POLITICS/02/21/port.security/.

109. Ibid.

110. "Dubai Company Gives Up on Ports Deal," CBS News, March 9, 2006, www.cbsnews.com/stories/2006/03/09/politics/main1385030.shtml.

111. For information about the drill, see "Avian Flu Drill," County of Yolo, Health Department, June 10, 2004, www.yolocounty.org/org/health/avianfludrill.asp.

112. "Confirmed Human Cases of Avian Influenza A," World Health Organization, www.who.int/csr/disease/avian_influenza/country/en/index.html, May 2, 2007.

113. Information about the avian flu and pandemic flu can be found at "PandemicFlu.gov," managed by the United States Department of Health and Human Services, http://pandemicflu.gov/.

114. "Pandemic Planning Assumptions," PandemicFlu.gov, www.pandemicflu.gov/plan/pandplan.html, May 2, 2007.

115. "Economic Impacts," PandemicFlu.gov, http://pandemicflu.gov/impacts/index.html, May 2, 2007.

116. E. J. Mundell, "Outbreaks Show Bird Flu Virus Is Changing," *Washington Post,* November 22, 2006.

117. "National Strategy for Pandemic Influenza," Homeland Security Council, Washington, D.C., November 2005, www.whitehouse.gov/homeland/nspi.pdf, May 2, 2007; *National Strategy for Pandemic Influenza: Implementation Plan* (Washington, D.C.: Homeland Security Council, May 2006), www.whitehouse.gov/homeland/nspi_implementation.pdf, May 2, 2007.

118. *National Strategy for Pandemic Influenza: Implementation Plan,* 2.

119. Newt Gingrich and Robert Egge, "To Fight the Flu, Change How Government Works," *New York Times,* November 6, 2005, Sec. A.

120. Donald G. McNeil Jr., "States and Cities Lag in Readiness to Fight Bird Flu," *New York Times,* February 6, 2006, Sec. A.

121. Rick Weiss, "Bush, Executives Consider Strategies to Ramp Up Vaccine Production; Spurred by Concern about Avian Flu, Officials Focus on Capacity to Fight Possible Pandemic," *Washington Post,* October 8, 2005, Sec. A.

122. Sebastian Mallaby, "A Double Dose of Failure," *Washington Post,* November 7, 2005, Sec. A.

123. A fact sheet for *National Strategy for Pandemic Influenza: Implementation Plan* can be found at "Fact Sheet: Advancing the Nation's Preparedness for Pandemic Influenza," White House, Washington, D.C., May 3, 2006, www.whitehouse.gov/news/releases/2006/05/20060503-5.html, May 2, 2007.

124. "Avian Flu Drill."

125. "Lessons Learned from the Avian Flu Outbreak and Vaccination Drill, June 10, 2004," Yolo County Health Department Emergency Preparedness and Response, September 2004, www.yolocounty.org/org/health/AvianFluDrill/Yolo%20County%20Avian%20Flu%20Drill%20Exe%20Summary.pdf, May 2, 2007.

126. Rick Weiss, "Bush, Executives Consider Strategies to Ramp Up Vaccine Production; Spurred by Concern about Avian Flu, Officials Focus on Capacity to Fight Possible Pandemic," *Washington Post,* October 8, 2005, Sec A; M. Asif Ismail, "Prescription for Power: Drug Makers' Lobbying Army Ensures Their Legislative Dominance," Center for Public Integrity, Washington, D.C., April 28, 2005, www.publicintegrity.org/lobby/report.aspx?aid=685, May 2, 2007.

127. Rick Weiss, "Unknowns Pose a Challenge for Preparedness Plan; Report Highlights U.S. Weaknesses in Infrastructure, Vaccine Dispersal," *Washington Post,* November 3, 2005, Sec. A.

128. McNeil, "States and Cities Lag in Readiness to Fight Bird Flu."

129. *National Strategy for Pandemic Influenza: Implementation Plan,* 29–30.

130. Ibid., 29.

# Chapter 7

1. Cindy Skrzycki, *The Regulators: Anonymous Power Brokers in American Politics* (Lanham, Md.: Rowman and Littlefield, 2003), 4.

2. The Internet home page for the Federal Performance Project is www.govexec.com/fpp/index.htm. Researchers have also rated the performance of state and local governments. See the Internet home page for the Government Performance Project: www.maxwell.syr.edu/gpp.

3. *Government Executive,* February 1, 1999.

4. Jeffrey Pressman and Aaron Wildavsky, *Implementation* (Berkeley: University of California Press, 1973).

5. Its predecessor agency, known as the Health Care Financing Administration (HCFA), received a C in 1999.

6. "IRS Updates Tax Gap Estimates," IR-2006-28, Internal Revenue Service, February 14, 2006, www.irs.gov/newsroom/article/0,,id=154496,00.html.

7. Ibid.

8. *Debt Burden Four Years after College,* Statistical Analysis Report (Washington, D.C.: National Center for Education Statistics, August 2000), iii.

9. "National Student Loan Default Rates," U.S. Department of Education, www.ed.gov/offices/OSFAP/defaultmanagement/defaultrates.html.

10. James Q. Wilson, *Bureaucracy: What Government Agencies Do and Why They Do It* (New York: Basic Books, 1989), 158.

11. Jonathan Weisman, "Backers of Immigration Bill Optimistic; Lawmakers Cite Sense of Urgency," *Washington Post,* June 4, 2007, Sec. A.

12. Wilson, *Bureaucracy,* 158–171.

13. "Vision for Space Exploration," National Aeronautics and Space Administration, www.nasa.gov/mission_pages/exploration/main/index.html, May 2, 2007.

14. Columbia Accident Investigation Board, National Aeronautics and Space Administration, http://caib.nasa.gov/, May 2, 2007.

15. "STS-114 Return to Flight," National Aeronautics and Space Administration, www.nasa.gov/returntoflight/main/index.html, May 2, 2007.

16. Wilson, *Bureaucracy,* 168–171.

17. Susannah Figura, "Travel Advisory," *Government Executive,* April 1, 2001, 79.

18. Even destinations such as the Caribbean islands were affected by these new passport rules. Gary Lee, "Island Hoppers, Pack Your Passports," *Washington Post,* March 4, 2007, Sec. P.

19. Katherine Peters, "Trail of Trouble," *Government Executive,* April 1, 2001, 91.

20. "Operation Jump Start: Fact Sheet," U.S. Customs and Border Protection, www.cbp.gov/linkhandler/cgov/newsroom/fact_sheets/border/fact_sheet_jump_start.ctt/fact_sheet_jump_start.pdf, May 2, 2007.

21. "Getting to No," *Washington Post,* June 10, 2007, Sec. B (editorial).

22. Susannah Zak Figura, "Progress in the Parks," *Government Executive,* March 1, 2000, www.govexec.com/gpp/0300nps.htm, May 2, 2007.

23. Ibid.

24. "Policy for the Bay," Chesapeake Bay Commission, www.chesbay.state.va.us/.

25. David A. Fahrenthold, "A Revitalized Chesapeake May Be Decades Away; EPA Official Warns of Slow Progress toward 2010 Goals," *Washington Post,* January 5, 2007, Sec. A.

26. Craig W. Thomas, *Bureaucratic Landscapes: Interagency Cooperation and the Preservation of Biodiversity* (Cambridge: MIT Press, 2003), 267–268.

27. Theodore J. Lowi, *The End of Liberalism: The Second Republic of the United States,* 2d ed. (New York: W. W. Norton, 1979), 109.

28. Cathy Johnson, *The Dynamics of Conflict between Bureaucrats and Legislators* (Armonk, N.Y.: M. E. Sharpe, 1992), 71–73.

29. Ibid., 78–80.

30. William Gormley Jr., *Taming the Bureaucracy: Muscles, Prayers and Other Strategies* (Princeton: Princeton University Press, 1989).

31. "Four-Pronged, Comprehensive Approach," U.S. Department of Labor, Occupational Safety and Health Administration, 2002, www.osha.gov/SLTC/ergonomics/four-pronged_ fact sheet.html, May 2, 2007.

32. R. Michael, "Reaction to OSHA's Ergonomics Strategy," Ergoweb.com, April 8, 2002, www.ergoweb.com/news/detail.cfm?id=510, May 2, 2007.

33. Ibid.

34. W. Anthony Rosenbaum, "Escaping the 'Battered Agency Syndrome': EPA's Gamble with Regulatory Reinvention," in *Environmental Policy,* 4th ed., ed. Norman Vig and Michael Kraft (Washington, D.C.: CQ Press, 2000), 176–181.

35. "John D. Graham Appointed Dean of Pardee RAND Graduate School," RAND Corporation, October 17, 2005, www.rand.org/news/press.05/10.17.html, May 2, 2007.

36. Gary J. Miller, *Managerial Dilemmas: The Political Economy of Hierarchy* (New York: Cambridge University Press, 1992).

37. Kenneth J. Cooper, "Higher Ed: Department of Education; 'Customer' Service, the New Frontier," *Washington Post,* October 22, 1999, Sec. A.

38. Stephen Burd, "Top Aide to Gore Is Named to Revamp the Delivery of Federal Student Aid: Greg Woods Will Try to Replace Federal Bureaucracy with a 'Performance-Based Organization,' " *Chronicle of Higher Education,* December 11, 1998, Sec. A; Stephen Burd, "Federal Panel Lambastes Education Department's Plan on Computer Modernization," *Chronicle of Higher Education,* December 17, 1999, Sec. A.

39. Dipka Bhambhani, "Greg Woods, Early E-Gov Advocate, Dies," GCN, November 25, 2002, www.gcn.com/online/vol1_no1/20568-1.html, May 2, 2007.

40. Stephen Burd, "Rift Emerges over Independence of Federal Financial-Aid Office: College Officials Cry Foul as Education Dept. Seeks to Rein in 'Performance-Based' Agency," *Chronicle of Higher Education,* October 19, 2001, Sec. A; Stephen Burd, "Impending Departure of Education Department Official Worries Many Student-Aid Administrators," *Chronicle of Higher Education,* May 31, 2002, Sec. A.

41. "Advice on Student Loan Options Takes on Added Importance; Investigations Reveal Ties between Lenders, Campus Aid Officers," *Washington Post,* May 17, 2007.

42. Amit R. Paley, "Financial Aid Group Adopts Conduct Code After Loan Scandal," *Washington Post,* June 1, 2007, Sec. A.

43. Amit R. Paley, "Federal Student Loan Chief Will Step Down; Resignation Comes as Probes Intensify," *Washington Post,* May 9, 2007, Sec. A.

44. Matthew Brelis, "Earning Her Wings: When Jane Garvey Took the Controls, the Federal Aviation Administration Was Having a Bumpy Flight. Can She Smooth It Out?" *Boston Globe Magazine,* September 6, 1998, 12; Michael Skapinker and Charles Batchelor, "Aviation Chief Puts Faith in Flight: FAA Head Jane Garvey Will Be Airborne When the Millennium Midnight Hour Strikes. But Not in a Third World Airliner," *Financial Times,* November 27, 1998, 8.

45. Rene Sanchez, "L.A.'s New Top Cop Undertakes Tough Task; Style Lauded, but Reform Is Daunting," *Washington Post,* November 3, 2002, Sec. A.

46. "About SFAF—History," Success for All Foundation, n.d., www.successforall.net/about/about_history.htm, May 2, 2007.

47. Geoffrey Borman et al., "Comprehensive School Reform and Student Achievement: A Meta-Analysis," *Review of Educational Research* 73 (2003): 125–230; Geoffrey Borman et al., "The National Randomized Field Trial of Success for All: Second-Year Outcomes," *American Educational Research Journal* 42 (2005): 673–696.

48. Robert Slavin and Nancy Madden, " 'Success for All' and African American and Latino Student Achievement," in *Bridging the Achievement Gap,* ed. John Chubb and Tom Loveless (Washington, D.C.: Brookings Institution Press, 2002), 74–90.

49. Paul C. Light, "The True Size of Government," *Government Executive,* January 1, 1999, 18; Paul C. Light, "The Total Federal Workforce," *Government Executive,* January 1, 1999, 12; Paul C. Light, "Fact Sheet on the New True Size of Government," www.brookings.edu/gs/cps/light20030905.htm, May 2, 2007.

50. Light, "Fact Sheet," 4.

# INDEX

*Alphabetization is letter-by-letter (e.g., "Children" precedes "Child welfare").*

AABC bill, 65–66
AARP, 116
Aberbach, Joel D., 226n25, 229n45, 232n54, 233nn84–85, 238n79
Abraham, Spencer, 124
Abramowitz, Michael, 231n47, 247n96
Abshire, David, 244n8
Accountability, 11–15, 200–201
  bureaucratic, 11, 45
  contracting out and, 144
  defined, 11
  in education, 1–4
  evaluating, 25
  evolution of, 13
  Executive Branch and, 12
  legal, 11, 45
  limits of, 14–15
  of networks, 135–136
  political, 11, 56
  post-9/11, 183
  professional, 11
  in public bureaucracies, 8–11
  theories and applications, 24–27
Achievement gap, 1
Acid rain, 63
ACLU (American Civil Liberties Union), 70
Administration for Children, Youth, and Families, 121
Administrative Conference, 84
Administrative deference, 89
Administrative law, 87–89
Administrative Procedure Act (APA)
  judicial review and, 86, 88
  notice and comment process, 104, 106, 209, 210
  participation in decision making, 8
Administrative procedures, 80–82
Adoption, 142
Adverse selection, 58–59, 195
Advisory committees, 106–109
Advocates, 42
Afghanistan war, 183

Afghanistan war veterans, 153
AFL-CIO, 213
Agency loss, 59
Agent, defined, 57
Agranoff, Robert, 131, 239nn5–6
Agriculture Department (USDA), 100, 101, 106, 114
Agriculture policy, 62, 100, 101
Air quality/pollution, 34, 35, 88–89, 160, 162
Air travel
  explosive detection system, 56, 61, 91, 220
  security screening, 174
Akerlof, George, 227n10
Alameda-Contra Costa Transit Authority (AC), 33, 49–50
Allbaugh, Joe, 170–171, 176
Allen, Mike, 242n82
Allen, Thad, 178
All hazards approach, 170
Alter, Catherine, 155, 239n13, 240nn15–16, 242n87
Altman, Lawrence K., 241n46
American Bar Association, 90, 122
American Civil Liberties Union (ACLU), 70
American Trucking Association, 98
American Wildlands, 95
Anthrax, 16, 143
APA. *See* Administrative Procedure Act
Appointments, presidential, 70–73, 90, 213–214
Approximations, 50–52
Arlington County Fire Department, 181
Army Corps of Engineers
  Dickey-Lincoln School hydroelectric power project, 52
  Florida Gulf Coast University permit, 110
  NEPA's impact on projects, 82
  projects' impact on Hurricane Katrina effects, 175–176
  report cards, 201, 202
  water storage project, 118
Arnold, R. Douglas, 230n7

Association of Trial Lawyers of America,
115–116
Atlas, Mark, 244n122
Atomic Energy Commission, 97
Attainment areas, 34
Automaticity, 134
Availability heuristic, 45
Avian flu pandemic, 190–197
  national strategy, 192–193
  theoretical frameworks, 193–197
Aviation security
  explosive detection system, 56, 61, 91, 220
  security screening, 174
Axelrod, Robert, 157, 228n17, 242n73, 242n91
Azerbaijan, 116

Babington, Charles, 231n29
Baggage screening
  explosive detection system, 56, 61, 91, 220
  security screening, 174
Bailey, Michael, 158, 243nn98–99
Baker, James, III, 46, 72, 83, 116, 150
Baker, Peter, 247n96
Baldauf, Scott, 234n1
Balla, Steven J., 226n22, 233n74, 233n76,
    233n81, 233n89, 235n22, 235nn27–28,
    236n41, 236n46, 237n49, 237n68,
    239n106
Ban, Carolyn R., 231n41
Banks, Christopher, 233nn92–94, 234n97
Bardach, Eugene, 157, 229n61, 242n89
Barr, Nevada, 52, 229n59
Barr, Stephen, 232n57, 244n8, 246nn59–61
Batchelor, Charles, 250n44
Baumgartner, Frank R., 227n9, 234n7, 235n14
Bawn, Kathleen, 226n28
Bay Area Rapid Transit (BART), 33, 49–50
Bazelon, David, 88
Bazelon Center for Mental Health Law, 123
BCA (Bureau of Consular Affairs), 202, 207
Beam, David, 160, 243n104
Begala, Paul, 69
Behn, Robert, 225n16, 228n24
Beierle, Thomas C., 237nn72–73
Bendor, Jonathan, 50, 228n12, 229n53
Benefit-cost ratios, 41, 50–52, 103–104
Benefits
  concentrated, 96–97
  diffuse, 96–97
  perceived, 103–104
  of public policy, 96–99
Bennett, William, 154–155
Berends, Mark, 225nn11–14
Berenson, Robert, 240n27
Bernstein, Carl, 241n70

Berry, John M., 226n30
Bhambhani, Dipka, 249n39
BIA. See Bureau of Indian Affairs
Bianco, William T., 236n41
Bibby, John F., 233n83
Biodiversity, 209
Bird flu pandemic, 190–197
Birnbaum, Jeffrey H., 238n76
Bitterroot National Forest, 94–95, 125–127
Blind Descent, 52
BLM (Bureau of Land Management), 209
Block, Robert, 244n7, 244nn15–20, 245n27,
    245nn35–36, 245n46
Block grants, 158
Blum, Justin, 226n34
Blustein, Paul, 231n42
Bohlen, Charles, 45
Borman, Geoffrey, 250n47
Bounded rationality, 41
  approximations, 50–52
  avian flu pandemic forecast, 193–194
  consequences of, 49–53
  decision making and, 31–33
  defined, 24
  evaluating accountability and
    performance, 25
  Hurricane Katrina response analysis, 173–176
  narrow range of options, 49–50
  problem disaggregation, 50
  standard operating procedures, 52–53
Boutrous, Helen, 238n97, 242n74
Bowles, Chester, 44
Bradford, David, 243n101
Bratton, William, 216–217
Brehm, John, 42, 226n23, 228n35, 234n107
Brelis, Matthew, 250n44
Brinkley, Douglas, 244n6, 245n21,
    245nn28–32, 245nn39–41, 245n43,
    245nn53–54, 246n58, 246n63
Broder, David S., 231n29, 242n83
Brooks, Rick, 241n64
Brown, Michael, 168, 171, 172, 174
Browner, Carol, 214
Budgeting, 17
Burd, Stephen, 249n38, 250n40
Bureaucracies. See also Public bureaucracies
  authority of, 219
  congressional control of, 78–85
  perceptions of, 21–24
  as policymaking organizations, 1–27
  politics of bureaucratic structure, 79–80
  rationale for, 59–67
  size of, 59–60
Bureaucratic accountability, 11, 45
Bureau of Consular Affairs (BCA), 202, 207

Bureau of Indian Affairs (BIA), 202, 207–208, 211–212
Bureau of Land Management (BLM), 209
Bureau of Medical Devices, 8
Burger, Warren E., 89
Bush, George H. W., 46, 66, 121, 141
Bush, George W.
  Allbaugh appointment, 170
  appointees, 90
  cabinet, 71–72
  Card memorandum, 117
  education issues, 1–4
  ergonomics rule, 55, 117, 212–213
  Executive Office of the President, 74
  Federal Docket Management System (FDMS), 114
  Homeland Security Department, 74–75, 155–156
  mental health issues, 123
  National Energy Policy Development Group, 108
  Office of Homeland Security, 154–155
  PART, 19
  post-9/11 acts, 182–183
  regulatory review, 77
  task force on Iraq and Afghanistan war veterans, 153
  unilateral actions, 69–70
Business organizations, 117–119

Cabinet departments, 5, 149–150
Cable television industry, 82
Camissa, Anne, 238n96
Capture, 48
Card memorandum, 117
Carney, Eliza Newlin, 231n46
Carpenter, Daniel P., 227nn54–55, 227n57
Caruson, Kiki, 247nn100–101
Carwile, Bill, 244n19
Casework, 61
Catalytic control, 212–213
Categorical grants, 158
CBC (Chesapeake Bay Commission), 209
Centers for Disease Control and Prevention (CDC), 16, 72, 143
Centers for Medicare and Medicaid Services (CMS)
  "full immunization," 19
  hospital payments, 105
  managed care, waivers, 141
  nursing homes, 128–129
  performance rating, 203–204
  physician payments, 11, 126
  report card, 202
Central Intelligence Agency (CIA), 180, 186

Centrality, 131–133
Chain of command, 172
Challenger space shuttle, 12, 22
Chemical releases, 162
Cheney, Dick, 150, 185
Chertoff, Michael, 171, 175
Chesapeake Bay, 140
Chesapeake Bay Commission (CBC), 209
Chevron U.S.A., Inc. v. Natural Resources Defense Council, Inc. (1984), 89, 234n101
Chicago public schools, 148–149
Child care
  agencies, 36–37
  inspectors, 28–29, 44
  legislation, 65–67
  policy, 121
Child Care and Development Block Grant, 65, 158
Child Care and Development Fund, 65
Child protection agencies, 36–37
Children's Defense Fund, 121
Children's Health Insurance Program (CHIP), 18, 22, 142
Child welfare, 146
Chisholm, Donald, 242n92
Chrysler Corporation, 39
Chubb, John E., 233n67, 250n48
CIA (Central Intelligence Agency), 180, 186
Circuit courts of appeals, 87–89
CIS (Citizenship and Immigration Services), 201, 202, 205, 208
CitiStat, 38
Citizenship and Immigration Services (CIS), 201, 202, 205, 208
Civil liberties, 70, 185
Civil Rights Division, 43
Civil Service employees, 47, 60
Civil Service reform, 73–75
Civil Service Reform Act, 74
Clark, Peter, 41, 228n34
Clarke, Richard, 180
Clean Air Act, 63, 88, 89, 138, 160
Clean Water Act, 138
Client politics, 97, 176
Clients, 89–90, 94–127
  advisory committees, 106–109
  benefits, costs, and politics of public policy, 96–99
  collaboration, 106–109
  government institutions and, 124–125
  influence on policymaking, 115–124
  Internet and, 110–115
  iron triangles, 99–104
  notice and comment process, 104–106
  political intervention, 109–110

political support, 210–211
variation in influence, 126–127
variation in participation, 125–127
venues of participation, 104–115, 126
Climate change, 166–167
Climbers, 42
Clinton, Bill
cabinet, 149
child care policy, 67, 121
environmental protection, 139
ergonomics rule, 55
Executive Order 12886, 76
executive orders, 69
health care policy, 141
health care task force, 108
midnight regulations, 117
waivers, 123, 141
Clinton, Hillary, 121
Clinton, Joshua D., 238n93
Clotfelter, Charles, 244n119
CMS. *See* Centers for Medicare and Medicaid
Services
Coast Guard, 177–178, 202
Coercive control, 212–213
Coerciveness, 134, 160
Coglianese, Cary, 236n45, 236n48, 237n61
Cohen, Jeffrey, 242n71
Cohen, Michael, 157, 242n91
Cohen, Sally, 238nn94–95
Colby, Charles, 243n96
Collaboration, 106–109
Collective bargaining, 75
*Columbia* space shuttle, 22, 207
Comfort, Louise, 245nn48–49, 245n52
Committee hearings, 84
Commodity policy, 62, 100, 101
Communication
avian flu pandemic, 192
disaster management, 197
emergency systems, 172
first response to 9/11 attacks, 30, 181
Hurricane Katrina response, 172–173, 175
relationships and, 208–209
Community Development Block Grant, 159
Community peer review, 111–112
Complexity, 62–63, 131–132
Compromise, political, 80
Concentrated benefits and costs, 96–97
Congress
administrative procedures, 80–82
control of EPA, 63
control of the bureaucracy, 78–85
intergovernmental relations, 137
Iraq war sentiment, 183

judicial review, 85–89
oversight, 82–85
politics of bureaucratic structure, 79–80
post-9/11 acts, 182–183
Congressional Review Act, 55
Conlan, Timothy, 160, 243n104
Connect the dots, 183
Conservers, 42
Constituencies. *See* Clients
Constitution, U.S., 68, 69, 85
Consumer Product Safety Commission
(CPSC), 78, 79–80
Contracting out, 128, 144–145
no-bid contracts, 176
Cooper, Christopher, 244n7, 244nn15–20,
245n27, 245nn35–36, 245n46
Cooper, Kenneth J., 249n37
Co-optation, 148
Coordinated control, 68
Coordination. *See* Interagency coordination
Coping organizations, 207–208
Corrections, 39–40, 147
Corrections Corporation of America, 147
Corwin, Edward S., 230n22
Cost-benefit analysis, 41, 50–52, 103–104
Costs
concentrated, 96–97
diffuse, 96–97
perceived, 103–104
of public policy, 96–99
sunk costs, 38–39
Council of Economic Advisors, 74
Counterbureaucracy, 75
Counterterrorism Security Group, 180
CPSC (Consumer Product Safety
Commission), 78, 79–80
Craig, C. S., 243n116
Credible commitments, 214–216
Crisis situations
anthrax contamination, 16
avian flu pandemic, 190–197
czars and, 153
Hurricane Katrina, 168–179
management, 166–167
National Response Plan, 171
September 11, 2001, 29–30, 179–190
Croley, Steven, 232n60
Cropper, Maureen, 238n87
Crowd out hypothesis, 159
Customs and Border Protection, 33, 104
performance rating, 208, 211
Customs Service. *See now* Customs and
Border Protection
Czars, 153–155, 214

Daniels, Benjamin M., 235nn27–28, 237n68
Daschle, Tom, 16
Davies, J. Clarence, 228n14, 243n110
Davis, David Howard, 242n78
Day, Kathleen, 227n51, 235n11
Day care centers, 28–29, 160
D.C. Circuit, 87–89
Decision making, 28–54
  Administrative Procedure Act, 8
  bounded rationality model, 31–33
  consequences of bounded rationality, 49–53
  implications for policy analysis, 40–49
  policy analysis and, 28–54
  problem solving, 34–40
Dedekorkut, Ayşin, 240nn39–41
Dee, Thomas, 229n40
Deering, Cristopher J., 233n89
Defense Intelligence Agency (DIA), 186
Delegation, 57–58
  avian flu pandemic, 195
  congressional control of bureaucracy, 78–85
  EPA delegation of authority to states,
    137–140
  fragmenting authority, 193
  Hurricane Katrina response, 174–175
  judicial review, 85–89
  managing, 67–68
  presidential power and, 68–78
  variation in, 62–65
Democracy, 10, 200
DeMuth, Christopher C., 232n60
Density, 131–133
Department of ___. See other part of name
Deregulation, 82, 161
Devolution, 137
Dewar, Helen, 229n1, 234n105, 242n86
DeWitt, Jeff, 236n33
DeYoung, Karen, 247n97
DIA (Defense Intelligence Agency), 186
Differential monitoring, 37
Differential response, 37
Differentiation, 132
Diffuse benefits and costs, 96–97
Digital divide, 115
Dillon, Sam, 225n4
Dimock, Michael, 244n122
Diplomacy, 207
Direct lobbying, 118–119
Directness, 134
Director of national intelligence, 186
Disaster management, 166–199. See also Crisis
  situations
Discovery space shuttle, 207
Dismissals, 73

Divided government, 64
Dockets, 113
Dodd, Lawrence C., 230n19
DOE. See Energy Department
DOJ. See Justice Department
DOT. See Transportation Department
Downs, Anthony, 42, 228n36
Drew, Joseph, 227n2
Drinking water, 81, 107
Drotning, Lucy, 230nn10–11
Drug czar, 153, 154
Drug industry, 194–195
Drug policy, 35
Drug trafficking, 36
Drug use discouragement, 162
Dubai Ports World, 189–190
Dubnick, Melvin, 225nn19–20, 226n24
Dudley, Susan E., 238nn80–82
Dunne, Finley Peter, 238n90

Eavesdropping, 69–70
Ebbert, Terry, 172
Economic rationality, 41
Economic regulation, 135, 160–161
Economists, 12, 32, 48–49
Education
  accountability, 1–4
  achievement gap, 1
  Bureau of Indian Affairs, 207–208
  emergency response, 189
  iron triangles, 99
  performance, 1–4
  policymaking challenges, 1–4
  reform, 217–218
  vouchers, 135
  waivers, 123
Education Department (U.S.), 123
Efficiency, 17
Egge, Robert, 247n119
Eggen, Dan, 231nn31–32, 231n49, 232n50,
  246n86
Eichel, Henry, 239n104
Eisenhower, Dwight, 159
Eisinger, Peter, 248n104
Eisner, Neil, 236n37
Elementary and Secondary Education Act
  (1965), 2
Ellig, Jerry, 244nn10–14
Elliott, E. Donald, 232n61
Emancipation Proclamation, 68
Embryonic and fetal research, 103
Emergency communications, 172
Emergency response calling system, 53
Emission standards, 88

Emissions trading, 160
Empathy, 42–43
Endangered species, 109, 120, 148
Energy conservation, 162
Energy czar, 153
Energy Department (DOE), 124, 145
Energy policy, 145
English as a Second Language (ESL), 3
Enron, 21, 99
Entrepreneurial politics, 98
Environmental groups
  Bitterroot National Forest revitalization, 95,
    125–127
  BLM and, 209
  EPA constituencies, 210
  habitat conservation plans, 148
  spotted owl controversy, 120–121
  Toxics Release Inventory, 162
Environmental impact statements, 81
Environmental protection, 137–140, 148
Environmental Protection Agency (EPA)
  administrative procedures, 81
  approximations, 52
  Browner as head, 214
  bureaucratic motivation, 43
  business organizations and, 119
  congressional control of, 63
  creation of, 68
  guidance documents, 91–92
  independent agency, 8
  intergovernmental relationships, 19,
    137–140
  judicial review, 88
  notice and comment rulemaking, 105
  online dialogue, 115
  organizational chart, 51
  performance rating, 210
  pesticide label review, 166
  policymaking by, 16–17
  problem disaggregation, 34, 50
  report card, 201–202
  reputation of, 21
  role, 96
  rulemaking, 123
  Toxics Release Inventory, 162
EPA v. American Trucking Associations, Inc.
  (2001), 88–89, 234n100
Epstein, David, 226n28, 230n3, 230nn17–18
Equity, 17
Equivalence, 133
Ergonomics rule, 55, 91, 117, 212–213
Escalante, Jaime, 50
Ethnicity, 44
Everglades, 109–110, 118

Executive branch
  forms of accountability, 12
  organizational chart, 6–7
  reversed or remanded actions, 85–86
Executive Office of the President, 73–74
Executive orders, 69
  12291, regulatory review, 75
  12886, regulatory review, 76
Executive Service Corps, 148
Exit, 46
Export control reform, 152

FAA. See Federal Aviation Administration
FACA (Federal Advisory Committee Act),
  107–108
Fahrenthold, David A., 249n25
Fairfax County, Virginia, 3
Fairness, 8
Faith, Roger, 237n55
Farm issues, 62, 100, 101
Farquhar-Pilgrim, B., 243n117
FBI (Federal Bureau of Investigation), 22
FCC. See Federal Communications
  Commission
FDA. See Food and Drug Administration
Federal Advisory Committee Act (FACA),
  107–108
Federal Aviation Administration (FAA)
  amateur rocket licensing, 115
  flight and duty time, 106–107, 108
  Garvey as head, 216
  report card, 202
Federal Bureau of Investigation (FBI), 22
Federal Communications Commission (FCC),
  82, 119
  website, 113
Federal Emergency Management Agency
  (FEMA)
  evolution, 169–172
  Hurricane Katrina response, 172–179
  report card, 201–202
  scorn in aftermath of Hurricane Katrina,
    168–169
  theoretical framework application to
    Hurricane Katrina response, 173–179
Federal Energy Regulatory Commission, 82
Federal Highway Administration, 96
Federal Insecticide, Fungicide, and Rodenti-
  cide Act, 119, 139
Federal Performance Project, 201–202
Federal Railroad Administration (FRA), 81,
  82, 109
Federal Register, 60, 61, 104

Federal Reserve, 5, 40
Federal Trade Commission (FTC), 48–49, 110, 161–162
Fee-for-service, 141
Feigenbaum, Harvey, 239n3
Feldman, Martha, 41, 228n32, 229n62
FEMA. *See* Federal Emergency Management Agency
Fenno, Richard F., Jr., 233n86
Fetal tissue research, 103
Figura, Susannah Zak, 249n17, 249nn22–23
Financial Crimes Task Force, 124
Fiorina, Morris P., 230n6, 230n19, 230n21, 232n66
Fire alarm oversight, 84, 86, 90
Firefighting, 40
    first response to 9/11 attacks, 180–182
Firestone, David, 239n105
Firings, 73
First responders, 180–182
Fish and Wildlife Service, 110, 120–121
Fisher, Linda L., 231n40
Florida Gulf Coast University, 110
FOIA. *See* Freedom of Information Act
Food and Drug Administration (FDA)
    nutritional labeling, 161–162
    organization, 9
    product seizures, 71
    role, 8
    tobacco products and juveniles, 105
    user fees for new drug applications, 22
Food and Nutrition Service, 43, 48
Food safety, 78
Foreign Service, 44–45, 46
Forest Service
    Bitterroot National Forest revitalization, 94–95, 125–127
    conflicting goals, 18
    environmental groups and, 120–121
    Hurricane Katrina response, 178
    personnel management, 47–48
    public image, 22
    Smokey Bear, 23
    spotted owl, 120
Forsythe, Dall, 226n37
*Fortune* magazine, 115–116
Fountain, Jane E., 238n74, 242n94
FRA. *See* Federal Railroad Administration
Fragmenting authority, 193
Frank, Thomas, 245n33, 245n47, 248n105, 248n107
Frederickson, David, 225n18, 226n40
Frederickson, H. George, 225n18, 226n40, 240n30

Freedom of Information Act, 13, 120
Freedom Support Act, 116
Freeman, A. Myrick, III, 229nn57–58
FTC. *See* Federal Trade Commission
Full immunization, 19, 20
Fung, Archon, 241n67
Furlong, Scott R., 235n28, 236n36

GAO (General Accountability Office), 18
Gao, Ling, 225n2
Garvey, Jane, 216
Gates, Scott, 42, 226n23, 228n35, 234n107
Gender, 43–44
General Accountability Office (GAO), 18
General Electric, 220
Gerberding, Julie, 143
Gilmour, John, 20, 226n43, 227nn44–47
Gingrich, Newt, 193, 247n119
Ginsburg, Douglas H., 232n60
Giuliani, Rudy, 217
Glasser, Susan, 245n44
Glickman, Dan, 48, 62, 78, 101, 111, 118, 120, 127
Global warming, 166–167
Glod, Maria, 225nn5–6, 225n9
Golden, Marissa Martino, 228n38, 235nn29–30, 236n33
Golden, Olivia, 121
Goldstein, Amy, 233n87
Go native, 71
Gonzales, Alberto R., 70, 73
Goodsell, Charles, 226n33
Gormley, William, Jr., 225n1, 225n21, 226n26, 226n28, 227n1, 227nn3–4, 228n18, 229n41, 229n60, 230nn8–9, 232n59, 238n84, 238n88, 239n3, 238nn99–101, 240n36, 240n42, 243n100, 243n105, 243n109, 244nn118–119, 249n30
Government
    divided, 64
    organizational chart, 6–7
    scope of, 59–62
    state and local, 121–124
    third-party, 135–136
Government corporations, 7
*Government Executive* magazine, 201
Government institutions, 124–125
Government in the Sunshine Act, 13, 120
Government Performance and Results Act (GPRA), 17–19, 219
Graham, Bob, 110, 170
Graham, John D., 214
Granovetter, Mark, 239n7
Grants-in-aid, 137, 158–160, 164

Gray, Wayne, 243n108
Greater Boston Television Corp. v. FCC (1970),
   88, 234n95
Great Lakes Basin, 140
Greenberg, Saadia, 227n2
Greene, Judith, 241n63
Greenspan, Alan, 14, 40
Greenspan, Martin, 228n31
GreenWorld, 120
Griffin, Ben Hill, III, 110
Griffin, Michael D., 22
Grimaldi, James V., 235n11
Group identification, 43–44
Grunwald, Michael, 237nn53–54, 245nn44–46
Gugliotta, Guy, 227n52
Guidance documents, 91–92
Guinnessy, Paul, 235n15
Gulf Coast, 168–179
Gumbel, Andrew, 234n1

Hage, Jerald, 155, 239n13, 240nn15–16, 242n87
Halberstam, David, 241n69
Hall, Thad, 240n29
Hamilton, James T., 234n106, 244nn120–123
Hamilton, Laura, 225nn11–14
Hamnett, Chris, 239n3
Hankin, James, 243n114
Hanushek, Eric, 225n3
Hard look doctrine, 88
Harrington, Winston, 236n33
Harter, Philip J., 236n35, 236n44
Harvey, Francis, 73
Hayes, Arthur Hull, 71
Hazard Analysis and Critical Control Point, 78
Hazardous wastes, 91–92
HCFA (Health Care Financing Administra-
   tion). See now Centers for Medicare and
   Medicaid Services (CMS)
Head Start, 158, 159
Health, Education, and Welfare Department,
   79
Health alert network, 143–144
Health and Human Services Department
   (HHS)
  avian flu pandemic, role in, 192
  child care policy, 65–67, 121
  coordination of agencies, 72
  iron triangles, 99
  performance measurement, 18, 19
Health Care Financing Administration
   (HCFA). See now Centers for Medicare
   and Medicaid Services (CMS)
Health care task force, 108
Health policy, 136, 141–144

Hearings, oversight, 78
Heclo, Hugh, 231n41, 235n17
Helburn, Suzanne, 243n107
Henig, Jeffrey, 239n3
Hermann, Alexis, 151
Hermanson, Judith A., 232n64
H51N virus, 190–197
HHS. See Health and Human Services
   Department
High-stakes testing, 1, 3
Hill, Kevin A., 237n63
Hirschman, Albert, 46, 229n49
Hodges, Jim, 124
Holistic perspective, 50
Hollander, Jack M., 235n16
Hollings, Ernest "Fritz," 169
Hollow state, 128
Homeland Security Advisory Council, 74
Homeland security czar, 154
Homeland Security Department
  agencies comprising, 156
  authority, 219–220
  avian flu pandemic, role in, 192
  cabinet department, 5
  creation, 182–183
  FEMA incorporation, 171, 174
  limited authority, 154–155
  organization, 184
  personnel management, 74–75
  website, 113
Homeland security grants, 189
Homeland Security Threat Advisories, 187–188
Hoover, J. Edgar, 22
Hortatory control, 160, 212–213
Hospitals, 162
Housing and Urban Development Depart-
   ment (HUD), 18
  notice and comment rulemaking, 105–106
Hovanyetz, Scott, 238n77
Howard, Robert M., 236n33
Howell, William G., 230n22
Hsu, Spencer, 245nn37–38, 245nn55–56
Huber, John D., 230n4, 230nn13–15
HUD. See Housing and Urban Development
   Department
Hughes, John E., 237n63
Humphrey's Executor v. United States (1935),
   231n49
Huntington, Samuel P., 235n12
Hurricane Andrew, 169
Hurricane Hugo, 169
Hurricane Katrina, 168–179
  National Weather Service, 206
Hurricane Pam, 173–174, 197

Hurricane Rita, 172
Hurricane superhighway, 176
Hussein, Saddam, 185

Illegal immigration, 208
Immigrants, 3
Immigration, 208
Immigration and Naturalization Service
    (INS). *See now* Citizenship and
    Immigration Services (CIS)
Immunization, 19, 20
    avian flu pandemic, 193, 194–195, 197
Implementation, 16
    tasks, 204–205
Incentives, 41–42, 160
Incident command, 181
Incrementalism, 32
Independent agencies, 5, 7
Influenza, 190–197
Information flow, 47, 137–138
Information sharing
    disaster management, 197
    homeland security information, 187–188
    Hurricane Katrina response, 173, 175
    Iraq war, 186
    network theory and, 161–163, 164, 165
    pre-9/11 information, 180
Ingraham, Patricia W., 231n41, 232n53
Ingram, Helen, 148, 241n66, 241n68
INS (Immigration and Naturalization
    Service). *See now* Citizenship and
    Immigration Services (CIS)
Inspectors general, 13
Institutional design, 59
Institutional uncertainty, 132
Institutions, 124–125
Intelligence community, 180, 185, 186–187
Interagency coordination
    avian flu pandemic, 195–196
    importance in relationships, 208
    network theory and, 136, 151–153, 164
    prevention of future terrorist attacks, 188
Interagency networks, 149–151
Interagency task force, 152–153
Interest group mobilization, 124–125
    defined, 26
    evaluating accountability and performance,
    25
    prevention of future terrorist attacks, 189
Interest group politics, 98
Interest groups
    business organizations, 117–119
    influence on policymaking, 115–124
    iron triangles, 99–104

number of, 101
Intergovernmental relationships
    avian flu pandemic, 195–196
    challenges, 18–19
    communication within, 208–209
    environmental protection, 137–140
    health policy, 141–144
    network theory and, 136, 137–144
    prevention of future terrorist attacks, 188
    variations in performance, 202
Interior Department, 113
Internal Revenue Service (IRS)
    mistreatment of taxpayers, 79
    perceptions of, 21
    performance rating, 204
    report card, 201, 202
    tips, reporting income, 52
    website, 113
Internal Revenue Service Restructuring and
    Reform Act, 204
*International Harvester Co. v. Ruckelshaus*
    (1973), 88, 234n96
International Space Station, 207
Internet, 110–115, 157–158
    patent applications, 111–112
Interorganizational networks, 130–131
Interstate Commerce Commission, 13, 98, 210
Interstate highway system, 159
Iraq war, 183, 185–187
Iraq war veterans, 73, 153
Iron triangles, 99–104, 120, 125, 210
IRS. *See* Internal Revenue Service
Isett, Kimberley R., 241n58
Ismail, M. Asif, 248n126
Issue networks, 102–103

Jaffe, Greg, 241n64
Jelinek, Pauline, 231n47
Jennings, Edward, 157, 242n90
Johnson, Cathy, 249nn28–29
Johnson, Lyndon, 149, 159
Johnson, Ronald N., 232n51
Johnson, Stephen M., 237n62
Jones, Bryan D., 227n2, 227n6, 227n9, 234n7,
    235n14
Jones, Charles O., 235n16
Judgeship appointees, 90
Judges vs. politicians, 86–87
Judicial review, 85–89
    administrative law, 87–89
    circuit courts, 87–89
    judges vs. politicians, 86–87
    Supreme Court, 89
Justice Department (DOJ), 35, 79, 85, 181

Kagan, Robert, 229n61
Kahneman, Daniel, 229n46
Kamarck, Elaine Ciulla, 237n63, 242n94
Kane, Paul, 231n49, 232n50
Kaplan, Fred, 247n95
Karkkainen, Bradley, 241n67
Katzmann, Robert, 229n51
Kaufman, Clifford, 227n2
Kaufman, Herbert, 47–48, 229n50
Kaufman, Marc, 227n53
KBR, 176
Kearney, Richard, 247nn98–99
Keep Committee, 73
Kelman, Steven, 241n51
Kerry, John, 85
Kerwin, Cornelius M., 225n17, 233n72,
     235n20, 235n22, 235n28, 236n33,
     236n36, 236n47
Kettl, Donald F., 145, 229n55, 241n52,
     241nn55–57, 246n74, 246n77,
     246nn81–82, 248n106
Khademian, Anne M., 226n31
Kickert, Walter J. M., 239n10
Kiewiet, D. Roderick, 230n5
Kiley, Kevin, 73
Kilroy, Richard, Jr., 247nn98–99
King, Anthony, 235n17
Kingdom, John, 227n9
Kissinger, Henry, 46
Kliljn, Erik-Hans, 239n10, 240nn17–18,
     240n30
Klinenberg, Eric, 245n33, 245n47, 248n105,
     248n107
Knight, Brian, 243nn101–102
Knoke, David, 239n8
Koenig, Louis W., 230n22
Kolata, Gina, 241n46
Koppenjan, Joop F. M., 239n10, 240nn17–18,
     240n30
Kovach, Bill, 238n90
Kraft, Michael E., 229n55, 240n35, 250n34
Krause, George A., 236n46
Krebs, Valdis, 134, 240n21
Krueger, Gary, 243n98
Krupnick, Alan J., 236n33

Labeling, 161–162
Labor interests, 110
Ladd, Helen, 244n119
Laird, Melvin R., 233n83
Lake Okeechobee, 118
Lamott, Anne, 50, 229n54
Lane, Charles, 234n100
Langbein, Laura I., 236n47
Laumann, Edward O., 239n8

Law enforcement. *See* Police
Lawyers, 48–49
Layzer, Judith, 238nn85–86, 238n91
Lead, 34–35, 38, 52
Leadership, 202, 212–217
     Hurricane Katrina response, 174–175
Leavens, Donald, 237n55
Lee, Gary, 249n18
Legal accountability, 11, 45
Legislative clearance, 150
Legislative professionalism, 64
Legislative veto, 13
Leonnig, Carol D., 231n27, 231n30, 233n87
Leventhal, Harold, 88
Lewis, David E., 20, 227nn46–47, 238n93
Lewis, Eugene, 227n56
Libecap, Gary D., 232n51
Liberation management, 13
Lichtblau, Eric, 231nn26–28
Light, Paul C., 226n27, 232n52, 241n55,
     248n102, 250nn49–50
Lindblom, C. Edward, 32, 227n8, 238n83
Lindsey, Duncan, 228nn20–21
Linzer, Dafna, 231n31
Lipsky, Michael, 38, 228n16, 241n54
Lobbying, 118–119, 120–121
Local governments, 121–124
Localism, 48
Logging, 94–95, 120–121, 125–127
Loomis, John, 238n92
Loosely connected network, 176
Los Angeles Police Department, 217
Louisiana Purchase, 68
Love, John, 153
Loveless, Tom, 250n48
Lowi, Theodore J., 249n27
L-3 Communications, 220
Lubell, Mark, 240nn37–38
Mack, Connie, 110
Mackenzie, G. Calvin, 231nn35–37, 231n40
MacManus, Susan A., 247nn100–101
Madden, Nancy, 250n48
Magat, Wesley A., 236n33
Mahler, Jonathan, 246n73
Mail delivery. *See* Postal Service (USPS)
Majoritarian politics, 98–99
Major rules, 105
Mallaby, Sebastian, 248n122
Managed care, 64, 136, 141, 145–146
Management by objectives, 17
Mandates, 137
Manor Care, 129
Mansbridge, Jane, 228n33
Margolis, Michael, 237n63
Market incentives, 160

Marshall, Bryan W., 246n83
Mass transit, 33, 49–50
Mateja, Jim, 243n113
May, Peter, 243n112
Mayfield, Brandon, 185
Mayfield, Max, 173
Mazurek, Jan, 228n14, 243n110
McAllister, Bill, 234n4
McAuliffe, Christa, 12
McCarthy, Catherine, 238n92
McCarthy, Kevin F., 245n24
McCubbins, Mathew D., 230n5, 232n64,
    233n75, 233n77, 233n79, 233n88
McGarity, Thomas O., 232n62
McGinnis, J. Michael, 231n45
McMahon, Gerard, 236n43
McNeil, Donald G., Jr., 247n120, 248n128
Mead, Lawrence, 241nn60–61
Meddling, political, 110
Media, 101–102, 119
Medical devices, 8
Medicare/Medicaid
  coordination with CHIP, 142
  financial incentives and, 142–143
  "full immunization," 19
  goals, 18
  hospital payments, 105
  managed care, 64, 123, 141
  mental health, 145–146
  nursing homes, 128–129
  performance rating, 203–204
  physician payments, 11, 126
  report card, 202
  results of program, 159
Meier, Kenneth J., 228n39, 229n42, 236n46
Mental health, 123, 145–146, 157
Menzel, Donald, 245n25, 245n34
Michael, R., 249nn32–33
Midnight regulations, 117
Military recruitment, 162
Miller, Gary J., 249n36
Miller, Jason, 237n70
Miller, Pamela, 246n85
Milward, H. Brinton, 128, 155, 157, 239n2,
    239n9, 239n11, 240n14, 240n19, 241n58,
    242n88, 245n50
Missions, 205–206
Mississippi River Gulf Outlet, 175
Mitka, Mike, 241n50
Mobilization, 90. See also Interest group
    mobilization
Moe, Terry M., 226n32, 230n4, 230n22,
    232nn67–70, 233n90
Monetary policy, 14
Monopolies, 98–99, 161

Montana Wood Products Association, 95
Moral hazard, 58–59, 82
Morgan, Dan, 235n15, 241n44
Morgan, James, 244n9
Morial Convention Center, 173
Moses, Robert, 50
Motivations, 41–49
  attitudes toward risk, 44–45
  empathy, 42–43
  organizational advancement, 45–46
  organizational cohesion, 47–49
  representative bureaucracy, 43–44
  self-interest, 41–42
Motor Vehicle Manufacturers Association of the
    U.S. v. State Farm Mutual Automobile
    Insurance Co. (1983), 234n99
Moussaoui, Zacarias, 180
Multiplexity, 131–132
Mundell, E. J., 247n116
Murray, Frank J., 230nn23–24

Nader, Ralph, 98
Nagin, C. Ray, 173
Nakashima, Ellen, 230n2
Narrow range of options, 49–50
Nathan, Richard, 226n37
National Advisory Committee on Ergonomics,
    212
National Advisory Committee on Meat and
    Poultry Inspection, 107
National Aeronautics and Space Administra-
    tion (NASA), 12, 22, 202, 206–207
National Assessment of Educational Progress, 2
National Association of Attorneys General,
    122
National Center for Education Statistics, 205
National Commission on Terrorist Attacks
    Upon the United States, 180
National District Attorneys Association, 122
National Drinking Water Advisory Council,
    81, 107
National Energy Policy Development
    Group, 108
National Environmental Performance
    Partnership System (NEPPS), 139–140
National Environmental Policy
    Act, 81–82, 120
National Geospatial-Intelligence Agency, 186
National Governors Association, 117, 122
National Highway Traffic Safety
    Administration, 43
National Institutes of Health, 72, 103
National Park Service (NPS), 202, 208
National Response Plan, 171, 177
National Rifle Association, 115

National Security Agency (NSA), 69, 186
National Security Council, 74
National Strategy for Pandemic Influenza, 192–193, 194
National Weather Service (NWS), 178, 202, 205–206, 211
Native Americans. *See* Bureau of Indian Affairs (BIA)
Natural monopolies, 161
Negotiated rulemaking, 108
Nelson, Michael, 230n22
NEPPS (National Environmental Performance Partnership System), 139–140
Network failures, 177
Networks, 128–165
   accountability of, 135–136
   avian flu pandemic, 195–196
   czars, 153–155
   disaster management, 198
   effectiveness of, 155–158
   grants-in-aid, 158–160
   Hurricane Katrina response, 176–177
   information, 161–163
   intelligence community, 186–187
   interagency coordination, 151–153
   interagency networks, 149–151
   intergovernmental relations, 137–144
   network theory, 130–134
   9/11 attacks, 182
   nursing homes, 129
   partnerships without contracts, 147–149
   prevention of future terrorist attacks, 187–189
   public-private partnerships, 144–147
   regulation, 160–161
   tools, 158–163
   tools approach, 134–137
Network theory, 130–134, 164
   defined, 26
   evaluating accountability and performance, 25
Neustadt, Richard E., 230n20
New Deal, 59
New Mexico, 123
New Orleans, 168–179
New York Fire Department, 29–30, 180–181
New York Police Department, 29–30, 180–181, 217
New York Port Authority, 30, 181
New York Public Service Commission, 162
*New York Times,* 155
Nicholson-Crotty, Jill, 229n42
9-11 attacks. *See* September 11, 2001 terrorist attacks

9-11 Commission, 180
911 system, 53
Nitz, Lawrence, 243n98
Nixon, David C., 236n33
Nixon, Richard, 74, 79, 141, 149, 153
Nixon, Willliam H., 232n65
No-bid contracts, 176
No Child Left Behind Act, 1–4
Noll, Roger G., 232n64, 233n75, 233n77, 233n79
Nonattainment areas, 34
Nondelegation doctrine, 88–89
Non-English-speaking students, 3
Nongovernmental organizations, 219
Nonpoint sources, 34
Notice and comment process, 104–106, 220
Notice of proposed rulemaking, 104
NPS (National Park Service), 202, 208
NSA (National Security Agency), 69, 186
Nuclear power, 97–98, 101–102
Nuclear Regulatory Commission, 102
Nuclear weapons, 145
Nursing homes, 128–129
NWS. *See* National Weather Service
Nye, Joseph S., Jr., 237n63, 242nn94–95

Oates, Wallace, 243n101
Observability, 206–208
Occupational Safety and Health Administration (OSHA)
   ergonomics rule, 55, 91, 117, 212–213
   impositions on business, 61–62
   monetary penalties, 160
   political meddling, 110
   report card, 202
   workers' compensation, 37
Offeror process, 80
Office of Faith-Based and Community Initiatives, 74
Office of Federal Student Aid, 204–205
   Shaw as head, 216
   Woods as head, 215
Office of Homeland Security. *See now* Homeland Security Department
Office of Information and Regulatory Affairs (OIRA), 75–78, 214
Office of Management and Budget (OMB), 19–21, 75–78, 150–151
Office of National Drug Control Policy, 153
Office of Personnel Management (OPM), 114
Office of Student Financial Assistance (OSFA). *See now* Office of Federal Student Aid
Ogul, Morris S., 233n82
O'Halloran, Sharyn, 226n28, 230n3, 230nn17–18

OIRA (Office of Information and Regulatory Affairs), 75–78
Olson, Mancur, 234n104
Olson, William J., 230n25
O'Malley, Martin, 38
OMB. *See* Office of Management and Budget
O'Neill, Paul, 71–72
OPM (Office of Personnel Management), 114
Oppenheimer, Bruce I., 230n19
Optimize, 32
Options, narrow range of, 49–50
Organic food, 106
Organizational advancement, 45–46
Organizational cohesion, 47–49
Organizational identification, 46
Organizational report cards, 162, 201–202
OSFA (Office of Student Financial Assistance). *See now* Office of Federal Student Aid
OSHA. *See* Occupational Safety and Health Administration
O'Toole, Laurence, 130, 136, 239n4, 239n9, 240nn28–29, 240n31
O'Toole, Tara, 241n45
Outcomes, 15, 206–208
Outputs, 15, 206–208
Outsourcing, 189–190
Oversight, 59, 82–85
Oversight hearings, 78

Pacelle, Richard L., Jr., 246n83
Paige, Rod, 215
Paley, Amit R., 250nn42–43
Parallel systems, 49
Parasuraman, A., 243n96
PART (Program Assessment Rating Tool), 19–21, 159
Participation, 104–115, 125–127
Partnerships without contracts, 147–149
   education, 148–149
   environmental protection, 148
Patent and Trademark Office (PTO), 110–112
Patients' Bill of Rights, 151
Patriot Act, 182
Payan, Luis, 242n79
Pear, Robert, 232n56
Peer review, 111–112
Pentagon, first response to 9/11 attacks, 181–182
Perceived benefits and costs, 103–104
Performance, 15–23, 200–201
   defined, 15
   in education, 1–4
   evaluating, 25

Government Performance and Results Act, 17–19
   indicators, 10
   perceptions of, 21–24
   post-9/11, 185
   in public bureaucracies, 8–11
   rating, 201–202
   theories and applications, 24–27
   variations in, 202–217
Performance Measurement Partnership Project, 18
Performance measures, 38
Performance partnership agreement (PPA), 138–140
Perlman, Ellen, 228n25
Perrow, Charles, 45, 228n27, 229n47, 229n63
Personal Responsibility and Work Opportunity Reconciliation Act, 17
Pesticides. *See* Federal Insecticide, Fungicide, and Rodenticide Act
Peters, Katherine, 249n19
Peterson, D. J., 245n24
Peterson, Paul E., 233n67, 243nn97–98
Petracca, Mark P., 236n40, 236n42
Pfiffner, James, 231nn33–34, 242n72
Pharmaceutical industry, 194–195
Pianin, Eric, 234n5, 242n83
Pildes, Richard H., 232n58, 232nn60–61
Pitt, Harvey, 21
Plutonium, 124
Point sources, 34
Police, 44, 132–134
   first response to 9/11 attacks, 180–182
   patrol oversight, 84
Policy entrepreneurs, 98
Policy images, 101–102
Policymaking
   business organizations and, 117–119
   client influence on, 115–124
   defined, 16
   public interest groups, 119–121
   state and local governments, 121–124
   tasks, 203–208
   trends, 219
Political accountability, 11, 56
Political compromise, 80
Political intervention, 109–110
Political meddling, 110
Political support, 202, 209–213
Political uncertainty, 79–80
Politicians vs. judges, 86–87
Politics
   of bureaucratic structure, 79–80
   client politics, 97

entrepreneurial politics, 98
interest group politics, 98
majoritarian politics, 98–99
of public policy, 96–99
Pollard, Michael, 245n24
Pollution
air quality, 35
emissions trading, 160
Everglades restoration, 118
problem disaggregation, 34, 50
Toxics Release Inventory, 162
water pollution, 19
Popely, Rick, 243n113
Port running, 33
Port security, 189–190
Posner, Paul, 135, 239n10, 240n26
Postal Rate Commission, 213
Postal Service (USPS)
anthrax contamination, 16
outputs and outcomes, 206
performance rating, 211
postal savings system, 22
report card, 201, 202
Potter, John, 16
Powell, Michael, 227n5
PPA (performance partnership agreement),
138–140
Presidential appointees, 70–73, 90
Presidential power, 68–78
appointments, 70–73
Civil Service reform, 73–75
firings, 73
regulatory review and OMB, 75–78
President's Daily Brief, 186
President's Management Agenda, 114
Pressman, Jeffrey, 248n4
Principal, defined, 57
Principal-agent theory, 57–59, 124
agency clients and, 89–90
avian flu pandemic forecast, 195
contracting out, 129
defined, 26
disaster management, 198
evaluating accountability and performance,
25
Hurricane Katrina response, 176
prevention of future terrorist attacks,
189–190
Principled agents, 92
Prisons, 39–40, 147
Privatization, 129, 144–145
Problem disaggregation, 34–35, 50, 194
Problem solving, 34–40
problem disaggregation, 34–35, 50

simulations and tests, 39–40
standard operating procedures, 35–38
sunk costs, 38–39
Procedural requirements, 86, 88
Professional accountability, 11
Professional associations, 121
Professionalism, legislative, 64
Professionals, 48–49
Program Assessment Rating Tool (PART),
19–21, 159
Progressives, 13
Project XL, 214
Promiscuity, discouragement of, 162
Provan, Keith, 155, 157, 239n9, 239n11,
240n19, 241n58, 242n88, 245n50
PTO (Patent and Trademark Office), 110–112
Public bureaucracies
accountability and performance in, 8–11
contours of, 5–8
defined, 5
Public Citizen, 101
Public health network, 143–144
Public hearings, 109
Public housing, 106
Public interest groups, 101–102, 119–121
Public meetings, 109
Public policy, 96–99
Public-private partnerships, 136, 144–147
avian flu pandemic, 195–196
contracting out, 144–145
corrections, 147
energy policy, 145
mental health policy, 145–146
welfare policy, 146
Purposive incentives, 41
Purpura, Paul, 246n57
Putnam, Robert, 229n45

al-Qaida
deterrence of further attacks in U.S., 187
flying lessons, 197
infiltration into U.S., 183
network, 134, 157
prediction of pending attack, 180

Rabe, Barry, 140, 229n55, 240n35, 243n97
Race, 43–44
Radin, Beryl, 225n10, 226n41
Rahman, Omar Abdel, 179
Railroads, 98, 109
RAND Corporation, 4
Rational choice model, 32–33, 40, 41
Rauch, Jonathan, 238n75
Raymond, Margaret, 225n3

Reagan, Ronald
  bureaucratic motivation under, 43
  drug policy, 154
  FDA product seizures, 71
  ideological congruence, 149
  regulatory review, 75, 76
Reform movements, 13, 73–75
Regulation, 160–161
  deregulation, 82, 161
  economic, 135, 160–161
  social, 161
Regulatory agencies, 14
Regulatory czar, 214
Regulatory impact analysis, 151
Regulatory review, 75–78
Relationships. See Intergovernmental
  relationships
Reorganization Act, 73
Repetitive motion injuries, 55, 91, 117, 212–213
Report cards, 162, 201–202
Representative bureaucracy, 43–44
Resnick, David, 237n63
Resolution of disapproval, 55
Resource Conservation and Recovery Act,
  91–92, 138
Resource dependency theory, 155
Revolving door, 118
Ridge, Tom, 124, 154–155, 171
Ringquist, Evan, 238n89, 243n106
Risen, James, 231nn26–27
Risk, 44–45
Risk averse, 44–45
Robbins, Jim, 234n2, 234n5
Roberts, Alasdair, 241n45
Rockefeller, John D. IV, 69
Rocketry, 115
Rockman, Bert A., 229n45, 232n54, 233n82,
  238n79
Rockwell International, 145
Rocky Flats, Colorado, 145
Rom, Mark, 146, 241n59, 243n98
Romzek, Barbara, 225nn19–20, 226n24
Roosevelt, Franklin D., 73, 179
Roosevelt, Theodore, 73
Rosenau, Pauline, 241n59, 241n64
Rosenbaum, W. Anthony, 249n34
Rosenstiel, Tom, 238n90
Roth, William V., Jr., 232n65
Rothenberg, Lawrence S., 230nn10–11, 234n8
Rothenberg, Richard, 134, 240n22
Rothstein, Richard, 3, 225n10
Roy, Railton, 237n51
Rubin, Barry, 229nn43–44
Rulemaking, 104, 108, 113, 122–123

Sabatier, Paul, 238n92
Sabel, Charles, 241n67
Safe Drinking Water Act, 81, 139
Salamon, Lester, 134, 239n1, 240n10,
  240nn23–25, 241nn51–52, 243n104,
  244n114
Salience, 62–63, 119
Sanchez, Rene, 250n45
Sanger, David E., 231n28
San Joaquin Valley biodiversity plan, 209
Sastry, Narayan, 245n24
Satisficing, 24, 32–33, 194
Savas, E. S., 239n3, 241n53
SBA (Small Business Administration), 114
Scavo, Carmine, 247nn98–99
Schachtel, Marsha, 228n23
Schattschneider, E. E., 239n103
Scheberle, Denise, 240n32
Schlozman, Kay Lehman, 235n13, 235n23
Schneider, Anne, 241n62
Schneider, Greg, 230n2
Scholz, John, 237n56, 241nn39–41, 241n65,
  243n108
Schrag, Peter, 243n111
Schram, Sanford, 243n98
Schroeder, Christopher H., 234n106
Schwartz, Thomas, 233n88
Scientific management, 13
Scope of conflict, 123
Scott, John, 239n12
Scowcroft, Brent, 150
Screening mechanisms, 59
Seatbelts, 161
Second Federal Savings Bank, 148
Securities and Exchange Commission (SEC),
  14, 21, 105
Seelye, Katharine Q., 234n4
Seidenfeld, Mark, 232n60
Seidman, Harold, 153, 242n77
Self-interest, 41–42, 58
Semansky, Rafael, 239n102
Sen, Amartya, 43, 228n37
Senate confirmation, 70–71
Senior Executive Service, 74
Separation of powers, 80
September 11, 2001 terrorist attacks, 179–190
  Coast Guard role in response, 178
  communication failures, 30
  FEMA in wake of attacks, 171
  first response, 180–182
  post-9/11 acts, 182–185
  prevention of future attacks, 187–190
  standard operating procedures and, 29
Serafini, Marilyn Weber, 231n43

Shadow government, 219
Shalala, Donna, 32, 45, 67, 76, 80, 99, 105, 121, 142, 151, 153
Shane, Peter M., 237n64
Shapiro, Stuart, 232n62
Sharp, Elaine B., 235n18
Shaw, Theresa, 216
Shaw Group, 176
Sheehan, Reginald, 234n102
Sherman Antitrust Act, 98–99
Shipan, Charles R., 230n4, 230nn13–15
Shlonsky, Aron, 228nn20–21
Shogren, Elizabeth, 234n4
Shortcuts, 32
Shulman, Stuart W., 236n31
Sierra Club Legal Defense Fund, 120
Simmons, Melvin K., 235n16
Simon, Herbert, 30–33, 38, 40, 45, 53, 227n7, 227n11, 228n15, 228n29, 229n48, 229n52
Simulations and tests, 39–40, 197
  Avian flu pandemic, 190–191, 194
  Hurricane Pam, 173–174
Sipress, Alan, 237n57, 237nn59–60
Size, 131–132
Skapinker, Michael, 250n44
Skrzycki, Cindy, 229n1, 248n1
Slavin, Robert, 250n48
Sloppy hexagons, 102–103, 125
Small Business Administration (SBA), 114
Smith, Steven R., 148, 241n54, 241n66, 241n68
Smokey Bear, 22, 23
Smuggling, 33
Social regulation, 161
Social Security Administration (SSA)
  benefits and costs, 96
  Hurricane Katrina response, 178
  implementation, 16
  outputs and outcomes, 206
  performance rating, 203, 211, 217
  report card, 201, 202
  website, 113
Social Services Block Grant, 159
Sociology, 131
Solidary incentives, 42
Sostek, Anya, 248n103
South Carolina, 124
Space shuttle, 12, 22, 207
Sparrow, Malcolm, 133, 228n13, 228n22, 229n56, 240n20
Spellings, Margaret, 3
Spence, David B., 233n71, 233n78, 233n80
Spotted owl, 120–121

Spriggs, James F., II, 233n91
SSA. See Social Security Administration
Standardized testing, 1–4, 162
Standard operating procedures, 28–30, 35–38, 52–53, 178–179
State and local governments, 121–124
  avian flu pandemic, role in, 192–193
  Children's Health Insurance Program, 18, 22
  EPA delegation of authority, 137–140
  Medicaid, 141
  Web resources, 222–224
State Department, 46, 150, 207
Statesmen, 42
Stecher, Brian, 225nn11–14
Stem cell research, 103
Stiftel, Bruce, 241nn39–41
Stone, Deborah, 40, 228n28, 228nn30–31
Stovepipe mentality, 50
Strategic uncertainty, 132
Street-level bureaucrats, 35, 53
Strickland, Jim, 172–173
Student loans, 204–205, 215–216
Student testing, 1–4, 162
Substantive uncertainty, 132
Success for All, 217–218
Sugar industry, 118
Sullivan, Louis, 66
Sunk costs, 38–39
Sunstein, Cass R., 232n58, 232nn60–61
Supreme Court, 86–87, 89
Surveillance, warrantless, 69–70
Susskind, Lawrence, 236n43
Sustainable multiple-use management, 94
Suwannee River Project, 140
Suzuki-Orff School of Music, 148

Task environment, 30
Task Force on Export Control Reform, 152
Tasks, 202, 203–208
Tax gap, 204
Teachers, 4
Teach to the test, 3
Terrorism. See also Homeland Security Department
  anthrax contamination, 143–144
  Coast Guard role in 9/11 attack response, 178
  Customs Service performance rating, 211
  FEMA in wake of 9/11 attacks, 171
  networks, 134
  9/11 attacks, 179–190
  prevention of future attacks, 187–190
  standard operating procedures and, 29–30

warrantless surveillance, 69–70
Tessler, Mark H., 233n73, 237n49
Testing, 1–4, 162. *See also* Simulations and
 tests
Theoretical frameworks, 24–27
 avian flu pandemic, 193–197
 Hurricane Katrina response analysis, 173–179
 terrorist attack prevention, 187–190
Third-party government, 135–136
Thomas, Craig W., 249n26
Thompson, Tommy, 72–73
Thornburgh, Dick, 36, 43, 47, 85, 87, 122, 124,
 152, 154
Three Mile Island, 45
Tierney, John T., 235n13, 235n23
Timber industry, 95, 120–121, 125–127
Tip income, 52
Tobacco, 105
Tollison, Robert, 237n55
Tools approach, 134–137, 164
Toxics Release Inventory (TRI), 162
Training, 47
Transportation Department (DOT), 56, 61,
 113–114
TRI (Toxics Release Inventory), 162
Trucking industry, 98
True, James, 227n9
Trust-busting, 98–99
Turque, Bill, 225nn7–8
Tversky, Amos, 229n46

Uncertainty, 132
 institutional, 132
 political, 79–80
 strategic, 132
 substantive, 132
Unilateral actions, 60–70
*Unsafe at Any Speed* (Nader), 98
U.S. attorney firings, 73
U.S. Chamber of Commerce, 212–213
U.S. Climate Change Science Program, 166
U.S. Court of Appeals for the District of
 Columbia, 87–89
USA Patriot Act, 182
USDA. *See* Agriculture Department
User fees, 22
USPS. *See* Postal Service
Utility, maximizing, 41–42
Utility companies, 118, 161

Vaccinations. *See* Immunization
Vance, Cyrus, 150
Vasu, Michael, 244n122

*Vermont Yankee Nuclear Power Corp. v.*
 *Ruckelshaus* (1973), 88, 234n98
Veteran Benefits Administration, 202
Veto, legislative, 13
Vig, Norman J., 229n55, 240n35, 250n34
Virginia, 3, 181
Visibility, 134
Vision for Space Exploration, 206
Vogel, Steve, 231n47
Voice, 46
von Sternberg, Bob, 246n85
Vouchers, 135

Waitzkin, Howard, 239n102
Waivers, 123, 141
Waldfogel, Jane, 228nn19–21
*Wall Street Journal,* 172
Walsh, Edward, 242n80
Walter Reed Army Medical Center, 73
Warrantless surveillance, 69–70
Warren, Earl, 89
Washington, D.C. area, 181
Waterman, Richard W., 231n39
Water quality/pollution, 19, 34, 118, 140
Weak ties, 133
Weapons of mass destruction, 185–186
Web resources
 federal, 221–222
 state, 222–224
Wei, Feng Heng, 237n56
Weightman, George, 73
Weil, David, 243n115, 244n123
Weimer, David, 225n1, 244nn118–119
Weingast, Barry R., 232n64, 233n75, 233n77,
 233n79
Weisbrod, Burton, 227n10
Weisman, Jonathan, 231n30, 248n11
Weiss, Eric M., 232n57
Weiss, Janet, 163, 244n114, 244nn116–117,
 244n124
Weiss, Rick, 235n19, 248n121, 248nn126–127
Welfare magnet effect, 158
Welfare policy, 17, 146
Wermuth, Michael, 242n81, 242n84
West, Darrell M., 237nn65–66
West, William F., 232n58, 236n34
Wetlands, 110, 175
Whistle blower legislation, 13
White, Ben, 226n35
White, Josh, 242n76, 245n26, 246n62
Whoriskey, Peter, 245n26
Wildavsky, Aaron, 248n4
Wilderness Society, 95

Wildfires, 94–95, 125–127
Wilkinson, Todd, 234n2
Willging, Cathleen, 239n102
Williamson, Oliver E., 226n32, 233nn68–70
Wilson, James Q., 41, 225n18, 228n34, 234n6, 235nn9–10, 238n78, 248n10, 248n12, 249n16
Wisconsin Works, 146
Wise, Charles, 242n93
Witt, James Lee, 169–170, 244n9
Wohlstetter, Roberta, 180, 246nn71–72
Woll, Alan, 230n25
Wong, Kenneth, 243n97
Wood, B. Dan, 231n39
Wood, David O., 235n16
Woods, Greg, 215
Woodward, Bob, 226n29, 241n70, 246n87
Workers' compensation, 37
World Bank-International Monetary Fund, 181

World Trade Center
  car bombing (1993), 179
  communication failures, 30
  first response to 9/11 attacks, 180–182
  standard operating procedures and, 29
World War I, 35–36
World Wildlife Fund, 101
Wright, John R., 233n76, 234n103, 236n41, 236n46

Yackee, Jason Webb, 235n28, 236n32
Yackee, Susan Webb, 235n28, 236n32
Year 2000 (Y2K), 39–40, 216
Yolo County Health Department, 190, 194, 197

Zealots, 42
Zegart, Amy, 242n75
Zelman, Walter, 240n27
Zero-base budgeting, 17